OXFORD
UNIVERSITY PRESS

ASPIRE
SUCCEED
PROGRESS

Complete
Global Perspectives
for Cambridge IGCSE® & O Level

Second edition

Jo Lally

T0338053

Oxford excellence for Cambridge IGCSE® & O Level

OXFORD

OXFORD
UNIVERSITY PRESS

Great Clarendon Street, Oxford, OX2 6DP, United Kingdom

Oxford University Press is a department of the University of Oxford. It furthers the University's objective of excellence in research, scholarship, and education by publishing worldwide. Oxford is a registered trade mark of Oxford University Press in the UK and in certain other countries

© Oxford University Press 2015

The moral rights of the authors have been asserted

First published in 2015

All rights reserved. No part of this publication may be reproduced, stored in a retrieval system, or transmitted, in any form or by any means, without the prior permission in writing of Oxford University Press, or as expressly permitted by law, by licence or under terms agreed with the appropriate reprographics rights organization. Enquiries concerning reproduction outside the scope of the above should be sent to the Rights Department, Oxford University Press, at the address above.

You must not circulate this work in any other form and you must impose this same condition on any acquirer

British Library Cataloguing in Publication Data
Data available

978-0-19-836681-2

12

MIX
Paper from responsible sources
FSC® C007785

Paper used in the production of this book is a natural, recyclable product made from wood grown in sustainable forests. The manufacturing process conforms to the environmental regulations of the country of origin.

Printed in Great Britain by Bell and Bain Ltd., Glasgow

Acknowledgements

The publishers would like to thank the following for permissions to use their photographs:

Cover images: Shutterstock; **p6-7(Bkgrd): p8-9:** Incomible/Shutterstock; **p8-9(Bkgrd):** Duniascrap/Shutterstock;Bloomua/Shutterstock; p10(T)(B): Imagefactory/Shutterstock; **p10(CL):** Mtsaride/Shutterstock; **p10(CR):** Kozak Dmytro/Shutterstock; **p10(BL):** Edward Haylan/Shutterstock; **p10-11(Bkgrd):** Duniascrap/Shutterstock; **p13(BL):** Mega Pixel/Shutterstock; **p13(Bkgrd):** Lightspring/Shutterstock; **p13(B):** Pio3/Shutterstock; **p14(Bkgrd):** Marchello74/Shutterstock; **p15:** 89studio/Shutterstock; **p15(B):** Sheff/Shutterstock; **p15(T):** Imagefactory/Shutterstock; **p16(R):** Lyudmyla Kharlamova/Shutterstock; **p16(B):** Designsstock/Shutterstock; **p16-17(Bkgrd):** Binik/Shutterstock; **p17(B):** Bardocz Peter/Shutterstock; **p17(T):** Prill/Shutterstock; **p18-19(Bkgrd):** Woaiss/Shutterstock; **p20-21(Bkgrd):** Aluna1/Shutterstock; **p22(T):** Tobkatrina/Shutterstock; **p22(CL):** Jojoo64/Shutterstock; **p22-23(Bkgrd_T):** MaxyM/Shutterstock; **p22-23(Bkgrd_B):** Kusska/Shutterstock; **p24-25(Bkgrd):** Duniascrap/Shutterstock; **p25:** Lyudmyla Kharlamova/Shutterstock; **p26:** Viacheslav Nikolaenko/Shutterstock; **p26(Bkgrd):** Naci Yavuz/Shutterstock; **p26-27(Bkgrd):** Chantal de Bruijne/Shutterstock; **p28:** Tsekhmister/Shutterstock; **p29:** Bikeriderlondon/Shutterstock; **p30-31(Bkgrd):** Vetkit/Sutterstock; **p31:** Sherry Yates Young/Shutterstock; **p32-33(Bkgrd):** STILLFX/Sutterstock; **p34-35(Bkgrd):** Chantal de Bruijne/Shutterstock; **p36-37(Bkgrd):** Ilolab/Sutterstock; **p38-39(Bkgrd):** Robert Lucian Crusitu/Shutterstock; **p40(T):** Ilona Ignatova/Shutterstock; **p40(Bkgrd):** Duniascrap/Shutterstock; **p41(Bkgrd):** Koosen/Shutterstock; **p41(T):** Corbis; **p41(BL):** Vlad61/Shutterstock; **p41(BR):** Filip Fuxa/Shutterstock; **p43(BL):** KoQ Creative/Shutterstock; **p43(Bkgrd):** Twobee/Shutterstock; **p44-45(Bkgrd):** Binik/Shutterstock; **p46-47(Bkgrd):** Chantal de Bruijne/Shutterstock; **p49:** Stocklight/Shutterstock; **p47:** James Steidl/Shutterstock; **p48:** Mopic/Shutterstock; **p48-49(Bkgrd):** JPL/NASA; **p49:** Stocklight/Shutterstock; **p50-51(Bkgrd):** I3alda/Shutterstock; **p51:** Pasko Maksim/Shutterstock; **p52-53(Bkgrd):** Chantal de Bruijne/Shutterstock; **p54-57(Bkgrd):** Stillfx/Shutterstock; **p58-59:** Bestdesigns/iStockphoto; **p60-61(Bkgrd):** Binik/Shutterstock; **p60:** Lyudmyla Kharlamova/Shutterstock; **p62-63(Bkgrd):** Quang Ho/Shutterstock; **p64-65(Bkgrd):** Duniascrap/Shutterstock; **p66-67(Bkgrd):** Roman Rybaleov/Shutterstock; **p67(B):** Kak2s/Shutterstock; **p67(T):** Kuznetcov_Konstantin/Shutterstock; **p68:** Africa Studio/Shutterstock; **p68-69(Bkgrd):** SETI Institute/JPL-Caltech/NASA; **p70:** Iunewind/Shutterstock; **p70:** Olga Lebedeva/Shutterstock; **p71(T):** Vetkit/Shutterstock; **p71(B):** Lyudmyla Kharlamova/Shutterstock; **p72-73:** Evgeny Karandaev/Shutterstock; **p74:** Malchev/Shutterstock; **p74-75(Bkgrd):** Girafchik/Shutterstock; **p76:** Ann Precious/Shutterstock; **p77:** Mega Pixel/Shutterstock; **p78-79(Bkgrd):** Bloomua/Shutterstock; **p81-82(Bkgrd):** Verbena/Shutterstock; **p84-86(Bkgrd):** Duniascrap/Shutterstock; **p82-83(Bkgrd):** Ilolab/Shutterstock; **p88-89(Bkgrd):** Robert Adrian Hillman/Shutterstock; **p90:** Andrew Grossman/123RF; **p90-91(Bkgrd1):** Sanchai Kumar/Shutterstock; **p90-91(Bkgrd2):** Tonello Photography/Shutterstock; **p92-93(Bkgrd):** Retrorocket/Shutterstock; **p95:** Thomas Trutschel/Getty Images; **p94-95(Bkgrd):** Sritangphoto/Shutterstock; **p96-97(Bkgrd):** Nobeastsofierce/Shutterstock; **p98:** NYHQ2002-0148/Markisz/UNICEF; **p98-99(Bkgrd):** Nobeastsofierce/Shutterstock; **p100:** Ellagrin/Shutterstock; **p105:** Mdesignstudio/Shutterstock; **p104-105(Bkgrd):** Talashow/Shutterstock; **p106-107:** Benjamin Haas/Shutterstock; **p108-109:** Triff/Shutterstock; **p110-111:** Freer/Shutterstock; **p100-101(Bkgrd):** Allies Interactive/Shutterstock; **p102-103(Bkgrd):** Piotr_pabijan/Shutterstock; **p114-115(Bkgrd):** photocell/Shutterstock; **p115:** Anthony Kelly/Cartoonstock; **p116-117:** Aysezgicmeli/Shutterstock; **p118-119:** Ivosar/Shutterstock; **p120-121:** Flocu/Shutterstock; **p122-123(Bkgrd):** MaxyM/Shutterstock; **p122:** Andrey Armyagov/Shutterstock; **p123(L):** ©EPA; **p123(R):** ©EPA; **p124-125(Bkgrd):** Charles Harker/Shutterstock; **p126:** Alinute Silzeviciute/Shutterstock; **p127:** Flocu/Shutterstock; **p128-129:** Shutterstock; **p129:** Paresh Nath/Cagle Cartoons; **p130-131:** Adam Vilimek/Shutterstock; **p132-133:** Csaba Peterdi/Shutterstock; **p134-135:** baoyan/Shutterstock; **p136:** Chris Madden/Cartoonstock; **p136-137(Bkgrd):** Annareichel/Shutterstock; **p138-139:** Lukasz Janyst/Shutterstock; **p140-141:** Symbiot/Shutterstock; **p142-143(Bkgrd):** Tom Grundy/Shutterstock; **p143:** Mariyana M/Shutterstock; **p144-145:** Crop/Shutterstock; **p146-147:** Crop/Shutterstock; **p148:** Ratana21/Shutterstock; **p150-151(Bkgrd):** Kris Tan/Shutterstock; **p152-153(Bkgrd):** Rawpixel.com/Shutterstock; **p154-155(Bkgrd):** Poznyakov/Shutterstock; **p156-157:** Robert Adrian Hillman/Shutterstock; **p158-159(Bkgrd):** Memo Angeles/Shutterstock; **p158:** 9comeback/Shutterstock; **p159(L):** Aaron Amat/Shutterstock; **p159(R):** Michael Pitts/Nature Picture Library/REX; **p160:** Henrik Larsson/Shutterstock; **p160-161(Bkgrd):** Kozoriz Yuriy/Shutterstock; **p162-163:** Vlad61/Shutterstock; **p164-165:** Microvector/Shutterstock; **p166-167:** VLADGRIN/Shutterstock; **p168-169:** Andrey Yurlov/Shutterstock; **p170-171(B):** Rvika/Shutterstock; p**170-171(T):** Photocell/Shutterstock; **p173:** Mark Graham/Stefeno De Sabbata/Oxford Internet Institute/University of Oxford; **p172-173(Bkgrd):** Shutterstock; **p174-175:** VKA/Shutterstock; **p178-179:** Nowik Sylwia/Shutterstock; **p180(TL):** Randy Glasbergen/Glasbergen Cartoon Service; **p180(TR):** Jeff Stahler/Cartoonstock; **p180(B):** Christopher Barnes/Alamy; **p180-181(Bkgrd):** MaxyM/Shutterstock; **p182-183(Bkgrd):** RTimages/Shutterstock; **p184-185:** Chantal de Bruijne/Shutterstock; **p186-187:** Eka Panova/Shutterstock; **p189:** Christian Musat/Shutterstock; **p190:** Thomas Marent/Minden Pictures/Corbis; **p194-195:** GiSpate/Shutterstock; **p196(T):** © 2015 OAS1S™ - R.A. de Hullu; **p196(B):** © 2015 OAS1S™ - R.A. de Hullu; **p197:** © 2015 OAS1S™ - R.A. de Hullu; **p198-199:** Chantal de Bruijne/Shutterstock; **p202-203:** Zygotehaasnobrain/Shutterstock; **p204(T):** www.polyp.org.uk; **p205:** www.polyp.org.uk; **p204(B):** www.polyp.org.uk; **p206:** Bardocz Peter/Shutterstock; **p208-209:** Donvictorio/Shutterstock; **p210:** Chantal de Bruijne/Shutterstock; **p212-213:** Arthimedes/Shutterstock; **p220-221:** Cherries/Shutterstock; **p222-223:** Woaiss/Shutterstock; **p224-225:** Chantal de Bruijne/Shutterstock; **p234:** Theresa McCracken/Cartoonstock; **p236-237:** Nrqemi/Shutterstock; **p238:** BP Statistical Review of World Energy 2015; **p238-239(Bkgrd):** Johan Swanepoel/Shutterstock; **p239:** Asmaa Waguih/Reuters; **p240-241:** Kstudija/Shutterstock; **p246:** Bardocz Peter/Shutterstock; **p251(T):** Karsten Schley/Cartoonstock; **p251(BL):** Fran/Cartoonstock; **p251(BR):** Len Hawkins/Cartoonstock; **p254:** Christian Mueller/Shutterstock; **p255:** Evlakhov Valeriy/Shutterstock; **p254-255(Bkgrd):** Ilolab/Shutterstock; **p256-257:** corgarashu/Shutterstock; **p258-259:** Chantal de Bruijne/Shutterstock; **p262-263:** Igor.stevanovic/Shutterstock; **p244-265(Bkgrd):** Ilolab/Shutterstock; **p264:** Christian Mueller/Shutterstock; **p264:** Simon Kneebone; **p266:** Malcolm Chapman/Shutterstock; **p267:** Artindo/Shutterstock; **p272-273:** Stockphoto mania/Shutterstock; **p274-275:** Chantal de Bruijne/Sutterstock; **p276:** Governing Urban Futures, Urban Age conference newspaper, November 2014/LSE Cities.

Artwork by OUP and Q2A Pvt. Services Ltd.

®IGCSE is the registered trademark of Cambridge International Examinations.

All questions, examination practice and comments that appear in this book were written by the author.

The author and publisher are grateful for permission to reprint extracts from the following copyright mat

Sally Adee: 'Zap your brain into the zone: Fast track to pure focus' (Excerpt) (c) 2012 Reed Business Inforn UK. All rights reserved. Distributed by Tribune Content Agency

Ian Birrell: 'Corrupt, ineffective and hypocritical: Britain should give less aid, not more' *Independent*, 2 Ma Copyright *The Independent*, www.independent.co.uk. Reprinted by permission of the Independent.

Rupert Blackstone: with contributions from Roger Middleton, Brian Robinson and Ian Arbon 'How do w achieve a sustainable lifestyle?' from http://www.imeche.org/knowledge/industries/energy-environment-an sustainability/news/Sustainable-Lifestyles. Reprinted by permission of The Institution of Mechanical Engine

Paul Cappon: 'Social Implications of Globalization: Can New Ways of Learning Humanize our Global Institutions?' from http://www.21learn.org/archive/. This work is licensed under a Creative Commons Attri Non-Commercial-NoDerivs 3.0 Unported License.

Andy Coghlan: 'Myths make measles soar' from *New Scientist*, 14 February 2015. © 2015 Reed Business Information – UK. All rights reserved. Distributed by Tribune Content Agency.

Nick Cumming-Bruce: 'U.N, Warning of Migrant Crisis in Greece, Urges Europe to Act' © 2015 *The New Yo* Reprinted by permission of the New York Times.

James Cusick: 'Michael Gove determined to scrap the Human Rights Act – even if Scotland retains it', 31 2015 from http://www.independent.co.uk/news/uk/politics/ copyright *The Independent*, www.independent.co. Reprinted by permission of the *Independent*.

Patrick Kingsley: 'Libya's people smugglers: inside the trade that sells refugees hopes of a better life', *The Guardian*, 24 April 2015. Copyright Guardian News & Media Ltd 2015.

Sherryl Kleinman: 'Why sexist language matters' from http://www.alternet.org/story/, originally publishe Center Line, a newsletter of the Orange Country Rape Crisis Center, North Carolina.

Kenneth Lau: 'Exam pressure has primary pupils flocking to tutorials', *The Standard*, July 06, 2015 from ht www.thestandard.com.hk. Reprinted by permission of The Standard.

Anna Leach: '2015 challenges: demographic shifts', theguardian.com, 16 March 2015. Copyright Guardian & Media Ltd 2015.

Zhang Lihua: Reprinted by permission of the publisher from *China's Traditional Cultural Values and National I* (Washington, DC; Carnegie Endowment for International Peace, 2013). www.CarnegieEndowment.org

Charles C. Mann: 'What if we never run out of oil?' © 2013 The Atlantic Media Co., as first published in *T Atlantic Magazine*, 1 May 2013. All rights reserved. Distributed by Tribune Content Agency.

Brian Orend: "War", The Stanford Encyclopedia of Philosophy (Fall 2008 Edition), Edward N. Zalta (ed.), ht plato.stanford.edu/archives/fall2008/entries/war. Reprinted by permission of Stanford University and Brian

Jonathan Paige: 'British public wrong about nearly everything, survey shows', *Independent*, 17 February 20 Copyright *The Independent*, www.independent.co.uk. Reprinted by permission of the *Independent*.

Luke Patey and Zhang Chu: 'China, trade, aid and Africa', *Financial Times* 11 March 2014. Reprinted by permission of the *Financial Times*.

Helen Pidd: 'UK's north-south divide has widened', says thinktank, theguardian.com, 19 January 2015. Co Guardian News & Media Ltd 2015.

Paul Sargeant: 'How Fifa makes and spends its money', BBC News, 29 May 2015 from http://www.bbc.co.uk/news/worldeurope-32923882 © bbc.co.uk/news.

Tiffany L. Shih and Joshua J Goldman: Extract from 'Recognizing and Resolving Ethical Dilemmas in R Medicine' Virtual Mentor, May 2011, Volume 13, Number 5: 291-294. The viewpoints expressed in the *AMA J of Ethics* are those of the authors and do not necessarily reflect the views and policies of the AMA.

Julie Turkewitz: 'Wyoming, Long on Pride but Short on People, Hopes to Lure Some Back' © 2015 *The New Times*. Reprinted by permission of the New York Times.

Lisa Yanovich: extract from 'Children Left Behind: The Impact of Labor Migration in Moldova and Ukraine' http://www.migrationpolicy.org/article/children-left-behind-impact-labor-migration-moldova-and-ukraine, Ja 23, 2015. Reprinted with permission of the Migration Policy Institute.

Graph from Allianz GI Global Capital Markets & Thematic Research Data as of March 2015. Reprinted by permission of Allianz Global Investors GmbH.

Extract from http://www.christianaid.org.uk/whatwedo/issues/trade.aspx. Reprinted by permission of Christi

The Guardian: 'A tale of four world cities London, Delhi, Tokyo and Bogotá compared' theguardian.com, 11 Fe 2015. Copyright Guardian News & Media Ltd 2015.

The Guardian: 'The key debates for sustainable living', theguardian.com, 27 October 2011. Copyright Guardia & Media Ltd 2015.

Extract from 'Syria air strikes conducted by UK military pilots' from http://www.bbc.co.uk/news/uk-3356242 bbc.co.uk/news.

Extract from http://www.givingwhatwecan.org/why-give/myths-about-aid. Reproduced by permission of givingwhatwecan.org.

Global Policy Forum (2011): Tables and Charts on Global Food Aid. New York. https://www.globalpolicy.org/world-hunger/. Reprinted by permission.

Global Policy Forum (2013): International Trade and Development. New York. https://www.globalpolicy.or social-and-economic-policy/international-trade-and-development. Reprinted by permission.

'Nuclear evacuees face dilemma over returning home' from http://www.japantimes.co.jp/news/2015/07/23/na social-issues/nuclear-evacuees-facedilemma-returning-home/#.Vbl_3_nCefg. Reprinted by permission.

Extract from the 'Universal Declaration of Human Rights' http://www.un.org/en/documents/udhr/ Article 3, 4 7, Copyright © United Nations 2015. All rights reserved. Reprinted with the permission of the United Nation

Extract and graphics from http://reports.weforum.org/outlook-global-agenda-2015/top-10-trends-of-2015/8-intensifying-nationalism/. Reprinted by permission of the World Economic Forum.

Extract and graphs from http://socialreport.msd.govt.nz/documents/cultural-identity-social-report-2010.pdfl. Reprinted by permission of the Ministry of Social Development.

Extract from 'Three ways communities are changing for the better' from http://www.socialenterprise.org.uk/ Reprinted by permission of Stickyboard Limited.

Global Youth Unemployment, % of Youth Ages 15- 24, Copyright (Year) by the Council on Foreign Relations. Reprinted with permission.

Extract from http://www.redpepper.org.uk/biomass-the-trojan-horse-of-renewables/. Reprinted by permission Pepper Magazine.

Extract from http://www.antislavery.org. Reprinted by permission of Anti-Slavery International.

Extract from http://www.nineteen48.com/about-us/our-values/. Reprinted by permission of Nineteen48 Ltd. Al rights reserved.

OECD (2008) Promoting Sustainable Consumption, Good Practices in OECD countries, OECD Publishing, Paris http://www.oecd.org/greengrowth/40317373.pdf. Reprinted by permission of OECD.

Quote from https://www.worldenergy.org/wp-content/uploads/2015/01/2015-World-Energy-Issues-Monitor.pdf. Copyright © 2015 World Energy Council. All rights reserved. Used by permission of the World Energy Counci London.

Extract from http://www.urbanknowledge.org/ur/docs/UR_Flagship_Full%20Report.pdf - World Bank. Planning Connecting, and Financing Cities—Now: Priorities for City Leaders. 2013. Washington, DC: World Bank. DOI: 10.1596/978-0-8213-9839-5. License: Creative Commons Attribution CC BY 3.0.

Extract from 'How to shrink a city' from http://www.economist.com/news/leaders/21652343-many-citiesare-los inhabitants-better-manage-decline-try-stop-it-how-shrink

Extract from 'Badly educated men rich countries have not adapted well' http://www.economist.com/news/essays/21649050-badly-educated-men-rich-countries-have-not-adapted-well-trade-technology-or-feminism.

Extract from Wet Your Whistle drinking water activity handbook. Reprinted by permission of Terrific Science

Extract from http://www.interpol.int/Crime-areas/Trafficking-in-human-beings/.

Extract from http://www.saudigazette.com.sa/. Reprinted by permission.

Extract from 'Turtle terror! Why Hong Kong should embrace its wild side' http://www.scmp.com/magazines/p magazine/article/. Reprinted by permission of South China Morning Post Publishers Ltd.

We have made every effort to trace and contact all copyright holders before publication, but if notified of any errors or omissions, the publisher will be happy to rectify these at the earliest opportunity.

Links to third party websites are provided by Oxford in good faith and for information only. Oxford disclaims responsibility for the materials contained in any third party website referenced in this work.

Contents

Introduction

Who is this book for?

This book is for:

- Teachers and students following the Cambridge International Examinations course in Global Perspectives, either at IGCSE® or O level.
- People who want to think independently about, and debate, important issues in the world.
- Anyone who wants to improve their thinking, reasoning, research, planning, teamwork, and presentation skills.

How do I use this book?

This book is structured so that you can choose your own route through it – it's a sort of "build your own learning adventure" book.

Skills development activities

Section A includes skills development chapters which concentrate on the skills that are used in Global Perspectives. Each skills development chapter is divided into three Levels.

- Level 1 introduces the skills.
- Level 2 develops and practises the skills.
- Level 3 extends and practises the skills.

It is best to work through the Level 1 skills from several chapters and apply them to some research, before going back to work through Level 2. You should apply Level 2 to some research before going back to work through Level 3. You will get more out of the skills practice this way, than if you simply work through all the skills levels at the same time.

It's best to work through the skills development chapters in order, rather than for example starting with Section 3.2, Level 3, however going back to an earlier chapter to revise a skill can be very helpful.

Sections B, C and D cover the topics from the Global Perspectives syllabus, helping you to put your skills into practice and to start your learning journey. Each topic chapter covers:

- Key issues
- Key language
- Stimulus material
- Skills practice activities
- Ideas for discussion, debate and practice

The topic chapters suggest one approach to developing your skills with relevant content. So long as you do practise your skills, you can choose other stimulus material and other ways of exploring the topics.

Team Project

Section B includes a chapter on each of the topic areas for the **Team Project**.

For your assessment, you will need to work with a team to organise an active project – a project where you set an aim and make that aim happen. You won't be able to simply gather information for this project. You will need to choose **one** of these eight topics as the general area for your project. You will also research different cultural perspectives on your chosen issue. Each chapter includes suggestions for aims and outcomes to help you.

Individual Report

Section C includes a chapter on each of the topic areas for the **Individual Report**.

For your assessment you will need to write an individual report relating to **one** of these eight topics. You will be assessed on the skills that you use and demonstrate rather than on your subject knowledge. Each chapter includes suggestions for research to help you.

Written Paper

Section D includes a chapter on each of the topic areas for the **Written Paper**.

For your assessment you will have to take a written examination paper, which will assess your skills. The written examination paper will be based around these topics. Each chapter includes examination practice to help you.

Choosing topics

You may have to negotiate with your teacher to let you choose topics for your Team Project and Individual Report that you find interesting (rather than ones your teacher finds interesting). Good luck – it will improve your presentation and reasoning skills!

But be prepared to listen to your teacher too – listening is also an important skill in Global Perspectives. Furthermore, you have to choose the right moment to strike out independently. Your teacher will have a valuable, informed opinion about whether you are ready for this. And you may be ready sooner, or later, than your classmates.

It is possible to work through some of the discussion and activities in a topic chapter without completing the whole chapter or producing your Individual Report or Team Project.

What will I learn

You will be able to choose – or at least negotiate – quite a lot of what you learn. You will discuss and learn about a number of important global issues.

More importantly, however, you will develop, practise and apply the skills you need to research, plan and take action. You will learn to understand different perspectives on complex global issues, and you will learn to see the world differently.

1.1 Searching for information

Level ①

What kind of information do I need?

Before you do an internet search, you need to think about what sort of answers, information and ideas you need. They might be:

- Definitions
- Facts
- Opinions
- Value judgements
- Predictions

Let's look at some examples:

Question	Type of answer
What is a family?	Definition
What proportion of families are extended families?	Numbers, statistics, facts. You will also need to define "extended".
How are families in China and the UK different from one another?	Facts and opinions; possibly values.
Why are families in China and the UK different from one another?	Requires an explanation which discusses causes and consequences. Facts will help, but you have to consider how they link together as well.
Will changing divorce rates have a negative effect on the country?	Prediction. This is a question about the future. You will need to think about complex causes and consequences. You will need to weigh up opinions and values too.

Activity ①

1. What sort of answers do you need for the following questions? Which question is most interesting?

   a) What is a national sport?

   b) What is the national sport of Bhutan?

   c) What is education?

   d) Why is education necessary? (Think carefully about this one – is it really a simple definition?)

   e) How many migrants to the EU were there in 2013?

   f) Is migration likely to be beneficial?

   g) What would be the best sort of education?

   h) What other species live in your country?

   i) Why does it matter if a species becomes extinct?

   j) What are the effects of unemployment on a community?

> You will think about answers to these questions later. For now, just think about the kinds of question they are and the sorts of answer they will need.

Level 2

Internet search terms

You have thought about what sort of information you want. This will help you to structure your internet search to find this information.

- Be precise.
- Target your search terms to what you want to know.
- Add the name of a country, e.g. "family values + Singapore" or "family values + USA".
- Change your search terms if necessary.
- Look at the titles of the pages you find. Do they look as if they will answer your questions? If not, change your search terms.

Only read a page or site if it looks useful.

Activity 2

In this activity, do not read the sites you find in detail.

1. a) Put "family" into your search engine. What sort of sites do you find?

    b) Put "family values" into your search engine. What sort of sites do you find?

    c) Put "effect divorce family values" into your search engine. What sort of sites do you find?

2. Which of the following sets of search terms would best help you answer the question, "Who cares for children (parents, mothers, or grandparents, etc.)?"

    a) "Who cares for children?"

    b) "Caregiver"

    c) "Family structure + country"

    d) "Men + women + childcare"

3. What search terms would help you to find information and ideas to answer these questions?

    a) What is the unemployment rate among young people in the UAE?

    b) What effect is globalisation having on Pakistan?

    c) How can we prevent species extinction?

    d) Do the Olympic Games successfully promote peace?

    e) How are communities changing in Vietnam?

    f) Is it possible to have a truly fair sports competition between nations?

Discussion

1. Discuss the opinion that, "Divorce is killing family values."

    a) Which of your searches produced the most useful sites?

    b) What other search terms could you use to find relevant information and ideas?

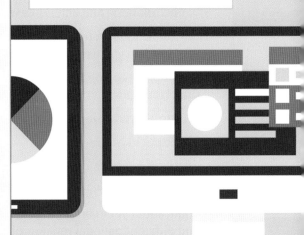

Level 3

Advanced search skills

How to improve your search results:

- Search within organisations such as NGOs – charities, international organisations, etc.
- Use the advanced search function in search engines.
- Compare different search engines.

> Use these strategies after your first search, when you already know a little bit.

Activity 3

1. You need to find out about human rights abuses around the world. Which of these organisations is likely to be useful?

   a) http://www.worldbank.org

   b) http://www.wwf.org

   c) http://www.amnesty.org

   d) http://www.unesco.org

   e) http://www.un.org

2. You need to find out what some of the key issues are in education in Pakistan.

   a) Go to http://www.oxfam.org and search "education + Pakistan". What sort of information, ideas and perspectives do you get?

   b) Go to http://www.oecd.org and search "education + Pakistan". What sort of information, ideas and perspectives do you get?

   c) How did (a) and (b) compare with just using a search engine such as Google?

3. Think about your current research. Which organisations and charities are likely to help you? What different perspectives are they likely to have?

Activity 4

1. Go to http://www.google.com/advanced_search. This tool helps you to refine your search and be more specific.

   a) You want to look for the effects of rising sea levels on turtle conservation. How will you fill in the advanced search?

   b) You want to look for social consequences of the 2008 recession in Indonesia and Italy. How will you fill in the advanced search?

   c) Think about your current research. What do you need to know? How can you use an advanced search to help you?

2. Look up, "changing communities + Beijing" on the following search engines:

   a) http://www.google.co.uk

   b) http://hk.yahoo.com

   c) http://www.baidu.com

3. Consider the different perspectives these sites offer.

4. Think about your current research. Use different search engines and different national versions of search engines. Consider the different perspectives they offer on your topic.

Reflection

- How has your ability to search for information improved?
- What new skills have you learned?
- Are there any aspects of this that you struggle with?
- How can you improve?

> Different search engines can give you different results. This can be a way of getting different perspectives.

1.2 Reading and recording

Level 1

When you are searching for information, you do not have to read everything you find. You only need to skim read to see if it is relevant. If it does seem relevant, you can then read it in more detail.

- Look for key words.
- When you find the key words, read the sentence that they are in to see if it is relevant.
- Read for gist – ask yourself what the article or paragraph is about.
- Don't worry if there are some words you don't know. You can probably understand enough without them. At this stage, only look up words if you really need to.

Key words

Activity 1

1. For each of these questions, decide which key words to look for.

   a) Are single-parent families a recent change to family structures?

   b) Is it possible to have a truly fair sports competition between nations?

   c) How can we prevent species extinction?

   d) How can we combat international crime?

   e) Is investing in the future more important than preserving traditions?

Skim read

Activity 2

1. Skim read each of the passages on the right. Will any of them help to answer the questions in Activity 1?

   Look for key words. Read for gist.

1 International sport is fundamentally not fair. Rich nations can afford to spend more resources on finding and training elite sports people than poor nations. This inevitably means that they have an advantage in international sporting competitions.

2 People stereotype single mothers because they believe that unmarried mothers are living on welfare, have too many children and don't want to work. They also believe that single mothers will destroy family values. Yet only half of US mothers on welfare are divorced. Furthermore, a woman can pass on good values to her children, even if their father has left.

3 Perhaps the greatest threat that faces many species is the widespread destruction of habitat. Deforestation, farming, overgrazing and development all result in irreversible changes such as soil compaction, erosion, desertification, or the alteration of local climatic conditions. Such land-use practices vastly alter or even eliminate wildlife habitat. In areas where rare species are present, habitat destruction can quickly force a species to extinction. We therefore need to find ways of protecting these wildlife habitats.

4 During the years of slavery in the US, children usually stayed with their mothers when their fathers were sold. So women tended to be the head of the family. In the decades after slavery, single-mother families continued to be formed because of hard economic times, and men and women moving to look for work. Between 1880 and 1895, about 30% of urban black families in the US were headed by single mothers.

5 For years, there has been a noticeable rise in sports side-line fights between parents, the most infamous being the death that occurred when two fathers of hockey players fought after a pickup game in 2000 in Reading, Massachusetts, USA. Youth sports experts are well aware of a trend toward a new category of confrontations. In Canton, Texas, a 45-year-old father, who had been barred from attending the local high school football games for shoving and verbally abusing his son's coaches, shot and critically wounded the head coach.

Level 2

Making notes

Do:

- skim read looking for relevant and important ideas
- identify short passages to read carefully
- write key words or phrases
- use diagrams to show causes, consequences, perspectives, etc.
- write your own questions – about things you don't understand, about things you need to know, about differences of opinion, etc.
- use different colours – if your own questions are in different colours, you'll be able to find them. If causes and consequences are in different colours, you might be able to spot a pattern
- copy one or two significant sentences that you might want to quote
- cut and paste the website URL into your notes, along with the date
- write down the title and author of a book, with the page number(s) by each idea.

Do not:

- read everything on every website you find
- write down everything
- copy and paste everything, or
- use other people's work without quoting and referencing.

Activity 3

1. The Australian Great Barrier Reef is disappearing. Research the causes and consequences of this.

2. What are the most important causes and consequences of globalisation?

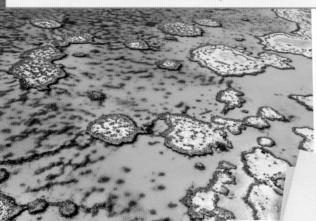

- Think about your search terms.
- Make structured notes of no more than 100 words. You may use diagrams.
- Keep a list of sources and make a note of which ideas are related to which sources.

Level 3

References

It is important to provide references for quotations, ideas and information from sources.

- Make a note of your sources.
- Be consistent with references.

You should make sure you include the following:

> Research the Harvard Referencing system and the APA referencing system.

Website	• URL
	• Date you accessed the website
	• Author (if one is given)
	K. Gammon, 2012. "Half of Great Barrier Reef Lost in Past 3 Decades" in *LiveScience*. Available at: http://www.livescience.com/23612-great-barrier-reef-steep-decline.html, accessed 04.01.16.

Book	• Author(s) • Publisher
	• Date of Publication • Place of publication
	• Title • Page number(s)
	A. Imeson, 2011. *Desertification, Land Degradation and Sustainability*, Wiley-Blackwell, UK, p.211

Article in Journal	• Author(s) • Title and volume of journal
	• Title of paper • Page number(s)
	L.E. Venegas and N.A Mazzeo, "Traffic Pollution Modelling in a Complex Urban Street," *International Journal of Environment and Pollution*, Vol.48/2, pp.87–95

Activity

1. Which of the following use proper referencing? Can you find the documents that the information was taken from?

   a) Vietnam's growth in the last two decades has been spectacular. The OECD says it has reached 7%.

   b) Hong Kong has all along adopted an open immigration policy. http://www.gov.hk/en/about/abouthk/factsheets/docs/immigration.pdf

   c) There are few effective mechanisms at national or international level to prevent corporate human rights abuses or to hold companies to account. Amnesty International is working to change this. http://www.amnesty.org

2. Choose one book and one website. Show how you would reference each of them.

3. Look at your own research. Make sure that you have properly referenced your sources.

Reflection

- How has your ability to search for information improved?

- What new skills have you learned?

- Are there any aspects of reading and recording that you struggle with?

- How can you improve?

1.3 Setting up research

Level 1

Asking questions

One way of starting research is to ask as many questions as you can think of. You can do this by

- having a class discussion
- working with a partner
- working on your own.

For example, what questions can be asked on the topic of family?

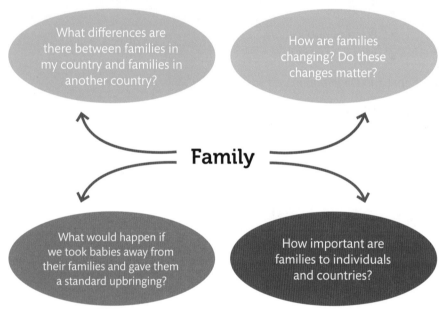

Figure 1a What questions can I ask?

Activity 1

1. Raise questions in a class discussion.

   a) Decide on some rules for class discussions. For example, one rule might be "we must listen to other people's ideas."

   b) "What differences are there between families in my country and another country?" Have a class discussion. What questions can help you? Make a class diagram on the board.

   c) "What would happen if we took babies away from their families and gave them a standard upbringing?" Discuss what you think would happen. How is this question different from part **(b)**?

2. Work with a partner. Start with a one-word topic, e.g. migration. Think of lots of questions together. Draw a diagram like the one above.

More specific questions

In this diagram we have some more specific questions that will help us to search for information and ideas.

How important are families to individuals and countries?

One parent

Who looks after children?

Both parents

Who earns the money?

Grandparents

Who supports education?

No one

What happens to values?

Role models

How does this affect the country?

Attitudes to work

On children

What effect does divorce have?

On the economy

Figure 1b What information do I need?

Activity 2

1. Choose one of the following questions about the topic of sport and recreation. In your class or group decide what information you might need to help you answer it. You could draw a diagram or table to help you.

   - What do national sports say about a country?

   - Is sport only for men?

   - Can darts, motor racing and chess be considered sports?

   - Can international sporting competitions help improve understanding between nations?

2. Choose any other topic. Work in your group to break the topic down into smaller questions. Think about the sort of information you might need to help you answer the questions. Use diagrams or tables to help you.

Rules for class discussions apply in group discussions too! Be respectful and polite to each other. Listening and thinking about what you hear can be more important than talking.

Level 2

Asking lots of questions

You can use diagrams like this to ask questions and break a topic into smaller issues.

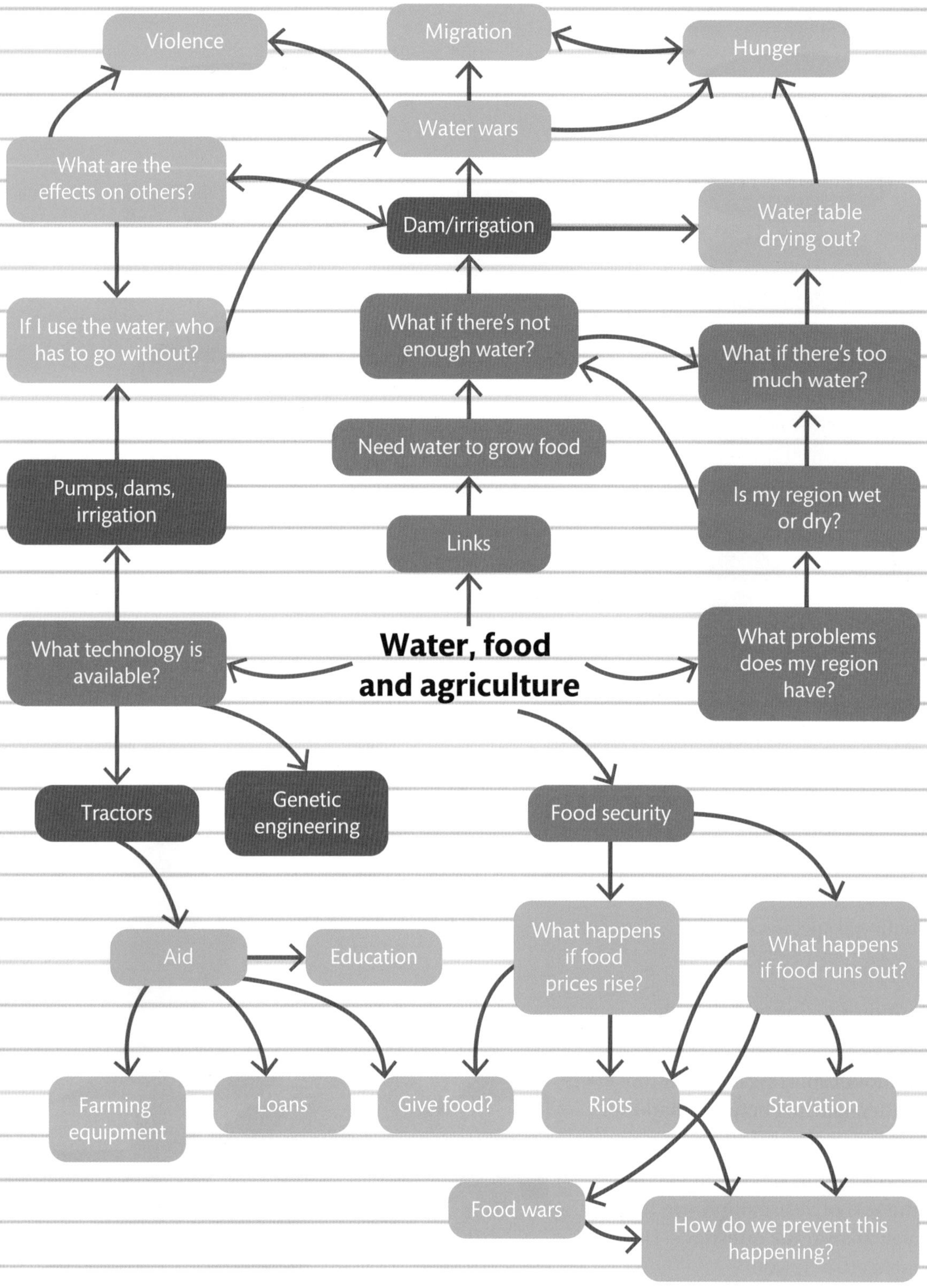

Violence

Migration

Hunger

What are the effects on others?

Water wars

Water table drying out?

Dam/irrigation

If I use the water, who has to go without?

What if there's not enough water?

What if there's too much water?

Need water to grow food

Pumps, dams, irrigation

Is my region wet or dry?

Links

Water, food and agriculture

What technology is available?

What problems does my region have?

Tractors

Genetic engineering

Food security

Aid

Education

What happens if food prices rise?

What happens if food runs out?

Farming equipment

Loans

Give food?

Riots

Starvation

Food wars

How do we prevent this happening?

Figure 1c Some first ideas about the topic "Water, food and agriculture". What other ideas do you have?

Activity 3

1. Look at Figure 1c.

   a) Identify three questions in the diagram that require different kinds of answers – one that needs a fact, one that needs a prediction, and one that needs an *opinion* or *value judgement*.

   b) Which of the questions in Figure 1c is most interesting to you? Give your reasons.

   c) What sort of answers – facts, predictions, opinions, value judgements – does this question require?

   d) What search terms would you use to find information and ideas to help you answer this question? Think of three or four different ways of searching. See which produces the most useful results.

   e) What other questions would you like to ask about the topic "Water, food and agriculture?"

Discussion

1. Discuss the topic "Sustainable living" in class. Ask lots of questions to break the topic into smaller issues.

2. Work in groups of four or five. Choose a topic of your own. Ask lots of questions in your group to break the topic down into smaller issues.

When you are breaking down a big topic, you can use three strategies:

- Ask all the questions you can think of in a class or group discussion and write down as many ideas as possible

- Ask, "what are the really important, key issues?"

- For each idea or key issue, ask, "What are the personal, local/national and global perspectives?"

Activity 4

1. Look at figure 1b on page 9 again.

   a) What are the key issues highlighted here?

   b) Organise the ideas into personal, local/national and global perspectives.

   c) Is there anything you want to add when you think about personal, local/national and global perspectives?

2. Look at the questions you asked about the topic of sustainable living.

   a) What are the key issues?

   b) Organise the ideas into personal, local/national and global perspectives.

   c) Is there anything you want to add when you think about personal, local/national and global perspectives?

3. Look at the questions you asked about your own choice of topic.

   a) What are the key issues?

   b) Organise the ideas into personal, local/national and global perspectives.

   c) Is there anything you want to add when you think about personal, local/national and global perspectives?

Level 3

Planning a line of inquiry

Research is not *only* about collecting as much information as you can find. It's also about planning a line of inquiry which involves asking:

- What are the key issues?
- What are the main problems in this area? Are these problems personal, local/national or global?
- What are the causes and consequences of the problems?
- What are the personal, local/national and global problems and perspectives?
- What are the possibilities? Are they personal, national or global?
- How does this link with what I already know?
- Which bits are most interesting?

Use these questions to guide your search for information. When you find information, try to classify it: is it a key issue or is it unimportant? Is it global or local? Is it a problem or a solution? Is it interesting enough to research more?

Activity 5

1. Work in groups. Write a list of questions to start your thinking on the following topics. Draw diagrams to help you as your ideas develop or you add more questions. Classify the ideas.

   - Unemployment in the Middle East
   - Effects of digital technology on the brain
   - Water wars
   - International drug smuggling

2. Work with a partner. Choose a topic you would like to research. Write a list of questions to start your thinking. Draw diagrams to help you as you follow ideas or add more questions. Classify the ideas.

3. Which specific questions are interesting?

Setting a question

Question:		
Does my question help me to:	**Yes/no**	**How to improve**
Focus		
Develop a line of reasoning (argument and explanation)		
Consider a current problem or issue		
Consider causes and consequences (positive and negative) of the problem/issue		
Consider personal, local/national and global perspectives		
Think of possible solutions/courses of action		
Consider the consequences (positive and negative) of these possible solutions		
Decide on the best course of action		
Answer within the word limit		

Question	Comment
"The Three Gorges Dam."	This is not a question! It won't help you to write a good research report.
"In the long term, is the Three Gorges Dam likely to be beneficial overall?"	This question meets the criteria. It will help you to write a good research report.

Activity 6

1. Use the table to help you decide whether these questions will help you to write a focused report:

   - What are the key issues in poverty and inequality?

   - Should we build a new airport in my area?

   - What is the quality of life like in Delhi, Mexico, Hanoi, or Dubai?

   - What are the effects of urbanisation on people's quality of life? How can we deal with these effects?

   - How can we ensure that all children are vaccinated against serious diseases?

   - How can we create more jobs in my region?

   - What were the causes of the global economic crisis in 2008?

   - Should people in developed countries give their old computers to people in developing countries?

   - What is the best way to help struggling communities (in my region/in developing countries)?

   - Should we punish criminals?

   - What are the best ways to deal with international crimes such as smuggling?

   - The benefits of trade and aid.

   - In times of economic recession, should governments reduce the amount of aid they give to foreign countries?

   - What sorts of aid are there?

Discussion

Can you improve the questions you thought about in Activity 5?

2.1 Identifying information and trends

Level ①

Facts, opinions, predictions, and judgements

Four very important kinds of information and ideas are:

- facts
- opinions
- predictions
- value judgements.

Facts are pieces of information that are true. You can *verify* a fact – that is, you can find out whether it is true or not.

Opinions are beliefs, views, or judgements. You can disagree with an opinion but you can't check whether it is true.

Predictions are attempts to foresee or say what will happen in the future. We can't tell if predictions are accurate until the event happens, however we can think about whether they are likely or unlikely to happen.

Value judgements are a particular kind of opinion. They deal with values about what is good and bad, right and wrong. We can't check whether value judgements are true, but we can think about whether they are reasonable and whether we accept them (and why).

Activity ①

1. Are the following statements facts, opinions, predictions or value judgements? Explain why.

   a) There have been single-parent families for a long time.

   b) Single-parent families can be just as good for children as two-parent families.

   c) Sport should be fair.

   d) There are 11 people on a cricket team.

   e) It's selfish of humans to destroy natural habitats.

   f) Fighting shouldn't be part of the Olympic Games.

   g) Education is the most important part of a child's life.

   h) Brazil will win the football World Cup next year.

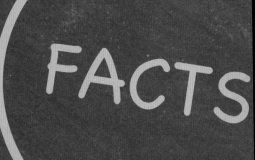

The International Labour Organisation recently released its 2015 *World Employment and Social Outlook* (WESO) report, and presented the findings to the United Nations.

The report finds that the worldwide unemployment rate among 15–24 year-olds (currently at 13 percent, or 74 million youths) is set to rise. Ekkehard Ernst, Chief of the ILO's Job-friendly Macro-economic Policies Team, said that slow economic growth was to blame for expected rises in youth unemployment rates.

> Does it matter whether you understand "Job-friendly Macro-economic Policies Team"? Can you understand enough without this?

OPINIONS

@Saira Samphire

This is very bad news for me. I have been looking for a job for over a year now. I have good qualifications, but there are no jobs.

@Hungry Fox

If young people wanted to work, they would find jobs. Their lives are too easy.

Activity 2

1. "The report finds that the worldwide unemployment rate among 15–24 year-olds (currently at 13 percent, or 74 million youths) is set to rise." Is this fact, opinion or prediction? Explain your answer.

2. Give one possible cause for the likely rises in youth unemployment rates.

3. Give one fact from @Saira Samphire.

4. Give one opinion from @Hungry Fox.

Level 2

Information from charts and graphs

Understanding information from charts and graphs is mostly about careful reading.

- Read the information on the axes.
- Read the captions.
- Is this a trend, showing how one thing has changed?
- Is this a comparison?

For example, the graph in Figure 2 shows the trend of unemployment. It shows how one thing – unemployment – changes over time. The graph about global youth employment shows a comparison. It compares the percentage of unemployed youth in different places at the same time.

Figure 1

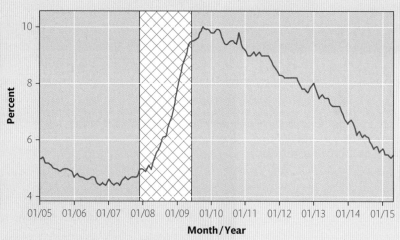

Source: US Bureau of Labor Statistics, Current Population Survey

Figure 2

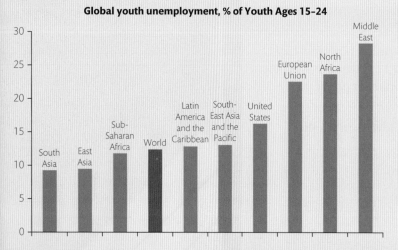

Source: ILO's *Global Employment Trends for Youth 2013* report. Regional data are from ILO's 2012 preliminary estimates; U.S. and E.U. data are from the OECD's second quarter 2012 data.

Activity 3

1. Look at Figure 1.

   a) When did unemployment peak in the USA?

   b) Describe the trends in unemployment in the USA between 2005 and 2015.

   c) "More people were unemployed in 2015 than in 2007." Is this true? Explain your answer.

2. Look at Figure 2.

   a) Figure 2 shows a trend of rising unemployment. Is this true? Explain your answer.

   b) What do you think are the likely causes of high youth unemployment rates in the Middle East?

   c) What do you think are the probable consequences of high youth unemployment rates?

   d) Can you find other graphs, charts or information about global youth unemployment rates now?

Level 3

Sometimes a passage does not give us enough information. We have to ask what else we need to know.

Activity 4

List what other information we need to know in these two passages.

1. Genetic engineering can make plants resistant to pests, cold, drought… These GE crops can save us from food shortages. The green movement should therefore stop its opposition to GE crops.

2. John and Jasvinder are setting up a company to manufacture environmentally friendly products. We should invest in their company.

Activity 5

1. Look at your own research. Identify facts, opinions, predictions and value judgements.

2. Look at any graphs, charts and tables in your research. Check that you have read the details carefully. Look for trends and comparisons.

3. Look through your research.

   a) Generally, what other information do you need to know?

   b) Are there any specific passages where you need more information to help you agree with a conclusion?

Reflection

- How has your ability to identify information improved?

- What new skills have you learned?

- Are there any aspects of this that you struggle with?

- How can you improve?

357.56
463.11
105.98
632.87
854.99
143.08
375.63
586.37
230.95
941.33
768.54
579.74

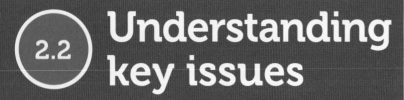

2.2 Understanding key issues

Level ①

Issues

Here are some examples of questions which raise issues, and questions which simply require facts:

> **"What should we do if drought/flooding means there is not enough food in my region?"**

This question does not raise an issue. The answer is factual and you do you not to debate it.

> **"How can we avoid water wars in dry regions?"**

This question does raise an issue. It's a real problem that can't be answered with facts. There isn't an easy answer, so there is a need for discussion and debate to find a solution.

This question does raise an issue. It's a real problem that needs to be discussed so that solutions can be found.

> **"Is my region wet or dry?"**

> **"How do you dig a well?"**

This question does not raise an issue. The answer is factual.

Activity ①

1. Which of these questions raise issues?

   a) What do we need fuel/energy for?

   b) How should we help migrants to integrate with society?

   c) Why does it matter if the coral reefs die?

   d) Is genetic engineering the best way to ensure food security?

   e) Is hydro-electricity efficient?

   f) Is it reasonable for developing nations to keep using oil to boost their economies, even though this contributes to global warming?

   g) Could we use some of the plants in the rainforest for medicines?

Language

An issue is a topic or problem that can be debated or discussed. Issues are usually matters of opinion, value judgement, or prediction. Facts are useful for making sure that the debate is realistic, but on their own, they are not issues.

Level 2

Going beyond facts to issues

There may be times when the questions you can think of are factual, and not about issues. Asking further questions can help you to move from the facts to the issues:

- Why do I need to know?
- What consequences could come from this fact?

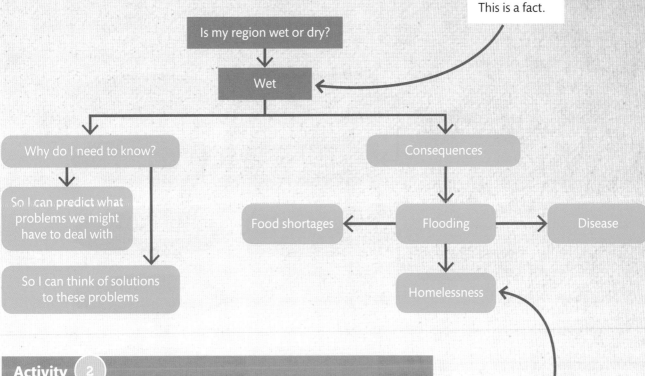

This is a fact.

Is my region wet or dry?

Wet

Why do I need to know?

So I can predict what problems we might have to deal with

So I can think of solutions to these problems

Consequences

Food shortages ← Flooding → Disease

Homelessness

One possible issue is how we cope with homelessness due to flooding.

Activity 2

1. For each of the following facts
   - ask why you need to know the fact
   - ask what the consequences could be.

   What issues do these questions lead you to? Draw diagrams if it helps you.

   a) We need fuel for factories, computers, travelling, lighting, and keeping our homes warm.

   b) Hydro-electricity is very efficient.

   c) Business people often have video conferences with partners around the world.

   d) The rainforest is the source of many plants that are used to make medication.

   e) Average salary increases with education.

Level 3

Key Issues

Key issues are the really important problems that need to be discussed. Some of the things that help to influence the importance of a problem are:

- consequences
- urgency
- severity
- perspectives.

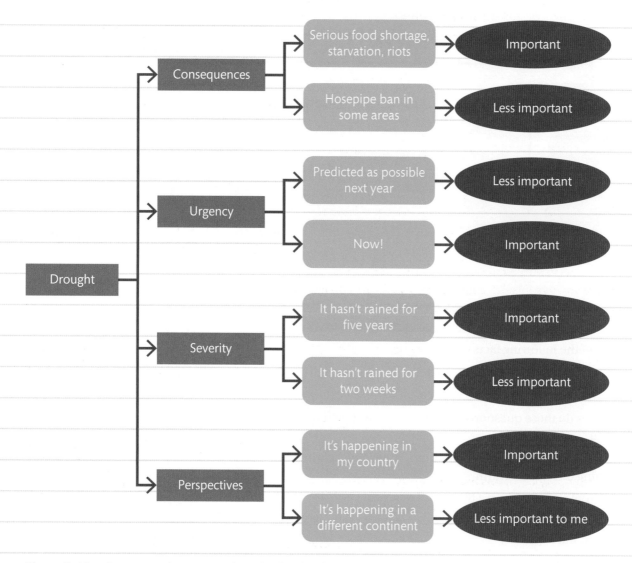

Figure 3 How important is a severe drought that leads to starvation in another country?

Activity 3

1. Consider the following facts.

   - What are the issues that come from these questions?

   - Consider these issues in terms of consequences, urgency, severity and perspectives. Which issues are the most important? What are your reasons?

     a) There has been a long running civil war in Syria.

     b) Youth unemployment is high around the world.

     c) Many young people spend more than six hours every day using digital technology.

     d) The polar ice caps are melting.

     e) Globalisation is leading to cities and cultures around the world becoming increasingly similar.

2. Look back at the diagram in Level 2 on p.23. Think about these issues in terms of consequences, urgency, severity and perspectives. Draw diagrams to show which issues are the most important? What are your reasons?

3. Look back at the questions you considered in Activity 2 on p.23 in terms of consequences, urgency, severity and perspectives. Draw diagrams. Which issues are most important? What are your reasons?

4. Look at the questions you have thought of during your own research in terms of consequences, urgency, severity and perspectives. Draw diagrams. Which are the most important? What are your reasons?

5. Are your answers influenced by the country you live in? For example, if you live in a dry country, are you more worried about problems related to drought than too much water?

6. Can you see how conflicts can arise from different national perspectives? Give examples of some possible conflicts.

Reflection

- How has your ability to understand key issues improved?
- What new skills have you learned?
- Are there any aspects of this that you struggle with?
- How can you improve?

KEY ISSUES

CONSEQUENCES

URGENCY

SEVERITY

PERSPECTIVES

2.3 Identifying causes and consequences

Level 1

One key skill is being able to read information and identify causes and consequences in that information.

Causes and consequences

Cause
Selima throws the ball

→

Consequence
The ball flies through the air

→

Further consequence
The ball breaks the window

You can also look at clues in the language to help you.

In this example, Selima did not intend to break the window, but she did cause the window to break. The ball only moves <u>because</u> Selima throws it. Selima's throw is the cause of the ball's movement, and the ball's movement is the cause of the broken window. The broken window is the consequence.

Look at what makes sense. It makes sense to say that Selima throwing the ball causes the window to break. It does not make sense to say that the window breaking causes Selima to throw the ball.

Language

Words that help to identify causes:

because   **as**   **since**

Words that help to identify consequences:

therefore   **so**   **that's why**   **as a result**

Key terms

Cause: something which produces a result; a person or thing which is responsible for a situation, action or event.

Consequence: an effect which follows logically from a cause; something which happens because of another situation, action or event.

Activity 1

1. **a)** Identify the causes and consequences in the following. Draw diagrams if it helps you.

   i) Dmitri stole $1 million. Dmitri went to jail.

   ii) Rich nations do better in international sporting events than poor nations because they can afford to find, develop, and train elite athletes.

   iii) People are no longer having as many children as they used to, therefore the nation's population is ageing.

   iv) There have been protests and riots because there is 50% unemployment amongst young men.

   v) Frank got a bad mark in his maths exam. So he believed he was bad at maths. So he stopped trying. So he became bad at maths. So when Frank opened his own business, he made a mess of the accounts. So his business failed.

   vi) Ilke got a bad mark in her maths exam. So she worked hard for her next maths exam. So she got a better mark. So she realised that hard work could lead to success.

   vii) People are living longer lives than they used to. They are also having fewer children. This means that a small number of adults are providing for a large number of older people.

   b) Fill in the gaps using 'because' or 'therefore'.

   a) My parents have worked hard to support me through school, _____ I will be happy to support them in their old age.

   b) Lots of people are migrating from country X to country Y _____ there is a war in country X.

   c) Lots of people are migrating from country X to country Y, _____ the international community must help country Y to provide for the migrants.

   d) I am not going to commit a crime _____ I don't want to go to jail.

   e) _____ we are losing habitats fast, we must take action to save species from extinction.

Possible consequences

Another important skill is identifying possible consequences of an event or situation. You can't do this just by reading – you have to think about it.

For example, Selima has thrown a ball through the window – what do you think the possible consequences of this are?

Activity 2

1. **a)** What might be the consequences of the following events? Discuss the possibilities in groups.

   - Imran put a frog in Selima's bed.
   - Petra says to the teacher, "Can we move onto something interesting, please?"
   - You trial for your national football team.
   - You work really hard at school for the next two years.
   - You spend more time doing household chores with your parents.
   - Your grandparents come to live with you.

   b) Are some of these consequences more likely than others?

   c) What other factors would you need to take into account? For example, are you good at football, and how will this affect the consequences of the third event?

Level 2

Complex causes and consequences

Think back to the example of Selima throwing a ball and breaking the window in Level 1. This seems like a simple chain of cause and consequence. It seems as if Selima throwing the ball is the cause, and the broken window is the consequence. However, the reality is more complex.

Selima's mother, Dr. Khan, sees only a broken window and a ball. Dr. Khan does not know that Selima's friend has stolen her phone. Dr. Khan does know that Selima's brother Imran loves cricket, and Selima thinks ball games are stupid. So Dr. Khan believes that Imran threw the ball. She shouts at Imran and tells him he's a bad boy. Imran thinks this is unreasonable so he puts a frog in Selima's bed.

Friend steals phone → Selima is upset → Selima throws ball

?

Ball breaks window   Dr. Khan's beliefs about her children

?

Dr. Khan shouts at Imran   Imran's mind

Imran puts a frog in Selima's bed

Can we say that Selima's friend caused Imran to put a frog in Selima's bed? There is a chain of causes, but these two events are quite a long way apart in that chain. And Selima and Imran could have reacted differently. So this is only a very indirect cause.

We don't know what caused Dr. Khan's beliefs about her children, or why Imran thinks putting a frog in his sister's bed is a good idea. We also don't know what caused Selima's friend to steal her phone. We can now see that what seemed like a simple cause and consequences is actually quite complex, with lots of contributory, partial causes.

Activity 3

1. Draw diagrams showing the causes, consequences and further consequences in these situations:

1 Ari and Harjanti Budiman are poor but have high hopes for their children, Ridwan and Liana. Ari is offered a government contract logging in the rainforest. He thinks that cutting down ancient trees is wrong, but the money allows him to send Ridwan and Liana to school. Ridwan and Liana do well at school, and eventually get good jobs with good money. However, logging in the rainforest has caused habitat loss and species extinction.

What would do if you were Ari? Why?

2 Deforestation, farming, overgrazing and development all result in irreversible changes such as soil compaction, erosion, desertification, or the alteration of local climatic conditions. Such land-use practices lead to habitat loss.

Some of these words are quite technical, and you might not be sure what they mean. Can you use other clues in the language to help you work out which are causes and which are consequences?

Discussion

Sometimes one action can have good and bad consequences. How do you think you should decide what to do if your actions might have both good and bad consequences?

Level 3

Possible causes

You may also need to think about possible causes. You can't do this by reading – you have to think about it.

For example, Jasper got a bad mark in his maths test – what might be the causes of this?

Activity

1. **a)** What do you think caused the following events? Do you think the causes are simple or complex? Discuss the possibilities in groups.

   i) Khalila got a detention.

   ii) Santiago's parents got a divorce.

   iii) Emily's grandparents came to live with her and her family.

   iv) Brazil did not win the football World Cup.

   b) How would you try to find out the real causes of these events?

> Think about what you have learned about research skills to help you answer (b). It's important to use all your skills together.

Recognising causes and consequences in more complex texts

When you are doing your own research, you will have to recognise causes and consequences in more complex texts. You can use the same skills that you used in simple contexts.

Activity

1. Identify the causes and consequences in the article on the next page. Draw a diagram to help you.

Myths make measles soar

Measles is exploding because parents are afraid to have their children vaccinated. That's the message emerging from the US and Germany this week. Anti-vaccination scaremongering is believed to be driving the outbreaks.

By the beginning of February, 486 cases had been reported so far this year to the Robert Koch institute in Berlin, which monitors the spread of infectious disease in Germany – up from 446 cases for the whole of 2014. In the US, the Centers for Disease Control in Atlanta, Georgia had reported 121 cases in the same time frame.

In both countries, health professionals are blaming parents who reject the triple MMR vaccine for their children, which protects against measles, mumps and rubella.

According to Mobeen Rathore, a member of the American Academy of Pediatrics' committee on infectious diseases, the upsurge is a sign that myths about vaccines need to be dispelled globally, including any link with autism. "We need to increase rates by educating people and having stronger laws that require childhood immunisations…" says Rathore.

In Germany, 344 of the cases have been in Berlin. "The main causes are low immunisation rates in toddlers, adolescents and younger adults, which results in missing 'herd immunity' for children too young to be vaccinated," says Dorothea Matysiak-Klose of the Robert Koch Institute.

–New Scientist, 14 February 2015 p.6

MMR
Measles Mumps
Rubella
Vaccine

20 ml   RX Only

> Think about what makes sense and use clues in the language.
> Learn to ignore irrelevant material and focus on the bits you need.

Hint:

- Think about your search terms.
- Make structured notes of no more than 100 words. You may use diagrams.
- Make a note of which ideas are related to which sources and keep a list of sources.

Activity 6

1. Choose one of the following issues and research its causes and consequences.

   - The Great Barrier Reef is dying.
   - Inequality is increasing
   - Cholera is killing people
   - Children from poor backgrounds do not do well at school.
   - People are migrating from less developed parts of the world to more developed parts of the world.

> Think about how you can use your research skills to help you. You will learn and work most effectively if you use different skills together.

2.4 Identifying and evaluating possible courses of action

Level 1

Who can take action?

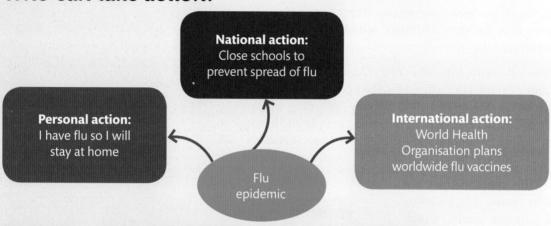

Personal action:
I have flu so I will stay at home

National action:
Close schools to prevent spread of flu

International action:
World Health Organisation plans worldwide flu vaccines

Flu epidemic

Activity 1

1. Your school is depressing and grey. The buildings are old, there are cracks in the walls and the paint is peeling. The computers are twentieth-century and the science labs are nineteenth-century. The toilets are always disgusting, and there is litter everywhere. There is an increasing problem with bad behaviour. Suggest appropriate actions for each of these people/groups of people:

   a) students
   b) teachers
   c) management
   d) parents
   e) government
   f) United Nations

2. There is a problem in your local area with gangs. Suggest appropriate actions for each of these people/groups of people:

   a) local children
   b) local youth leaders
   c) parents
   d) police
   e) social workers
   f) politicians

3. Look back at 1 and 2. Are there any other groups of people who could take action? What actions could they take?

4. We are using too much fossil fuel.

   a) Who can take action?
   b) What should those actions be?

Level 2

Possible consequences of future actions.

Activity 2

1. There is corruption in FIFA, the international governing body of football. Many of the leaders are arrested, others resign. What are the possible consequences of each of the following actions?

   a) Johann decides never to go to another international football match.

   b) Karim continues watching soccer matches.

   c) Tomas and Justina set up a campaign for fair football.

   d) A national government calls for a review of all FIFA's decisions in the last ten years.

   e) A major sporting broadcaster decides not to broadcast international football matches until FIFA has fixed its corruption.

2. Can you think of any other personal, local/national or global actions that could be taken?

3. Look back at the activities in Level 1 on the previous page.

   a) Do you agree with your decisions about who could take which action?

   b) What do you think the consequences of these actions will be?

Over time your thinking skills should develop and so your decisions may change.

Level 3

Weighing up possible consequences

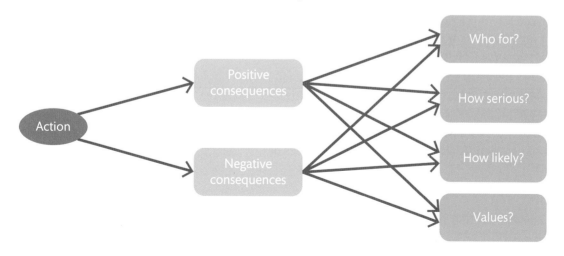

Activity 3

1. Zaki has to decide whether to drive a short distance on a cold, wet morning or whether to walk. He is worried that he will catch a cold and miss work. But he also worries about air pollution and climate change.

   a) What are the other probably or likely consequences of Zaki driving/walking? Are they mostly positive or negative?

   b) How likely is it that he will get a cold?

   c) How serious is a cold?

   d) How likely is it that Zaki driving will contribute to air pollution?

   e) How likely is it that Zaki driving will contribute to climate change?

   f) How big is Zaki's contribution to air pollution and climate change likely to be?

   g) What is more serious – Zaki getting a cold or Zaki contributing to air pollution and climate change?

   h) Is it wrong for Zaki to think his health is more important than the environment?

   i) What if Zaki is a government minister? Does this make his health seem more important?

   j) What if everyone made the same choices as Zaki? Would this change your perspective?

   k) What if Zaki is already seriously ill? How does this change your perspective?

   l) What if it is you making the decision? How does this change your perspective?

2. Your friend has asked for your help with a serious matter, but won't say what it is until you meet. Your friend seems very upset. Helping your friend means you will miss a football match.

   Consider possible and likely consequences of helping your friend and not helping your friend. Weigh them up using the questions in the diagram to help you.

3. Can one serious consequence sometimes outweigh several consequences? Think of examples.

4. You are a doctor. You have limited money. You can either treat one patient with terminal cancer, who is likely to die within six months. Or you can treat twenty children with less serious illnesses.

   a) What decision do you make?

   b) Does this decision change if you are a health authority?

5. Go back to your answers from Activities 1 and 2.

   a) Weigh up the consequences of the actions you considered using the questions in the diagram

   b) Decide on the best course of action.

   c) Write a case to support that course of action. Explain your thinking.

6. Consider the situations in your current research.

   a) What are the key problems?

   b) What are the possible personal, national and global actions?

   c) What are the probably consequences of those actions?

   d) Weigh up the consequences.

   e) Decide on the best course of action.

   f) Write a case to support that course of action. Explain your thinking.

Reflection

- How has your ability to identify and evaluate possible courses of action improved?

- What new skills have you learned?

- Are there any aspects of this that you struggle with?

- How can you improve?

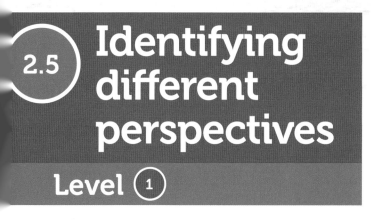

Identifying different perspectives

2.5

Level ①

Local, national and global perspectives

Most actions and events can be seen from personal, local/national and global perspectives. Even personal choices can be part of the cause of global events.

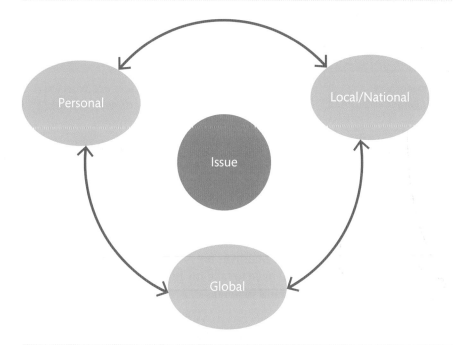

Personal perspectives: everyone has their own personal perspective. It is influenced by local and national perspectives, but also by the reflective thinking that each individual does.

Local perspectives can be related to a small part of a country, especially when there are differences within a country. Local perspectives can also relate to a region which is bigger than a country and which can share a common perspective on some issues: for example, Europe or North Africa and the Middle East would share local, regional perspectives.

National perspectives are related to a particular country as a whole. National perspectives include: issues relating to government policy, what is best for the country, or the way in which the people of that country see things.

Global perspectives are related to the world as a whole.

For every question in GP, we can think of Local, National and Global Perspectives. For example:

Local: Good for families and children in areas where parents struggle to pay for education. In the long term will benefit the local economy if workers are educated.

But what if educated young people leave the local area for the city?

Should education be free for all?

National: Who will pay? This policy will be expensive in the short term.

In the long term, an educated population will be good for the country.

Global: Children everywhere in the world should have the same opportunities, whether they are rich or poor, eastern or western.

Can you think of any more points to make about free education for all? Are your points local, national or global?

Activity

1. Think of local, national and global perspectives on these questions. You can think of points, questions, causes or consequences. Draw diagrams if it helps.

   a) Should I go to my training for the national Judo team tonight or revise for my exam?

   b) Should the government give extra money to married couples?

   c) Is it acceptable to eat meat from animals that have been kept in poor conditions?

   d) Should the country refuse to import wood from cleared rainforest?

   e) Should parents encourage their children to train hard at a sport?

   f) Should I spend more money to buy an ethically sourced engagement ring?

   g) Should we welcome refugees from war zones?

2. Do these comments express local, national or global perspectives? Do some of them have mixed perspectives?

   a) We have plenty of oil in our country, and we need to use it to develop our economy. Why should we use less because developing countries, who are already rich, are worried about climate change? Poverty will kill our people faster than global warming.

   b) Even a small rise in sea level will flood us in the Maldives, because 80% of our islands is less than 1m above sea level. People in the West have got to stop burning oil to make their lives more convenient – it's destroying my home.

   c) The Maldives are going to be flooded? Huh, I'll have to take my holidays on a Caribbean island instead.

   d) The UN has to work with national governments to reduce ecosystem destruction around the world. These ecosystems provide global benefits – for example the rainforest provides oxygen for us all to breathe. They also provide local benefits. Natural ecosystems such as forests, wetlands and coastal systems can provide barriers that prevent natural disasters from harming as many people. They also provide water, wood, food and medicines, which can help communities recover from natural disasters.

Level 2

Local, national and global perspectives

Activity 2

1. Fill in the box A, B and C in the diagram to show which are local, national and global perspectives.

2. Put the comments below into the right boxes on the diagram.

   a) Should the international community send aid? If so, what sort of aid?

   b) No direct effects on me – unless my Ethiopian coffee becomes more expensive.

Should I donate to a charity? What duties do I have to people less fortunate than me?

   c) Riots or civil war (is Ethiopia politically unstable?) leading to human rights abuses of local people?

   d) Ethiopian people? What effects will the drought have on local people? Rising food prices? Starvation?

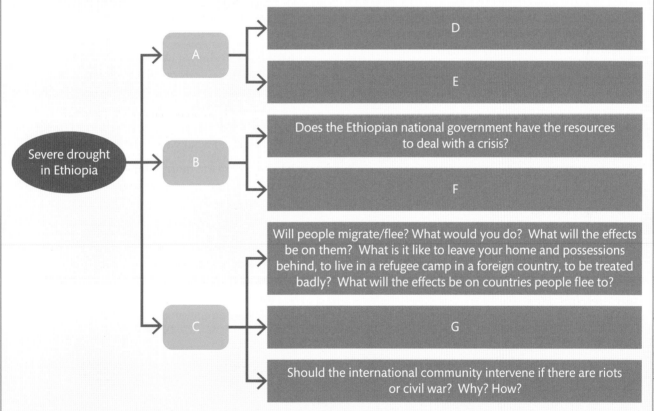

Figure 1 Different perspectives on a local drought.

Different cultural perspectives

Cultural perspectives are attitudes, values, beliefs and ideas that are shared by groups of people. Cultural perspectives can affect the way in which individuals behave.

Some cultural perspectives are specific to a particular nation. For example, Chinese people generally share a set of beliefs and values which are different from the beliefs and values which people in the UAE or Germany share.

Sometimes, though, a cultural perspective can link groups of people in different countries. For example, caring more about the environment than about money is a particular cultural perspective which is international.

Activity 3

1. Do you think the statements in the table are most likely to be part of the general cultural perspective shared by Europeans, by Arabs or by Chinese?

	European	Arabic	Chinese
Social stability is more important than individual freedom.			
The government should be separate from religious institutions.			
People should cover most of their body when they are in public.			
Honour and reputation are extremely important.			
Tradition and authority are revered.			

2. How would you describe the cultural perspectives of these people?

    a) I have studied at university in Oxford and Singapore, and travelled to most continents. It's really upsetting to see the way people live in the poorest parts of the world. I think that those of us who have opportunities in life should do what we can to help others.

    b) There are too many immigrants coming. They are going to swamp us – there will be nothing left of our way of life. Life's already hard for us. It's going to get harder if all these immigrants take our jobs.

    c) It's our responsibility to ensure that democracy reaches every corner of the world, and to keep the peace between less developed nations.

Level 3

Complex perspectives

Activity 4

1. Ethiopia wants to build a dam on the Nile near the border with Sudan and upstream of Egypt. What are the different local, national and global perspectives on this? What different cultural perspectives on this can you think of? Use internet searches and diagrams to help you.

2. Globalisation means that it is easier for people to move from one country to another to get work or sell products. What are the different local, national and global perspectives on this? What different cultural perspectives on this can you think of? Use internet searches and diagrams to help you.

3. Half of Australia's Great Barrier Reef, the world's largest coral reef ecosystem, disappeared between 1985 and 2012. What are the different local, national and global perspectives on this? What different cultural perspectives on this can you think of? Use internet searches and diagrams to help you.

4. Oil is getting harder to find and extract. This means that prices are rising. What are the different local, national and global perspectives on this? What different cultural perspectives on this can you think of? Use internet searches and diagrams to help you.

Reflection

- How has your ability to identify different perspectives improved?
- What new skills have you learned?
- Are there any aspects of this that you struggle with?
- How can you improve?

3.1 Questioning knowledge claims

Level 1

Activity 1

1. What can you remember about facts, opinions, predictions and value judgements?

2. Can we really claim to *know* any of the following?

   a) Malaysia is the best country to visit if you like beautiful scenery.

   b) Hong Kong is a Special Administrative Region of China.

   c) There are some beautiful buildings in the United Arab Emirates.

   d) Pakistan is going to develop considerably over the next fifty years.

   e) Vietnam should invest significantly in preserving its traditions.

Hint: You can verify a fact. Go back to section 1.1. on page 6 to remind yourself.

Quality of reasoning in source materials

When an author is expressing an opinion, or persuading the audience to accept a proposal, you can also ask if their reasoning works well. Think about:

Has the author given reasons for their opinion or proposal?

Are the reasons based on strong evidence?

Has the author used emotion instead of reason to make you agree?

Do the reasons support the opinion logically?

Are there gaps between the reasons and opinion?

Activity 2

1. Does the reasoning work well in the opinions given below? You have already thought about the local, national and global perspective of these opinions in Skills Section 2.5. Concentrate now on whether they are logical.

1 "We have plenty of oil in our country, and we need to use it to develop our economy. Why should we use less because developed countries, which are already rich, are worried about climate change? Poverty will kill our people faster than global warming."

2 "Even a small rise in sea level will flood us in the Maldives, because 80% of our islands are less than 1m above sea level. People in the West have got to stop burning oil to make their lives more convenient – it's destroying my home."

3 "The Maldives are going to be flooded? Huh, I'll have to take my holidays on a Caribbean island instead."

4 "The UN has to work with national governments to reduce ecosystem destruction around the world. These ecosystems provide global benefits – for example, the rainforest provides oxygen for us all to breathe. They also provide local benefits. Natural ecosystems such as forests, wetlands and coastal systems can provide barriers that prevent natural disasters from harming as many people. They also provide water, wood, food and medicines, which can help communities recover from natural disasters."

Level 2

Activity 3

1. Consider the values below. Do you agree with them? Give your reasons. Are some of them reasonable even if you disagree? Can you think of circumstances in which they should or should not apply?

   a) An eye for an eye, a tooth for a tooth.

   b) Killing is wrong.

   c) People should work for what they have.

   d) There is nothing wrong with some people being richer than others.

   e) Some people don't deserve to be helped.

   f) People are equal.

   g) The punishment for murder should always be death.

   h) Employers should treat their staff well.

   i) The law should protect all workers from bad employers.

   j) We have a duty to help those less fortunate than ourselves.

Activity 4

1. Read the passage.

   > Aid leads to dependency, corruption and waste. People who are given free things do not value them as much as people who work for what they have. Furthermore, giving people free things results in them believing they cannot achieve for themselves or that they have no reason to strive for success. Trade can lead to booming economies, higher unemployment and benefits for both developed and developing countries. So we should clearly promote trade not aid.

   How well does this passage reason? Think about:

   a) predicted consequences

   b) values

   c) how logical it is, and

   d) how emotive it is.

Activity 5

1. Are the following passages examples of good reasoning?

 According to the OECD, development aid fell by 4% in 2012, following a 2% fall in 2011. This shows that countries have recognised that aid isn't needed any more.

 We can't go on pouring billions of dollars into the pockets of foreign dictators who don't respect human rights. We are slashing the budgets for the armed forces, health and education in our own country. Projects to get our young people into work or training are being cut. So let's welcome the proposal to use aid money to get our national companies investing in infrastructure in developing countries instead of just giving it to corrupt governments.

 New technology is supposed to create employment, but I don't believe it. They brought new machines and robots into our factory, and now most of us are unemployed. We want to work, but they don't need us. What are ordinary people supposed to do? We're trapped between employers who'd rather use robots, a government that tells us to find work but doesn't help us, and people who believe we're lazy because we haven't got jobs.

Level 3

Activity 6

1. What strategies do you already know for questioning information, ideas, perspectives and sources? Write a list.

2. What aspects of questioning information, ideas, perspectives and sources do you need to improve on?

3. How will you improve?

More ways of being illogical

As you have learned, one important way of evaluating the quality of someone's reasoning is to ask:

Is it logical?

Look out for reasoning that isn't logical. All of the following are ways of being *illogical*:

- generalising
- poor use of facts
- contradiction and inconsistency
- not answering someone's argument
- attacking the arguer rather than the argument, and
- restricting the options.

> If you think someone's reasoning *is* logical, point that out too, and explain why.

Generalising

Generalising is moving from a small amount of evidence or from one example to a general claim. For example,

> That footballer spat in the referee's face. This just shows that all footballers are badly behaved, disrespectful and a bad influence on young people.

Here, there is one example of a footballer behaving badly, and it is used to make a general claim about all footballers. But this is illogical. There are many footballers who do behave well, and we can't judge their behaviour by one badly behaved footballer.

43

Poor use of facts

You have learned how important it is to support your opinions with facts and evidence. It is tempting to think that including facts and evidence is enough, but they have to be well used. We have to think about what the facts and evidence really mean. Let's look at two different uses of the same piece of evidence:

"About 75% of Hindus and Buddhists in America celebrate Christmas. This shows that traditions are completely meaningless and should be abandoned."

There is no logical connection between the fact given and the conclusion drawn from it. The conclusion is too extreme – there is no way that a single statistic could give support to such an extreme conclusion. This is very poor use of evidence.

This use of the fact is much more thoughtful. By exploring the reasons why Hindus and Buddhists celebrate Christmas, the writer has gained some understanding of what actually underlies the statistic. This allows a more meaningful interpretation of it. In addition, the conclusion here is a suggestion rather than an extreme claim. Of course, you could still argue against the interpretation and the conclusion – but you can't say that it is totally illogical, like the first example!

"About 75% of Hindus and Buddhists in America celebrate Christmas. They say that it is an opportunity to enjoy time with their own families and to share an experience with their Christian friends. So it looks as if sharing celebrations is beneficial. We could therefore consider encouraging Americans to join in with celebrations such as Diwali."

Contradiction and inconsistency

Sometimes people contradict themselves in their arguments. Contradiction is saying two (or more) things which are directly opposite (to each other). For example, let's look at two statements made by the same politician to different audiences:

1 Every primary age child should learn a second language because this is the age when you are best able to learn languages.

2 We should not be burdening 5, 6 or 7 year olds with learning other people's languages. They need to concentrate on mastering their own language at this tender age.

These statements are contradictory. It is not possible that all primary age children (ages 5 – 11) should learn a second language if 5 – 7 year olds should not learn a second language.

Inconsistency occurs when:

- Two (or more) things can't both be true at the same time.
- You change your perspective or view (without good reason). This is a random sort of change of perspective, often jumping about without thought. It is different from changing your mind because you've been persuaded by good reasons, or because you are trying to see someone else's point of view.

Let's look at some examples:

Statement 1: "We in Country Y support a peaceful outcome in the conflict between our neighbours, Country X and Country Z."

Statement 2: "Country Y is selling guns to Country X and tanks to Country Z."

These two statements cannot both be true, so they are logically inconsistent. You could say that it is illogical to claim that both of these statements are true.

Witness 1 and Witness 2 give contradictory accounts. Witness 1 states that the white car drove into the back of the red car which is the direct opposite of Witness 2's account (that the red car reversed into the white car).

Witness 1's account is inconsistent. If the witness was getting their phone out to text, they were presumably looking at the phone for at least some of the time, and not watching carefully.

Witness 1: "Yes Officer, I saw everything that happened. I was watching very carefully. I clearly saw the white car drive into the back of the red car, just as I was getting my phone out to text my sister."

Witness 2: "I was about the cross the road. The white car was driving along carefully, slowing down to stop at the lights. Then the red car reversed out of a side road, straight into the front of the white car."

Discussion

Which witness do you think is more reliable based on the evidence you have? What other questions would you want to ask the witnesses to find out if their accounts are reliable?

Not answering someone's argument

When people are having a serious discussion, they often use arguments and explanations to support their views. One really important skill here is answering the other person's arguments and points. Getting this wrong is another way of being illogical. Look out for attempts to counter an argument with answers that are just contradictions, disagreements or just don't make sense.

When you are showing that you disagree with a different point of view, make sure that you are answering the arguments, not just disagreeing with them or ignoring them.

Let's look at two different responses to an argument:

Argument: We should introduce Chinese lessons into schools so that our young people are prepared for the future. China is going to be an increasingly important economic and political power.

Response 1: We should teach Spanish. Spanish is easy to learn.

Comment: Response 1 is just a disagreement, and a reason that is irrelevant to the economic argument. If we need to learn Chinese for economic reasons, it is illogical to suggest that we should learn Spanish instead because it's easy.

Response 2: This would be a good idea, but we might have problems finding enough qualified Chinese teachers.

Comment: Response 2 is more logical. It suggests a practical problem with the proposal put forward in the argument. It does actually answer the argument.

> Response 3: The Chinese should learn English.

Comment: Response 3 is merely a disagreement, not an answer to the argument.

> Response 4: Actually, China's economy is declining at the moment, and economic predictions suggest that China will not grow as much or become as economically powerful as we thought. So the case for learning Chinese isn't so strong.

Comment: Response 4 addresses the prediction made in the argument about China's increase in power. It answers the argument by showing how it might not work if the prediction does not come true. Of course, we can't be sure which prediction is going to come true, so we could argue against this response, but we can't say that it is illogical.

Attacking the arguer not the argument

Another way of being illogical when you are having a discussion is to attack the person you are arguing against instead of answering their argument. Let's look at an example:

Language

A **pacifist** is someone who believes in peaceful negotiation and opposes war.

> Argument: We should stop fighting and start negotiating. We have lost too many of our people. Our nation is slowly dying with this war. Our lives and our futures are more important than a small strip of barren land.

Response 1: We must ignore the bleating of inadequate, fearful pacifists and fight our enemies to the death, spilling our blood if need be. We will not be defeated!

Response 1 attacks the arguer, saying they are "bleating" (like a sheep or goat) and an "inadequate, fearful pacifist," implying that the argument is based in fear and cowardice and that we should despise it for that reason. But it does not address the argument, or show why we should keep fighting. It just appeals to our emotions, not our reason. So this is an illogical response to the argument.

Response 2: If possible we should find a solution by negotiation, that's true. But it's not just a strip of barren land we are fighting over. It's a strip of mountain land that not only protects us from invasion, but also contains significant mineral wealth. So this bit of land is important to our future, as well as our people.

Response 2 answers the points in the argument. It acknowledges that it would be good to negotiate rather than fight, but shows the weak point in the original argument, by saying why the land is important (and therefore perhaps worth fighting for). So this is a logical response – although you could still argue against it. You could question the value that mineral wealth is worth dying for, or you could argue that these mountains clearly don't prevent war since we're fighting over them!

Activity 7

The National Film Association of Localia (NFAL) has $1million to support young film-makers and promote the national film industry. The leaders of the NFAL disagree over how to spend the money.

 A: What we want to do is support an energetic young producer who will make blockbuster Hollywood style action movies and really put our film industry on the global map. This will generate the revenue to support even more successful blockbuster movies, and then Localia will become the new Hollywood. We'll all be rich and all our economic problems will be solved.

B: You should spend less time thinking about money and more time thinking about our culture!

 C: The world already has Hollywood films. It seems to me that all we could offer would be a poor imitation. We need to do something new and different to captivate audiences.

 D: I agree with you that we shouldn't try to imitate Hollywood, but I don't agree that we need something new. We have our own traditions and our own language. These are being swept away by American language and values. So we should be investing in the development of traditional films which remind our young people that Localia is important.

 B: What's wrong with American language and values anyway? Do we want to be stuck in the past going on about ancient Localian traditions when we could be making real progress for a modern Localia?

 C: When I said new, D, I didn't mean completely different from our traditions. I believe that we should support films in Localian, films which emphasise Localian values. But Localia isn't the same place it was when our traditions developed, and I think our values and our films need to develop too. So we need a modern vision of our traditions and values: a fusion of old and new.

1. How effective is A's reasoning?
2. How well does B answer the points made by A and D?
3. How effective is C's reasoning?
4. How effective is D's reasoning?

Language

The sentence "How effective is the reasoning" means, "Does it work well to prove its point?" or "Is it good quality?" Remember to point out the parts that are logical as well as illogical.

Remember to think about the illogical patterns we have considered. But look for other ways of being illogical too. And remember to explain why the reasoning is illogical, if it is.

Reflection

- How has your ability to question knowledge claims and arguments improved?

- What new skills have you learned?

- Are there any aspects of this that you struggle with?

- How can you improve?

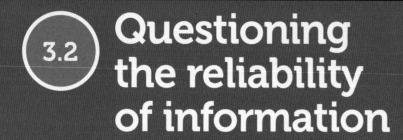

3.2 Questioning the reliability of information

Level ①

Reliable sources	Unreliable sources
Accurate facts – can be verified	Inaccurate facts
Opinions based on evidence	Speculations, unfounded assertions
Expert	Not expert
Has relevant information	Has irrelevant information
Has no reason to lie or mislead	Has a reason to lie or to mislead, including bias and vested interest

What sort of information can be reliable?

Activity 1

1. Which of the following are facts that can be verified?

   a) Eighty percent of people live on less than $10 a day.

   b) Living in a rural area is better than living in a city.

   c) It is wrong to cure sick people who can't afford to look after themselves.

   d) Eighty percent of poverty is due to laziness.

   e) Building the new airport will generate $3 million for the economy.

Activity 2

1. Which of the following do you think will be reliable sources? What are your reasons?

   a) You want to find information about the effects of climate change on mountainous regions of Pakistan. You find the following.

   - Sophie Maclean's blog, part of her high school project on Pakistan. She is a 15-year-old from Portland, Maine, USA.

   - Dr. A. Hamid's blog. He is a medical doctor who lives in Gilgit, Pakistan. He records weather conditions and comments on changes.

   - Dr. Jones' academic paper in the *Journal of Anthropology* on bridal customs in Pakistan's mountainous regions.

   - A report from the Pakistani Ministry of Climate.

   > Never heard of some of these places and sources? Look them up!

   b) You want to find information on changing communities in Vietnam. You find:

   - An article on the website http://www. migrationpolicy.org about the effects of migration on culture in Hanoi, Vietnam.

   - An Australian government backed research group's report on the effects of climate change on coastal communities in Vietnam.

   - The online diary of a rural migrant boy to Hanoi.

   - You talk to your Grandmother.

   c) You want to find information on FIFA corruption. You find the following.

   - A very rude article in a daily newspaper.

   - An article on Wikipedia.

   - A blog by "Football FanFanFantastica".

   - An article on http://www.forbes.com which provides in-depth reporting on specific financial issues relating to FIFA and World Cup bribery allegations.

Fakes, hoaxes, misunderstandings and mistakes

Richard Branson
Virgin blog

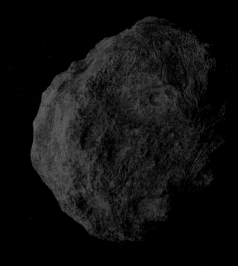

An extract from Richard Branson's blog, 01 April 2013:

> "I'm thrilled to announce that Virgin has created another world-first with the introduction of the technology required to produce the world's first glass-bottomed plane."

This seems like a genuine news story from a reliable businessman. However, it was in fact an April Fool's joke – a hoax.

Activity

1. a) Look at this website. It includes a number of internet hoaxes. http://urbanlegends.about.com/od/reference/a/top_25_uls.htm

    b) Is the extract about NASA on the right true or a hoax?

NASA is planning a $2.6 billion robotic mission to catch an asteroid in a giant bag and tow it to the Moon as part of a long-term programme that could one day lead to the permanent settlement of humans in space.

– The Times, 2013

Language

Bias: a tendency to support or oppose an idea, a proposal or a group of people in an unfair way. For example, we are biased in favour of our friends, and in favour of the cultural perspective we have grown up with.

Vested interest: having something to lose or gain by telling the truth, or a strong personal interest in a situation because you expect to gain advantage from that situation. For example, someone who has committed a crime has a vested interest to lie: to say that they are innocent in order to avoid prison. Or a politician who owns part of a renewable energy company has a vested interest to promote environmentally friendly government policies, in order to make more money through the company.

Level 2

Cross-checking facts

You need to cross-check facts from one source with other sources to make sure that they are correct. Sometimes a reliable source can make a mistake, or an unreliable source happens to get a statistic right.

- Put a fact or statistic into a search engine to see if other sources agree with it.

- Make sure that you find reliable, credible sources when you are cross-checking facts.

- Check where these sources found their information, and whether the origin is reliable.

Activity 4

1. Do you think the following facts have been sufficiently checked? What other sources could you check? What questions could you ask?

   a) Forty of your friends on a social networking site say that using a mobile phone can give you brain cancer.

   b) Forty of your friends say on a social networking site that the school will be closed due to snow.

   c) You read on a social networking site that there are now two Popes. You do an internet search and find many newspaper results saying, "The old Pope meets with the new Pope."

   d) A newspaper article claims that two billion people live on less than $1 a day. You believe it.

   e) A newspaper claims that, "The 100 richest people in the world earned $240 billion between them in 2012". You check, and find that many news organisations, including Al Jazeera and the BBC quote an Oxfam study which claims that, "the 100 richest people in the world increased their net wealth by $240 billion in 2012." You find the Oxfam report. It cites its source as http://www.globalresearch.ca/billionaires-gain-as-living-standards-fall/5318471 and Bloomberg Billionaires. You look up these sites to find out how they arrived at the figure.

2. Cross check the facts given in 1.(a). and 1.(d).

Checking facts, evaluating opinions, predictions and value judgements

You can verify a fact. You can't verify opinions, predictions or value judgements, but you can evaluate how well supported, likely or reasonable they are. For example:

"72% of men are over 1.75m in height."

If it's true, this is a **fact**. You can check this with several sources to verify it – or establish that it is false.

This is an **opinion** (or prejudice) which cannot be checked or verified. Instead of verifying them, you can consider whether opinions are well supported with reasons and evidence.

"Tall people are superior to short people."

"Vaccinating all the children will save 1 million lives."

This is a **prediction**, and hasn't happened yet, so it can't be verified. Instead, you can think about how likely it is to happen.

This is a **value judgement**, so it can't be verified. Instead, you can evaluate it by thinking about how reasonable it is, and testing it against other perspectives.

"It is wrong to let people die of curable diseases."

Be aware of opinions that are made to look like facts. Just because there is a number or statistic, doesn't mean it is a fact.

"The world's 100 richest people could end hunger." This has a number in it, but it is not a fact. It's an opinion based on predictions and facts.

"The world's 100 richest people increased their wealth by $240 billion in 2012" is a fact that can be verified. But whether they could use this amount of money to end hunger depends on other things. You can ask questions such as: How would the money be used? Would it be used for one year of food for everyone? What about the next year? Would it be used to help people develop businesses? What if these businesses fail? What if there is another drought?

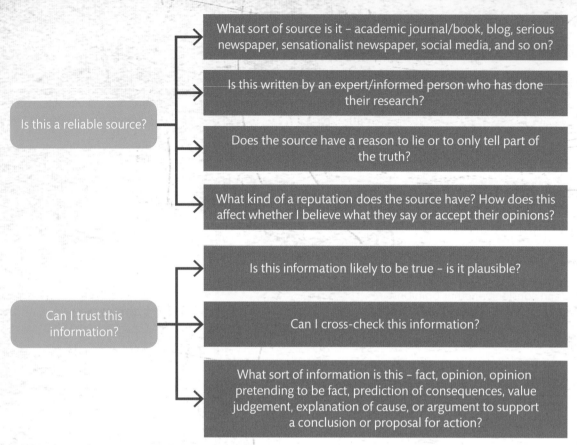

Figure 1 Questions to ask when cross-checking facts

The questions in Figure 2 are questions that you need to have in your mind all the time when you are researching, or even when you are just listening to the news or reading what people say on social media sites.

These questions are useful when you are deciding which sources to use. When you write your research report, it should be clear that you have chosen reliable sources. However, you do not need to write down the answers to these questions in your research report. It's a bit like an athlete – they do lots of different exercises when they are training, but they don't show this in the final performance!

Activity 5

1. In general terms, do you think the following types of source are likely to be reliable?

   a) Supranational organisations such as the UN, WHO, IMF.

   b) Government departments (in various countries).

   c) Large charity websites such as Oxfam, the Red Cross / Crescent or Amnesty International.

   d) The websites of small charities.

   e) Social media pages raising money for good causes.

   f) The websites of multinational corporations such as Shell, McDonald's or Apple.

   g) The websites of small local companies.

Language

Supranational organisations are large organisations which operate in many countries. Examples include the United Nations and the World Bank.

Level 3

Can I trust this information?

When you are deciding whether to believe information or to use it in your research, you need to question the source *and* the information itself. You can ask:

- Is this a generally reliable source?
- Could this be true – is it plausible?
- Can I verify or cross-check this?
- What sort of knowledge claims, information, ideas or perspectives are there here?

Activity 6

1. How reliable are the sources of the three documents below?

2. How reliable are the knowledge claims?

Remember: You should always question the opinions, predictions, proposals and value judgements you find in a source. Never accept these just because you think the source is reliable.

Document 1

Research indicates that the more foreign aid spent on health, the less the recipient spends – while nearly two-thirds of health spending in Africa was found to be diverted for other uses. One new study just found the biggest improvements in infant survival in Malawi was in areas that received less or no aid; meanwhile, Sierra Leone has just indicted its 29 top health officials after funds went astray, despite this being the world's third most dangerous place to give birth.

Source: http://www.independent.co.uk/voices/comment/corrupt-ineffective-and-hypocritical-britain-should-give-less-aid-not-more-8599403.html

Document 2

Too often, governments and international agencies have sought to fight the diseases of poverty with aspirational but impractical policies. Millions of dollars and countless working hours have been wasted on ill-conceived and poorly-run initiatives, needlessly costing lives.

Source: http://www.policynetwork.net/programs-policy-projects

Go back to your research. Check whether the knowledge claims in the documents you have selected are reliable.

Reflection

- How has your ability to question the reliability and trustworthiness of information improved?
- What new skills have you learned?
- Are there any aspects of this that you struggle with?
- How can you improve?

Document 3

Myth 4. "Aid is useless due to corruption in the governments who receive it"

The grain of truth:

Corruption is a big problem in many developing countries and it can sometimes lead to aid money being diverted from its intended purpose.

The full picture:

While corruption can lessen the impact of aid, it is important to understand that most aid money gets to its proper destination. This is especially true for money that is not given to a foreign government, but is instead directly spent on an aid project. Even taking corruption into account, you can realistically hope to greatly improve the lives of thousands of people through your donations, especially if you donate to programs which don't involve any valuable goods for corrupt officials to divert. Moreover, if you are particularly concerned about the effects of corruption, then you can donate to programs which fight corruption in developing countries.

Source: http://www.givingwhatwecan.org/why-give/myths-about-aid

3.3 Evaluating causes and consequences

Level ①

Two of the most important ways of evaluating reasoning about causes and consequences are:

- considering possible alternative causes and consequences.
- considering the likeliness of a consequence.

Possible alternative causes

Whenever a cause or consequence is suggested, think about whether there might be alternatives. For example:

Delilah arrives home after school sopping wet. Her mother says, "Oh, is it raining?"

Rain is one reason that Delilah might be wet. Other possible reasons include:

- Some other students threw water at Delilah.
- Delilah jumped in the river to cool off.

Activity ①

1. Suggest alternative causes to these situations.

   a) Toby failed his English exam because he has no talent for languages.

   b) Most old people in homes are there because their families do not care about them.

   c) There is a shortage of housing because migrants are taking all the houses.

   d) The main cause of disagreements about water use in the Nile basin is the growing population.

   e) The main cause of destruction of natural ecosystems is greed.

Activity ②

1. For each of the following events, think of all the possible consequences you can, and then decide which are the most likely, and why.

   a) We fly to the Maldives on holiday.

   b) We invest in methane hydrate.

   c) We drill down to the water table to get water to irrigate our crops.

   d) We invest in ways of harvesting more rainwater.

2. Play this game in teams:

   - One member of Team A describes an event.
   - Team B then has to think of a consequence.

   Award two points if Team C/the teacher thinks it is very likely, one point for likely, zero points for unlikely. Award one bonus point for being amusing.

Likeliness

When you are considering causes and consequences, you need to think about how likely a consequence is. To do this, you need to take lots of circumstances into consideration.

Let's look at a situation from school life first:

Cause	Possible consequences	Likely?
Adam hits the teacher.	The teacher respects Adam and stops giving him homework.	Highly unlikely in any well-run school.
	The teacher hits Adam back.	Unlikely in countries where teachers are forbidden from hitting students. More likely where there are no such laws.
	Adam is told off but is given no punishment.	This is quite unlikely because it doesn't reflect the seriousness of what Adam has done.
	Adam is sent on an anger management course.	This is quite likely in schools in some countries, especially if Adam often has problems controlling his temper. In other countries this might be less likely.
	Adam is given a serious punishment but allowed to remain in the school.	This is likely in many schools. It might depend on what Adam's behaviour was normally like.
	Adam is expelled from school.	This is likely in a strict school. In other schools it would be less likely if it was the first time Adam had misbehaved. It might depend on why Adam hit the teacher.

Possible alternative consequences

If we invest in nuclear power stations, we will significantly reduce our carbon emissions.

Predicted consequence: we will reduce our carbon emissions.

Other possible consequences:

- We might actually produce more carbon emissions because we are using more power in the belief that it is "clean".

- We might also produce significant quantities of radioactive waste.

Activity 3

1. Suggest alternative consequences to these situations.

   a) I am going to migrate to China. My children will be able to take advantage of China's economic growth and world power.

   b) If Toby doesn't go to school, he will be able to set up his own business and become rich and famous.

   c) There are two new sources of fossil fuels: "fracking" and methane hydrate. As a consequence we do not need to worry about fuel running out.

   d) If we build an offshore wind farm, the local residents will enjoy a cheap source of clean fuel.

Level 2

Exaggeration

Watch out for the following kinds of unrealistic predictions of consequences:

- exaggeration
- oversimplification
- ignoring other possibilities.

Watch out for unrealistic predictions of consequences in your own work, as well as in sources you find during research.

When people are predicting consequences, they often exaggerate. They overstate the possible consequences of an action. This can be either wishful thinking or disaster thinking.

Exaggeration

Problem	Example	Comment
Wishful thinking is too positive.	*If we vaccinate every child, we can wipe out disease and sickness, and everyone will grow up healthy and happy and have an economically productive life.*	This overstates the positive aspects so much that it is unrealistic. Vaccination can't wipe out *all* disease and sickness. But vaccinating every child might still be a good idea – we just need to be more realistic about the consequences.
Disaster thinking is too negative.	*If any more people move into the city, the city just won't be able to cope. The slum areas will grow, there will be piles of waste lying around, people will get sick and die. The gangs will recruit poor people who can't get work; they will attack the rich and take over, and it will end up being a lawless anarchy.*	There are real problems for many cities in the world, caused by more people moving in from the country (or other parts of the world), but this reasoning overstates the problems. So the consequences predicted here are too extreme.
Over-simplification.	*Poverty means having no money. If we give poor people money, we will solve poverty.*	This reasoning is oversimplified. It ignores the many causes of poverty, and the many different forms of poverty.
Ignoring other possibilities.	*If we build a factory, there will be work for the people.*	There may also be other consequences – the factory may pollute the water, take jobs away from independent businesses or it may never make money.

Activity 4

1. Explain why the following predicted consequences are unrealistic or unlikely, and suggest other possibilities.

   a) If we build a new ring road, the traffic will get very much better. This will bring more business to the city and should generate about $4 million in new revenue.

   b) If I borrow $1 m to invest in my business, I'll create employment for lots of local people.

   c) The government should set up a regional development agency. This will stop people from migrating to the cities.

   d) Donating money to help prevent malaria is pointless. These people will only make dresses out of the mosquito nets instead of using them to protect their children.

   e) We must make it a law that young people follow the old traditions. This will ensure that young people love our culture as much as our grandparents did.

Sometimes exaggeration, oversimplification and ignoring other possibilities can seem similar – or perhaps an argument contains all of these. Remember to explain why you think the predicted consequence is unrealistic or unlikely, and suggest other possibilities

Other possibilities?

Level 3

Oversimplification

What about the causes and consequences?

Considering causes and consequences in exam conditions is very much like considering them when you are engaging in research. You ask the same questions:

- Are there alternative possible causes or consequences?
- Are the predicted consequences likely?
- Is there any exaggeration, oversimplification or ignoring of other possibilities?

Underlying values

What do you think about the values that underlie these views?

Activity 5

1. How reasonable are the causes and consequences suggested in the passages below?

1 If we can get broadband internet access to everyone, the economy will improve significantly.

2 Aid leads to dependency, corruption and waste. People who are given free things do not value them as much as people who work for what they have. Furthermore, giving people free things results in them believing they cannot achieve for themselves or that they have no reason to strive for success. Trade can lead to booming economies, higher unemployment and benefits for both developed and developing countries. So we should clearly promote trade not aid.

3 Aid can be overused with the consequences of dependency, corruption and waste. This is true. However, this does not mean that we should abandon aid and rely on trade to improve people's lives. Trade can also lead to negative consequences. Trade is about money not about improving lives. It can lead to a small number of people becoming very rich whilst the majority remain poor. Trade often involves exploitation of the poor. So we need a third option – a humane option that helps people to improve their lives without becoming dependent on aid. If we use aid to provide small loans to businesses and to help people use and develop technology such as solar-powered computers, we will combine the advantages of aid and trade, without any of the disadvantages.

Use the internet to research these issues and to check whether the causes and consequences are likely.

Activity 6

Look at your current research.

1. Evaluate the causes and consequences that have been identified in the source material.

2. Evaluate the causes and consequences that you have suggested.

   - Are there alternative possible causes or consequences?
   - Are the predicted consequences likely?
   - Is there any exaggeration, oversimplification or ignoring of other possibilities?

Reflection

- How has your ability to evaluate causes and consequences improved?
- What new skills have you learned?
- Are there any aspects of this that you struggle with?
- How can you improve?

3.4 Questioning underlying beliefs

Level 1

Mia is upset because her little brother Amon keeps taking her toys. She thinks that he is being deliberately mean. So she hits him. Amon adores his big sister Mia and wants to share with her. Whatever she is playing with must be the best toy. He does not understand why she hit him. He feels she is being mean and unfair. Soon there is a big fight, and their mother tells them they are both bad children. They both think this is unfair, and each blames the other. As soon as their mother is not looking they start fighting again.

Unspoken beliefs

An action, view or opinion that makes no sense at all from the viewpoint of your own values and beliefs can begin to make sense if you understand the beliefs and values that underlie it. Look at the example of Mia and Amon above.

Culture is like an Iceberg

Visible behaviours

Values
Beliefs
Invisible sources
Assumptions

Activity 1

1. Match the beliefs to the things these people say. There may be more than one belief for some statements.

Statements:

a) "Let's go to the football on Saturday. Borussia Dortmund are playing Man United."

b) "Going to war is our only option."

c) "We should encourage more migrants to come and work here."

d) "Let's stay at home and read a book instead of watching grown men playing ball games."

Beliefs:

A. Ball games are for children.

B. Aggressive attack will protect us.

C. Watching football is an enjoyable thing to do.

D. Borussia Dortmund vs. Man United is likely to be an enjoyable match.

E. Reading is more entertaining than ball games.

F. Local people do not have the skills local businesses need.

G. Our neighbouring country is threatening us.

H. Migrants will improve our economy and look after our old people.

2. What do you think Mia and Amon's mother could do to help them resolve their conflict in the example above?

3. Identify some of the things that these people probably believe, based on what they say:

a) FBI agent: "This is a poor neighbourhood. The killer probably lived here."

b) Lady to her neighbour: "Don't you think you should stop filling your swimming pool with precious water?"

c) Amira: "No, I do not want to spend a whole day in the shopping mall with you."

Level 2

Beliefs underpinning perspectives

Behaviour and opinions that we see and hear are based on beliefs, values and assumptions that we cannot see or hear. So, when you consider different perspectives, it can be useful for you to question the beliefs and values that underlie each perspective.

Activity 2

1. In your country:

   a) Are individual rights more important than social stability? Give your reasons. What values, beliefs and assumptions underlie the attitude to individuals and society in your country? Do you agree with these?

   b) Are all people equal? Are young people equal to older people? Should young people respect older people? Give your reasons for each. What values, beliefs and assumptions underlie the attitude to equality and authority in your country? Do you agree with these?

Level 3

Activity 3

1. Think of a conflict happening at the moment. Do you think the different sides are misunderstanding each other's values?

2. The Localians are going to invest in a local film company. They are trying to decide what kind of films to make. List the beliefs and values that underlie the following passages.

   a) A: What we want to do is support an energetic young producer who will make blockbuster Hollywood-style action movies and really put our film industry on the global map. This will generate the revenue to support even more successful blockbuster movies, and then Localia will become the new Hollywood. We'll all be rich and all our economic problems will be solved.

   b) D: I agree with you that we shouldn't try to imitate Hollywood. But I don't agree that we need something new. We have our own traditions and our own language. These are being swept away by American language and values. So we should be investing in the development of traditional films which remind our young people that Localia is important.

Activity 4

1. Think of a personal situation recently where you have disagreed with someone or not understood them.

   a) What beliefs, values, assumptions and feelings might underlie their views and behaviour?

   b) What beliefs, values, assumptions and feelings underlie your own views and behaviour?

   c) Are any of your answers to parts (a) and (b) surprising?

   d) Can you see how your own subconscious perspective might have influenced the situation?

   e) Does understanding these help you to deal with the disagreement? If so, how?

2. Think of an international situation which includes a disagreement or lack of understanding. What beliefs, values, assumptions and feelings underlie this disagreement? Think about both/all parties to the conflict.

Reflection

- How has your ability to question underlying beliefs improved?

- What new skills have you learned?

- Are there any aspects of this that you struggle with?

- How can you improve?

4 Developing a line of reasoning

Level 1

Giving reasons for your opinions

Developing a line of reasoning starts with thinking about what reasons you can give for your own opinions. In Global Perspectives, it is important to think about your own opinions, and be prepared to change them.

You can ask the questions on the right:

Have i got good reasons for my opinion?

Is my opinion based on fact and thinking?

Can I check that my facts are true?

Where do my facts come from?

Is my opinion based on emotion or ignorance?

Activity 1

1. **a)** For each of the following opinions, give reasons why you agree or disagree.

    i) Family is more important than friends.

    ii) Sport is boring.

    iii) Everyone should stay at school until they are 18.

    iv) There is no point recycling things.

    b) Work with a partner who disagrees with you and discuss your reasons.

    i) Listen to what your partner is saying.

    ii) Think about what your partner is saying.

    iii) Examine your own thinking.

    iv) Would finding more information help? If so, what sort of information?

    v) Can you find a compromise? If not, why not?

Remember to respect your partner even if you disagree with their opinion.

You can ask the same questions about someone else's opinion. You can also ask:

Why do I disagree with this opinion?

Activity 2

1. Connect the following sentences using *because, so, therefore, also, in addition,* and *for example.* Think about which part of the sentence is the opinion and which parts are the reasons and examples.

   a) Ari should take the job. It will allow him to educate his children. Education for his children is the most important thing. If work is hard to find, you take what you can get.

   b) International sports competitions put different nations in opposition to each other. It is like a mini war. You are happy when the other country loses. You believe that your country winning is the most important aspect. During the Olympics, I really wanted the competitor from my country to win, even though the other competitor was better. International sports competitions actually make us less peaceful.

2. Answer the following questions with your opinion. Give reasons and examples.

   a) Do we have the right to use animals however we like?

   b) Should children always do what their parents want them to?

   c) Are some children better off working than in school?

   d) Should we have less sport on national television?

Level 2

Developing a line of reasoning

Reasoning is logical, connected writing. There are two main kinds of reasoning: argument and explanation.

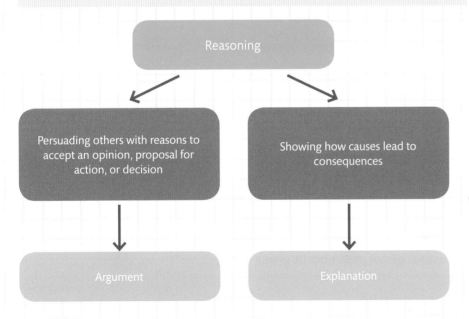

Reasoning

Persuading others with reasons to accept an opinion, proposal for action, or decision

Showing how causes lead to consequences

Argument

Explanation

Try the quiz in Activity 1 after you have been studying Global Perspectives for six months or a year. How have your scores changed?

Activity 3

Are these passages explanations or arguments? Explain your answer.

1. There are several major threats to the world's coral reefs. These include nutrient runoff from agriculture causing the population of crown-of-thrones starfish (which eat coral) to explode, rising sea-water temperatures due to climate change causing an effect known as 'coral bleaching', and tropical cyclones inflicting irreparable damage.

2. Climate change is threatening the Earth in many ways. We have a duty to protect it for future generations. Individually we cannot make big changes, but if each individual contributes, then together we can succeed. So we should work together as a community to reduce our consumption and recycle our waste.

Reasons and conclusions

To persuade someone to accept your opinion, value judgement or proposal for action, you use reasons. The opinion, value judgement or proposal for action becomes your conclusion.

For example, let's turn an opinion into an argument supporting a conclusion:

Opinion: People who don't recycle should have to pay a fine. Argument:

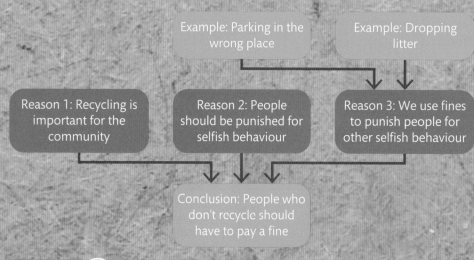

Activity 4

1. Turn these opinions and proposals into lines of reasoning by giving reasons and examples.

   a) You should take the part time job in the shop.

   b) The Government should increase funding for eco-friendly buses

   c) We should donate money to help victims of the earthquake.

Mini arguments and mini conclusions

In the argument about recycling, Reason 1 is also an opinion, and Reason 2 is a value judgement. This is OK, but you can make your line of reasoning better if you give reasons to support these opinions and value judgements. If you do this, it will turn your original reasons into mini conclusions. Let's look at supporting Reason 1 as an example:

Giving reasons for an opinion is also called "supporting" the opinion.

Reason 1: We share limited resources

Reason 2: If we recycle, we can preserve resources for our community in the future

Reason 3: Taking action (like recycling) together makes us bond as a group

Mini conclusion: Recycling is important for the community

Conclusion: People who don't recycle should have to pay a fine

Activity 5

1. How would you support the value judgement that, "People should be punished for selfish behaviour"?

   a) Can you think of specific circumstances when you would punish people for selfish behaviour?

   b) Can you think of specific circumstances when you would not punish people for selfish behaviour?

2. "Our school community needs to reduce consumption (of goods, energy, water, food, etc.) How can this be done?" Write an argument to persuade the school management to accept one proposal for reducing school consumption. Think about giving reasons. Do you need to support your reasons and turn them into mini conclusions?

Explanations

Explanations deal with causes and consequences.

Activity 6

1. Explain how climate change is caused and what its consequences are. Use diagrams.

2. Explain the advantages of migration.

3. Explain why we need to focus on sustainable living.

Level 3

Considering other perspectives

Considering other perspectives includes:

- trying to understand why someone might hold that perspective.

- being prepared to agree with all or some of that perspective.

- being prepared to negotiate a compromise position.

- giving reasons and evidence against that perspective if you can't agree.

Reflection in your reasoning

If you have reflected on the ideas and issues within a topic, this will show in your reasoning. Students who have reflected tend to:

- go beyond the source material, expressing personal thoughts on what the material means or implies

- come up with their own arguments and ideas, as well as using ideas from source material

- have a personal perspective which makes sense and is based on the evidence

- suggest compromises between different views or perspectives.

Personal perspective?

Own arguments and ideas?

Compromises?

What does the source material mean?

Activity 7

1. Consider the following opinions.

   a) Why might people hold these opinions? What perspectives might underlie them?

   b) Can you agree with all or part of the opinion?

   c) Is there a compromise position you could suggest?

   d) Give reasons and evidence against the following opinions.

      A. We should provide guns to the opposition to help them win the civil war.

      B. Our most important priority is developing the economy.

      C. Everyone ought to speak at least three languages.

      D. Our national identity is more important than international links.

      E. Democracy is the only acceptable form of government.

2. Argument tennis.

   Work in pairs or small groups to play this game:

   - Person/Team 1 makes a claim.

   - Person/Team 2 argues against it.

   - Person/Team 1 argues back again.

   - Keep going as long as possible. The last person/team to argue without repetition wins.

Activity 8

1. Is globalisation making the world a better place?

2. How important is it to look after natural habitats?

3. Are traditions just for older people?

For each question:

- state your conclusion

- give reasons and examples

- explain causes and consequences

- consider at least one other perspective.

Reflection

1. How has your ability to develop a line of reasoning improved?

2. What new skills have you learned?

3. Are there any aspects of this that you struggle with?

4. How can you improve?

5.1 Reflecting on issues and perspectives

Level 1

What is reflection?

Reflection is serious, considered thought. It involves:

- listening to or reading about issues and opinions
- making connections between ideas
- being open to new ideas
- taking other people's ideas seriously
- really thinking about other people's ideas
- really questioning your own opinions.
- being prepared to change your own opinions and beliefs.

Activity 1

How well do you know yourself?

1. Do the quiz and give yourself a score from 1 (very low) to 5 (very high). Be honest!

2. Do the quiz for friends, and get friends to do the quiz for you. Do your friends see you the same way as you do? What about class members who are not friends?

		5	4	3	2	1
1	I think deeply about things.					
2	I want to change the world but I don't know how.					
3	I think a lot about my place in the world.					
4	I am interested in other people's opinions.					
5	I am quite happy to change my opinion when I come across new ideas.					

Activity 2

1. In each case, which is more important to you? Give your reasons. Does your view change if your perspective changes?

   a) Keeping your parents happy or following your dream.

   b) Playing for the national team or getting good grades.

   c) Happiness or wealth.

   d) Success for your family, success for your nation or success for your favourite sports team.

   e) Helping people in bad circumstances or providing the best for your own family?

   f) Making sure that young people are prepared for work in a globalised world or making sure that young people love local and national traditions?

2. Think of some of the issues you've discussed in Global Perspectives. What aspects do you think are most important? Give your reasons.

Reflection

Think about the topics and issues you have studied so far in Global Perspectives.

1. Have you formed any new opinions? Give examples and say why.

2. Have you changed your mind about any issues? Give examples and say why.

> You need to reflect on ideas, issues and other people's perspectives. You also need to reflect on your own perspective, and develop it.

Level 2

Reflection is a way of examining your own thoughts. It should help you to spot patterns and links. It will help you to:

- make sense of an issue
- decide what your opinion is
- think about what the best course of action would be.

Different people have different ways of reflecting. Some people write and think, others paint and think, and yet others make music and think. Some people find that walking in a calm place helps them to sort out their thoughts. It is important to get away from distractions and give yourself space.

Activity 3

1. What strategies can you use to help you examine your thoughts? What can you do to help yourself spot patterns and links? Share ideas with your classmates.

2. Think about these questions. Let them float around in your mind over the next few days. Keep coming back to them

   a) What are the values that matter to you? Why?

   b) What sort of world do you want to live in? Why?

Activity 4

1. What connections can you see between

   a) law and criminality, and employment

   b) migration, transport systems, and demographic change

   c) education, globalisation and demographic change

   d) transport systems, globalisation, fuel and energy

   e) any other issues.

2. What issues and perspectives have you been dealing with in Global Perspectives?

   a) What new ideas have you come across?

   b) What do you think about the ideas and perspectives you have considered?

   c) How are they connected?

   d) Have you needed to question your value judgements?

   e) How do your personal perspectives link in with national and global perspectives on each issue?

   f) Write three questions for each topic you have studied to help you think more deeply about your opinions, value judgements and actions.

Reflection

After you have been doing the Global Perspectives course for a few months, try the quiz again. How has your score changed?

Level 3

Reflecting on what other people must feel, and understanding the world from their perspective is called empathy.

Language

Empathy is an emotional skill rather than a logical skill – but don't confuse this with emotive or illogical argument. When constructing logical arguments, it makes sense to try and understand how other people think and feel.

Empathy is an important part of understanding different cultural perspectives.

Activity 5

1. Consider the following scenario.

   Imagine there is a civil war in your country. The government is corrupt and only interested in money and power. The opposition started to fight two years ago, hoping for change and a fairer society, but now the opposition has broken down into five different groups who don't agree and there seems to be no prospect of a better future. Your home is rubble, and you have been separated from your family. You do not know if they are still alive.

   a) How do you feel?

   b) What options are available to you? Which one will you choose? Why?

   c) How would you like other people to treat you?

   d) Either,

      write a story or poem about your situation and your feelings

      or

      draw or paint a picture about your situation and your feelings.

Activity 6

1. Consider the following scenario.

> The Earth is dying due to humankind's poor choices. Scientists have found an Earth-like planet and have developed the technology to transport 1000 people to the new planet. There are just two problems: firstly, 25% of people will catch a local disease. With proper health care, 90% of these recover. Without healthcare, 60% are left with active minds but serious physical disabilities. Secondly, the settlers may have to deal with intelligent beings already living on the planet – scientists are not sure.

a) You need to decide how you are going to select 1000 volunteers – what characteristics do you want your settlers to have?

b) You need to decide what kind of society to have on the new world. You need to think about the values that will be important for your new society and then write three or four basic laws in each of the following areas:

Government
- What balance do you want between individual freedom and community strength?
- Democratic/autocratic/other form of government/community decision-making?
- Is equality important in your society? Do you want equal rights, equal wealth, or equal opportunity to do well?

Resources, energy
- Will all resources be jointly owned by all 1000 settlers?
- What precautions will you take to avoid overuse of resources?

Employment and economy
- Will everyone work for themselves? Will some of the settlers employ others? How will this be decided?
- Will you have a system of money? Give your reasons. If not, what sort of economy will you have?

Healthcare / aid
- What sort of healthcare provision will you have? Will people pay each time they need healthcare or will the community group together to ensure that everyone gets healthcare when they need it? Remember the local illness that strikes twenty five percent of people, and the likelihood of accidents.
- How will the community help those who have bad luck or who do badly? Will there be "aid" for those who struggle?

Crime
- What basic laws will you have to prevent crime?
- How will you deal with criminals?

5.2 Reflection on teamwork, outcomes and own performance

Level ①

Reflecting on teamwork

> **Activity ①**
>
> Look at the examples on the right. How would you advise these groups to improve their teamwork?

1 Carita and Kamal are doing all the work. Sophie is playing games on her phone. Akim and Chloe are competing to see who can throw most paper balls in the bin.

Reflecting on outcomes

2 Sonita, Mika and Xing Li are working on a project on fuel and energy. They all work hard, and they all find information about wind energy.

> **Activity ②**
>
> How successful do you think the groups in the table below have been?

3 Xu Fei and Natalie are both telling everyone else what to do. Kaya is cross and refusing to do anything. Simon and Ahmad are ignoring everyone and designing a computer game about fossil fuels.

Team	Intended outcome	Actual outcome
A	Raise awareness of a charity and earn money to donate to the charity through a school concert.	The best concert the school has ever had. No one noticed the charity poster. Ticket sales raised $100.
B	Gather some information about fossil fuels.	Copied and pasted some information about fossil fuels from the internet, and didn't bother reading it.
C	Produce a business plan for a school café using local organic produce and run by school cookery/catering students. Present it to the head teacher of the school.	Produced a business plan. Presented it to the head teacher. The head teacher has said that she will consider it.
D	Produce a photo display showing how globalisation has changed your city over the years.	Three photos and two sentences in the display.

Activity 3

Every time you work in a team, answer these questions:

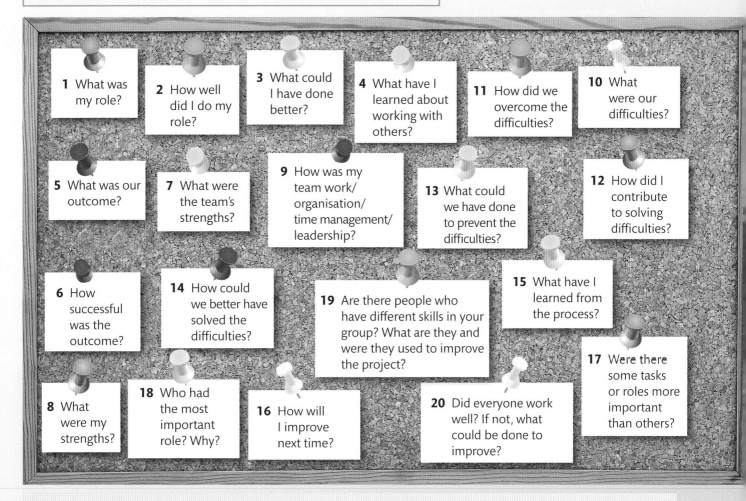

1 What was my role?

2 How well did I do my role?

3 What could I have done better?

4 What have I learned about working with others?

11 How did we overcome the difficulties?

10 What were our difficulties?

5 What was our outcome?

7 What were the team's strengths?

9 How was my team work/ organisation/ time management/ leadership?

13 What could we have done to prevent the difficulties?

12 How did I contribute to solving difficulties?

6 How successful was the outcome?

14 How could we better have solved the difficulties?

19 Are there people who have different skills in your group? What are they and were they used to improve the project?

15 What have I learned from the process?

17 Were there some tasks or roles more important than others?

8 What were my strengths?

18 Who had the most important role? Why?

16 How will I improve next time?

20 Did everyone work well? If not, what could be done to improve?

Does your outcome meet assessment criteria? It should:

- resolve an issue or problem
- involve actions – i.e. *not* an essay
- show that you have researched and thought about an issue
- allow you to show understanding of local, national, global and cross-cultural perspectives.

Activity 4

1. How successful has your teamwork been? Use the questions above to help you with your evaluation.

2. Did your outcome meet the assessment criteria?

3. How effectively did you achieve your outcome?

4. How would you improve the projects you have done if you could do them again?

5. What do you personally need to improve in your planning/ teamwork/time management/getting things done?

6. How will you go about making these improvements in the next project you do?

Reflection

- How has your ability to reflect on your teamwork improved?
- How has your ability to reflect on outcomes improved?
- What new skills have you learned?
- Are there any aspects of this that you struggle with?
- How can you improve?

5.3 Reflect on personal learning

Level 1

Activity 1

1. What kinds of learning did you engage in today?

2. How was Global Perspectives different from your other lessons?

3. How did you feel about it?

4. What was fun / interesting / exciting about today's lesson?

5. What are you good at in Global Perspectives? What is the person you sit next to good at? Tell them and see what they think you are good at. Does it match what you thought you did well?

6. What was difficult about today's lesson?

7. What can you do to improve your learning?

> It is useful to keep a learning log. After every lesson, make notes on *how* you have learned and how you felt about it. These questions can help you:

Level 2

Activity 2

1. Make a list of all the differences between GP learning and other learning you do.

2. What do you like about the GP way of learning? Why?

3. What do you find difficult? Why? How can you improve in this area?

4. How independent are you?

5. Can you plan a line of inquiry?

6. Can you find and record the right information?

7. Do you remember to use your information to answer a question or support a proposal or decision?

8. Do you select only relevant information?

9. How has your teamwork improved?

10. What do you need the teacher to help you with?

> Keep writing in your learning journal. Use these questions, but start to ask your own questions too.

Level 3

Activity 3

1. What strategies have you tried already to improve your performance?

   a) Which strategies were effective?

   b) Which were less effective?

2. Choose a topic to write about.

   a) What was interesting about this topic?

   b) How does your perspective on issues in this topic link to national and global perspectives?

   c) What else would you like to find out about?

   d) Do you view this topic differently now?

   e) If you wanted to find out more information on this topic, how would you go about it?

Keep writing in your learning journal.

Reflection

- How has your ability to reflect on your own learning improved?
- What new skills have you learned?
- Are there any aspects of this that you struggle with?
- How can you improve?

6.1 Planning a project

Level ①

Specific

Measurable

Achievable

Realistic

Time Bound

When you are planning a project you need to:

- Identify a specific issue.
- Set an aim – something you want to achieve.
- Identify an outcome – decide what action to take to achieve your aim.

Your action needs to be SMART:

Outcome	S	M	A	R	T
End world poverty	X	X	X	X	X
Design and make a set of t-shirts promoting family values to sell at the school open day.	Y	Y	Y	Y	Y

Activity ①

1. Are these outcomes SMART for a group of 14 – 16 year olds doing a school project?

   a) End world conflict.

   b) Produce a short video comparing the effects of drought and flooding on two different regions.

   c) Finding a solution to illness.

   d) Writing and performing a song about human rights to sing at a school event.

   e) Volunteering once a week with a local sports charity to help disabled children gain confidence.

2. Think of an action you'd like to take in each of the following areas. Is it a SMART outcome for a school project?

   a) Human rights

   b) Language and communication

   c) Tradition and culture

   d) Conflict and peace

   e) Poverty and inequality

   f) Water, food and agriculture

   g) Sport and recreation

   h) Disease and health

You'd probably need to be a superhero to end world poverty on a Saturday afternoon in between finishing your maths homework and starting your English!

Don't underestimate what you can do. Be ambitious – but be realistic.

When you actually decide on a project outcome, you will have done much more research and thinking!

Activity 2

1. Are these SMART outcomes for a project organised by a group of 14–16 year olds?

   a) Prevent conflict over water supplies in the Nile basin.

   b) Write a letter to the Egyptian and Ethiopian ambassadors in your country asking them to persuade their governments to cooperate over the use of Nile waters.

   c) Stop/reduce oil and water usage for a month, note the personal consequences and present your group's findings to the school.

   d) Design and produce t-shirts or mugs to show key issues in a topic you have studies.

   e) Design and produce a water saving device and present its advantages to your community.

Mini project plan

Project planning is about taking the ideas from your research, questioning and reflection and using them in the real world to make a difference. You need to work in a team to:

- choose an appropriate action (outcome) based on your research and thinking
- plan the tasks that need to be done
- carry out the action
- evaluate the effectiveness of your action.

Activity 3

1. You are going to organise a party or coffee morning with a theme to raise money for a charity. Use the bullets and the table to help you.

   Outcome: themed tea party or coffee morning to raise money for a charity

Task	Who	When	Comments
Decide on the menu	Group	Week 1	Chinese food and pizza

2. Hold the party or coffee morning.

3. Review:

   a) What went well?

   b) What problems did you come across?

   c) How did you solve them?

   d) What would you do next time to improve?

   e) How well did the team work together?

   f) How effective was your contribution to the team?

Reflection

- Which charity? Why
- Which theme? Why?
- What sort of food/drink will you serve – just coffee?
- Who will buy ingredients?
- Will there be music?
- What decorations will there be? Will you have decorations to reflect the theme and charity aims?
- How will you make sure you raise money?
- Who will be invited? Who will decide? How many people?
- Who will send invitations?
- What else?
- What roles should be given to team members?
- Are you being SMART?

Remember:

Specific, Measurable, Achievable, Realistic, Time bound.

Level 2

Choosing an action / outcome

Remember that when you choose an action or outcome, it needs to be SMART – Specific, Measurable, Achievable, Realistic, Time-bound. For Global Perspectives, your action/outcome also needs to:

- resolve an issue or problem
- involve actions – *not* an essay
- show that you have researched and thought about an issue
- allow you to show understanding of local, national, global and cross-cultural perspectives.

Activity 4

1. Think about these possible actions.

   - Cleaning a local river, together with members of the community.
   - Organising a project to vaccinate children in a village in Malawi.
   - Raising funds to support a charity that vaccinates children in Malawi.
   - Make a poster about poverty.
   - Produce a video campaigning for or against a local hospital project.
   - Make a poster to publicise a local sporting event.
   - Write a research report on urbanisation.

   a) Are they suitable for a GP project?

   b) Explain your thinking in terms of research and thinking, different cultural perspectives, appropriate actions and teamwork.

   c) What evidence would you send to CIE to prove you had engaged in an active project?

Project planning process

Let's look at the processes involved in planning and managing a project with an active outcome. Important things to remember are:

- A project is about managing practical tasks as well as research tasks.
- A project deals with teamwork and people as well as information.
- You need to be prepared to review and amend your plan.

You can think of the project process like the flow chart on the right.

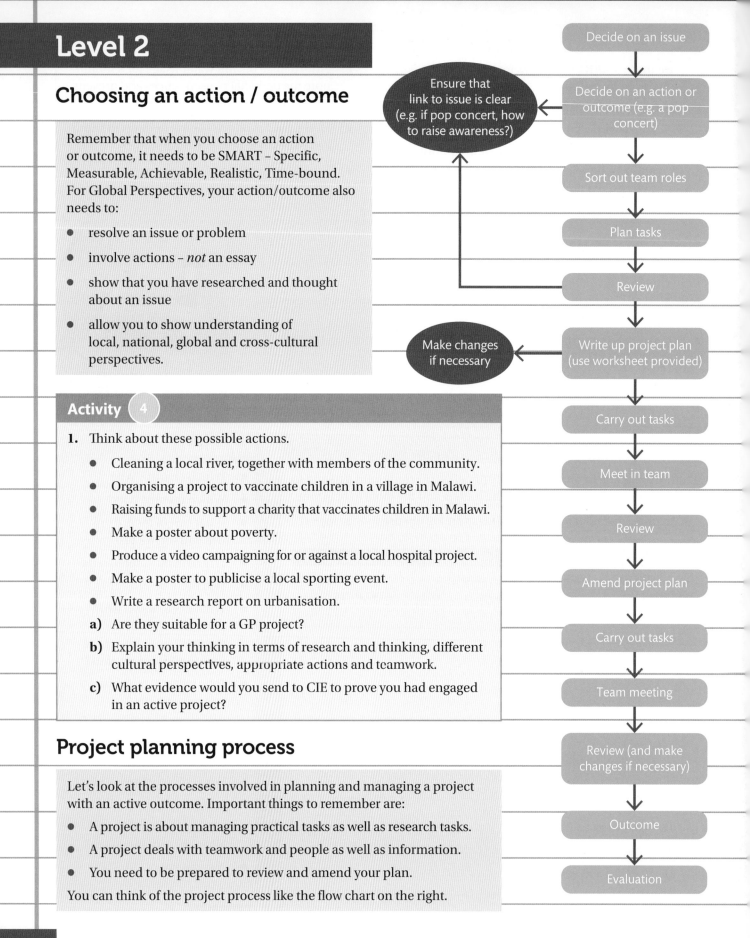

Decide on an issue

Decide on an action or outcome (e.g. a pop concert)

Ensure that link to issue is clear (e.g. if pop concert, how to raise awareness?)

Sort out team roles

Plan tasks

Review

Write up project plan (use worksheet provided)

Make changes if necessary

Carry out tasks

Meet in team

Review

Amend project plan

Carry out tasks

Team meeting

Review (and make changes if necessary)

Outcome

Evaluation

Some of the questions you can ask yourself at different stages of the project process include the following:

Stage	Questions to ask
Deciding on the issue	Is your teacher giving you the issue or do you choose it?
Deciding on an aim	Does it address an issue?
Deciding on the action or outcome	Is it SMART? Is it appropriate local action showing understanding of different perspectives? How will you collaborate with another culture, community, or country?
Sorting out team roles	Who is the project leader or will you rotate that role? Who is researching the issue? Who is liaising with other groups? How rigid will these roles be?
Planning tasks	What needs to be done? Who is doing which task? When does each task need to be done? Do some tasks need to be done before others can start? Do you need to revise team roles?
Review	Is the outcome possible or realistic? Does the outcome meet assessment criteria? Is the plan realistic? Are the tasks fairly shared out? Are you playing to your team's strengths? Have you thought of everything that needs to be done? What about money? What about publicity?
Team meeting	Check on progress, review, and make changes. What difficulties are you facing? How can these be solved?
Review	Are all team members working well? How will you deal with those who are not working well? Are the workloads fair? Do you need to add some more tasks? Who should do them? How is your team communication? How will you solve problems?
Outcome	How do you document the outcome? Do you need photos or a video to demonstrate that your project really took place? How will your documentation show your thinking about the issue? How will your documentation show your understanding of different perspectives? How will your documentation show your cross-cultural collaboration?
Evaluation	Did you achieve your aims? If not, why not? How well did you work in the team?

Activity 5

1. Your group has chosen to organise a concert to raise awareness of your issue and to raise money.

   a) How can you make a concert relevant to your chosen issue?

   b) What practical ways can you think of to make sure that the pop concert really does raise awareness of the issue?

   c) Make a list of everything you will need to organise your concert.

   d) Make a list of everything you will need to do to organise your concert.

   e) Plan a timeline.

> You could use Gantt charts to show your timeline. A Gantt chart is a visual representation of a project schedule. It uses horizontal lines to show how long each task in a project takes and when each task must be done.

Level 3

Planning and evaluating project work

When you do your assessed Team Project, you will need to submit:

- evidence of your outcome
- a group explanation, and
- a personal reflective paper.

You need to plan for this. You could:

- take photographs of meetings and activities
- record conversations
- print a copy of relevant emails, receipts or other documents, and/or
- keep a reflective journal – for example, if you argue with a team mate, ask, "how could I have dealt with that better? What strategies will I use if we have a similar situation again?" You could write your thoughts down, so that you have things to say when you have to write your individual evaluation.

> Remember that you also need to plan your exploration of different cultural perspectives.

Activity 6

1. What does SMART mean?

2. What are the different stages of the project planning and evaluation process?

3. You are producing a short play for your local community raising money to support a centre that counsels victims of human trafficking. What do you think would be useful evidence of:

   a) the planning and management process

   b) the outcome (the play/the raised money)?

> Refer back to Level 2 if you can't remember.

Activity

1. Think about your own Group Project.

    a) Use the questions in the table on the previous page to ensure that you have a clear plan.

    b) What evidence do you need to record?

    c) How well is your project going?

    d) What do you need to change?

Activity

1. a) What skills have you learned to help you plan and carry out an active project?

    b) Which of these skills do you need to improve?

    c) How will you improve these skills for your next project?

    d) Which of the following would make good project outcomes for a group of 14 – 16 year olds? Explain your answers. Suggest improvements where necessary.

        ● Make a film about the traditions of an immigrant group in your country.

        ● Learn a language.

        ● Work with a group of students from another country to investigate how language, culture and identity are linked, by learning a bit of each other's languages and considering important aspects of culture and identity.

        ● Visit a refugee camp and report back to other students and parents.

    e) Work in pairs or groups to think of good project outcomes for a group of 14–16 year olds.

Reflection

● How has your ability to plan improved?

● What new skills have you learned?

● Are there any aspects of this that you struggle with?

● How can you improve?

6.2 Teamwork and individual effort

Level 1

You will take action in teams during the Global Perspectives course. This will require different skills from doing homework or learning for exams (on your own). You will need to trust and cooperate with your team members.

Activity 1

1. The teacher will plan a route through your school. You will work in teams of three. One person will be blindfolded. One person will have a map of the route but will not be able to speak. One person will be able to speak, but will not be allowed to look at the map. The blindfolded person must arrive safely at the end of the route.

   a) What issues of teamwork does this exercise raise?

   b) What was your contribution to the teamwork?

2. Work in teams of three–five. You will have drinking straws, sticky tape and a plastic cup full of water. You have 15 minutes to build a structure that will support the cup of water.

   a) Which team was most effective? Why? How did their team work?

   b) How important were thinking and planning?

   c) What happens if no one takes the lead or makes decisions?

   d) What happens if everyone wants to make decisions?

   e) What was your contribution to the teamwork?

Level 2

Activity 2

1. You are going to work in a team to plan, design and produce a set of T-shirts illustrating issues relating to the topic of conflict and peace.

   a) Write a list of decisions that need to be made.

   b) Who makes decisions in your team?

   c) How are decisions made in your team?

   d) Will everyone play an equal role?

   e) How do you agree on who does which tasks?

   f) How do you make sure that each task is done at the right time?

> You do not have to actually produce the T-shirts. This is an activity in thinking about teamwork.

Level 3

Activity 3

1. You are the team leader. How will you resolve the following problems in your team?

   a) Bik isn't doing her share of the work, and it is holding up the team's progress. Bik claims that she has too much homework.

   b) Cara has lost her memory stick with all the team's work. She thinks she last used it on the library, but she did drop her bag on the bus.

   c) Chau and Karim won't listen to other people's ideas in team meetings. They just talk and give orders.

2. You are a team member. How do you respond to the following problems?

   a) No one in the team is doing any work. You are the only one who cares about getting a good grade.

   b) The team leader is disorganised and bossy. She keeps blaming you and one other team member for her own weaknesses.

   c) You have some good ideas, but no one listens to you.

   d) You hate the project the rest of the group has chosen and you really don't want to do the work.

3. What could be done to avoid these problems?

Activity 4

1. Who is more annoying – the person who takes over and does everything, or the person who does nothing?

   a) Why?

   b) What does your answer tell you about yourself?

Activity 5

Think about the team you are working in for the Group Project.

1. How well is your team working together?

2. Identify at least three things which are working well for your team.

3. What problems are you having?

4. What can you contribute to solving these problems?

5. What actions can the team take together to solve these problems?

6. What is annoying you?

7. What can you do to deal with your annoyance?

Reflection

- How has your ability to work in a team improved?
- What new skills have you learned?
- Are there any aspects of this that you struggle with?
- How can you improve?

7 Select evidence and present research

You need to select evidence and present your research in the Individual Report and in the Reflective Paper for the Team Project.

Level 1

Select evidence

You should only include relevant evidence in your work. Ask:

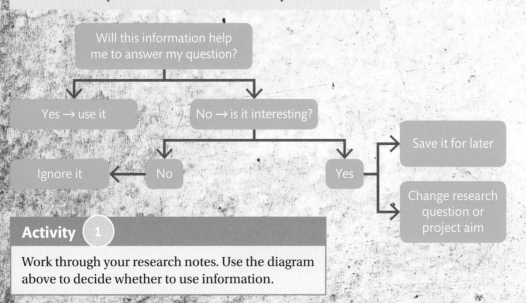

Will this information help me to answer my question?

Yes → use it

No → is it interesting?

Ignore it ← No

Yes → Save it for later

Change research question or project aim

Activity 1

Work through your research notes. Use the diagram above to decide whether to use information.

Clear English

It's important to write in your own words. You can summarise complex language into simple sentences that make sense to you. For example:

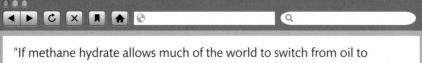

"If methane hydrate allows much of the world to switch from oil to gas, the conversion would undermine governments that depend on oil revenues, especially petro-autocracies like Russia, Iran, Venezuela, Iraq, Kuwait, and Saudi Arabia."

Methane hydrate fuel could cause problems for governments in oil-rich countries like Iran.

Activity 2

1. Write simple sentences that summarise these passages.

   a) "On a broader level still, cheap, plentiful natural gas throws a wrench into efforts to combat climate change. Avoiding the worst effects of climate change, scientists increasingly believe, will require 'a complete phase-out of carbon emissions … over 50 years.'"

   b) "Water scarcity is an issue exacerbated by demographic pressures, climate change and pollution," said Ignacio Saiz, director of Centre for Economic and Social Rights, a social justice group. "The world's water supplies should guarantee every member of the population to cover their personal and domestic needs."

   c) Recent scholars, including Thomas Homer-Dixon, have analysed various case studies on environmental degradation to conclude that there is not a direct link between scarcity and violence. Instead, he believes inequality, social inclusion and other factors determine the nature and ferocity of strife.

Presenting your research

You need to use clear English:

- use paragraphs
- use headings
- use bullet points
- use lists, tables and diagrams
- use references
- develop a line of reasoning.

Activity 3

1. Write a short practice research report of 500–550 words. Use diagrams and tables to help you to structure your ideas. Choose one of these options:

   a) How can we protect vulnerable ecosystems?

   b) What actions should the government take to help people adapt to changing urban communities?

   c) What should charities do to help people who are affected by changing coastal communities?

   d) Is trade a better way to help countries develop than aid?

   e) Choose a question of your own.

2. Check:

   a) Have I used clear English?

   b) Have I used paragraphs, headings and bullets?

   c) Have I included references?

   d) Have I explained causes and consequences?

   e) Have I developed a line of reasoning?

      i) Does my line of reasoning consider perspectives?

      ii) Does my line of reasoning propose and support a course of action?

> Remember to answer your question! You can often do this with your suggested course of action.

Level 2

Organising thoughts into a line of reasoning

- Write lists of reasons for and against your opinion/conclusion/proposal.
- Think about "mini" conclusions that come between your reasons and final opinion/conclusion/proposal.
- Think about evidence and examples to support and illustrate the reasons. This is usually where you can quote your research evidence.
- Use words like *because, so, therefore, also,* and *furthermore* to link your ideas.
- *Before* you start writing, you need to know what your final opinion, conclusion or proposal for action is. If you're not sure, go back to the Reflect and Plan stage!

Level 3

Causes, consequences, possible solutions

You can use causes, consequences and possible solutions to structure the reasoning in your research report:

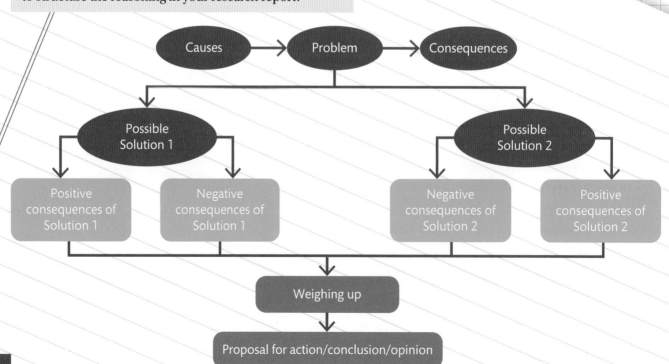

Activity 4

1. For each of these conclusions, write lists of reasons, evidence, examples and mini conclusions.

   a) We should build a new airport here.

   b) The government should invest in rural areas to prevent migration to the city.

   c) Giving people food does not help to end poverty.

   d) The best way to improve health is to improve sanitation.

Activity 5

1. Go to your research. Check:

   a) Have I used clear English?

   b) Have I used paragraphs, headings and bullets?

   c) Have I included references?

   d) Have I explained causes and consequences?

   e) Have I developed a line of reasoning?

      i) Does my line of reasoning consider perspectives?

      ii) Does my line of reasoning propose and support a course of action?

   f) Have I used words like *so, because, therefore* to show my line of reasoning?

Perspectives

Problems, causes, consequences and possible solutions can be personal, local, national or global. So another way to structure your reasoning is by thinking in terms of these perspectives.

1. Go back to the practice research report you wrote in Activity 3.

   a) Can you improve it by using causes, consequences and problems to structure it?

   b) Can you add a section using different perspectives to structure it?

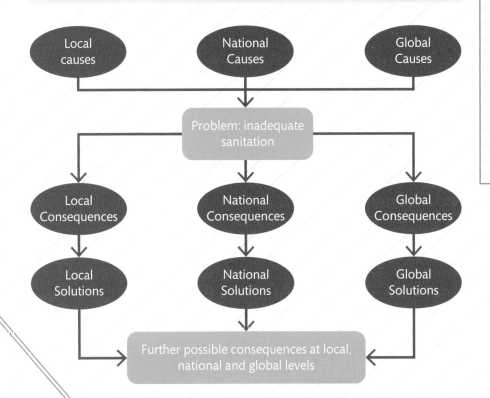

When you are presenting your research for the Team Project, you can use different cultural perspectives to help you structure your work.

Considering other perspectives

There other views or perspectives could be different personal, local/national or global perspectives. Or they could be different cultural perspectives.

When you present an argument, it is often useful to show why you disagree with other views or perspectives. When you do this you need to:

- take the other view seriously and respect the people who hold it
- look at the reasons or evidence for the other view
- say why you disagree, show why the other view is wrong or find a compromise.

You already know how to use words like *because, also, so, therefore* to link your ideas. When you are showing why you disagree with another view, you can use:

- Some people believe that...
- It is sometimes argued that...
- An alternative perspective on this issue is...
- However...
- On the other hand...
- This is true but...
- There is another way of seeing this...

Activity 7

1. Write a report on one of the following. Make sure you include phrases like, "An alternative perspective is..."

   a) Do you think Western governments should continue to give aid to developing countries? Give reasons for your answer and consider at least one different view.

   b) Propose one national and one international action that can be taken against human traffickers. Explain how they would work and write an argument to persuade your government to agree to them. Consider at least one different view.

   c) You are the leader of a remote village in an underdeveloped area. You are discussing with a charity how to invest in your community. The options under discussion are:

      - Providing small loans to women to operate small businesses.
      - Educating one child from each family in solar powered communications technology.
      - Cooperating with a multinational corporation in a large infrastructure project.

      Write an argument to persuade the villages to accept one of these options or another option of your choice. Explain why you do not support the other options.

Activity 8

1. Look at a piece of presentation work you have done so far in the course – this could be a spoken presentation, an exam-style argument, some project documentation, etc.

   a) How would you improve this piece of work?

   b) Actually improve the work – do it again, but better! Look at the difference.

   c) Work with a partner on a different piece of presentation work. Make (tactful and positive) suggestions about how each of you could improve your work.

   d) Work together to actually improve that piece of work.

Really think about how you could improve.

"I wrote a list of facts without using them to answer the question. I needed to write an opinion and use the facts to help me support my opinion."

"I didn't do the work very well. I didn't try hard enough. I will be better next time."

Redoing a piece of work is not wasting time. Is Usain Bolt wasting his time when he practises leaving the starting blocks *again* to get his start as fast as he can?

Reflection

- How has your ability to present research improved?
- What new skills have you learned?
- Are there any aspects of this that you struggle with?
- How can you improve?

Team project

Section B

How will I be assessed?

Together with a small group of two to five people, you will come up with and carry out a Team Project. Your Team Project is worth 70 marks. These marks will be awarded for your skills – mostly for your reflection, collaboration and communication skills, with some marks for your ability to research analyse and evaluate information.

You will submit:

1. Team Element (10 marks) – this is something you submit as a team and it must include:

   - Your aim.

   - A brief description of your outcome (what you did).

   - An explanation of how your research into cultural perspectives helped you produce your outcome.

2. Personal Element (60 marks) – this is something each team member must do on their own.

   It will be a reflective paper of 750–1000 words and should answer these questions:

   - How effective was my research?

   - What could I have done better?

   - What did I find out about different cultural perspectives on this issue?

   - What do I think about the different perspectives?

   - Have I changed my perspective?

   - Did we achieve our aim with our team project?

   - Why or why not?

   - What could we have done differently?

   - How well did we work as a team?

   - How well did I work within the team?

   - What have I learned from doing this project?

You will:

1 Decide on an active outcome (you will organise and do something, not just write about a topic).

2 Relate your outcome to one of the eight topics in this section.

3 Deal with different cultural perspectives.

4 Plan and carry out your project.

5 Reflect on your project's success.

The following section provides one possible way of approaching the topics, however many different approaches may be taken.

1 Conflict and peace

Some of the key issues include:

- Causes of conflict
- Consequences of conflict
- Paths to peace
- Solutions for peace

- Conflict resolution
- Roles of individuals, nations and NGOs in conflict
- Conflict driving progress
- The case for war

> Do some of these comments and questions raise more than one issue?

Activity 1

1. Match the comments and questions below to the issues in the diagram above.

   a) Since its establishment more than six decades ago, the United Nations has played a preeminent role in the peaceful resolution of armed conflict around the world.

   b) I think it's right to go to war. Our country has to defend itself from aggressive terrorists.

   c) This war is rooted in economic issues, but it has become linked to cultural and religious issues, so it will be difficult to find a solution.

   d) We need to take action to avoid water wars in the near future.

   e) Power and national security, realists claim, motivate states during wartime and thus moral appeals are strictly wishful thinking.

   Talk of the morality of warfare is pure bunk [nonsense]: ethics has got nothing to do with the rough-and-tumble world of global politics, where only the strong and cunning survive. A country should tend to its vital interests in security, influence over others, and economic growth–and not to moral ideals.

2. Do any of these comments come from particular cultural perspectives?

3. Choose an issue, comment or question that interests you and discuss it with a partner.

   a) Think about the possible different cultural perspectives on this issue.

   b) Research the issue and identify different cultural perspectives.

Key vocabulary and language exercises

Activity 2

1. What do you understand by the words below?

Moral ideals

War **Conflict** **Resolution**

Peacekeeping

The United Nations **Peace** **National security**

2. Use dictionaries and online resources to find definitions of these words and phrases. Concentrate on different ways in which these words can be understood – don't stop at the first dictionary definition.

> If English is not your first language, avoid using online translation tools. They are often not very good! Your language skills will develop better if you use dictionaries.

Activity 3

1. Complete the mind map below. Add as many ideas, events, thoughts and feelings that you associate with conflict and peace as you can think of. Use online resources and dictionaries as necessary. Some initial ideas are shown below.

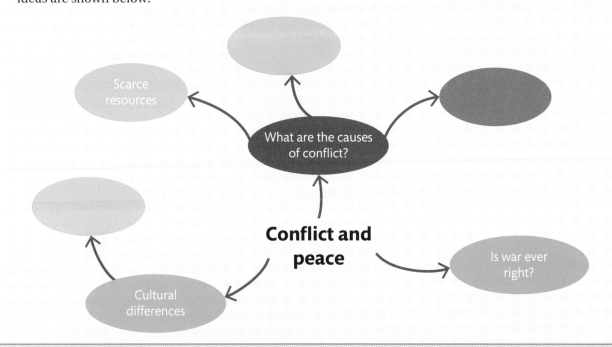

Stimulus material

UK pilots have been involved in air strikes over Syria against the Islamic State group. This is despite the UK Parliament voting against military action in Syria in 2013.

About 20 personnel, including 3 pilots, have spent time with the armed forces of allied countries such as Canada and the US. During this time they have taken part in military action including air strikes.

The Government defended this situation, saying it was normal. However, many Members of Parliament are outraged. They say that this is an undemocratic and possibly illegal involvement in someone else's war.

What different cultural perspectives can you identify in the documents? What attitudes and values underlie them?

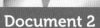

Document 2

Another successful session of conflict resolution.

Document 3

Liberia has experienced 3 decades of political unrest, changing governments and civil wars.

Historical context

In the 1800s, Liberia had a population of traditional tribes who followed traditional religions and Muslims who had migrated to Liberia. In the 1820s – 1840s, former US slaves settled in Liberia. Many of these settlers believed their ancestors had come from Liberia.

The settlers "bought" land from the tribes, but failed to understand that the tribes believed that land belonged to everyone, and could not be owned and passed down through one family. The settlers also established a constitution and a set of laws. But they did not recognise the traditional tribes as "citizens". Over time, this created economic and social differences between the groups, and quite a lot of resentment.

Over the years, a number of different ethnic groups from other countries in the region migrated to Liberia. Some of these people were fleeing from wars, famine and poverty.

So, by the 1980s, Liberia had several ethnic and religious groups, with different identities characterised by different levels of economic and political power, different languages, dress, family systems, land ownership and education.

Incompetent and corrupt governments used the money from natural resources such as diamonds to fund luxurious lifestyles. Eventually different groups started fighting to gain control of the country, and the ethnic and religious groups started to blame each other for the conflict. Money from diamonds was now used to fund warfare. $500 million was donated by foreign powers to support one military power or another.

As the institutions of the state disintegrated, poverty increased. Fighting in the civil wars became the largest employment opportunity. Child soldiers became adult soldiers who could not remember peace.

Document 4

Blood diamonds? No problem. It's your phone that is truly dripping with blood.

Blood diamonds – diamonds that are used to fund conflict in Africa – have received a great deal of attention in the media. It makes a great story, doesn't it? Sealing your love with a diamond ring steeped in the blood of child soldiers is a terrible beginning to a marriage. Yet conflict diamonds are a drop in the ocean of blood minerals. Minerals such as tantalum are far less well known than diamonds, but they are in every phone, tablet and laptop, and they are used in aeroplanes and cars. This report from Global Witness indicates the scale of the problem:

Armed groups including elements of the Congolese national army have played on the trade in tin, tantalum, tungsten and gold to fund a brutal war in Eastern Democratic Republic of Congo for more than 15 years. There were an estimated 2.7 million internally displaced people within the country due to ongoing armed conflict in the east, as of 2014.

The region's natural resource wealth is not the root cause of the violence, but competition over the lucrative minerals trade has become an incentive for some warring parties to continue fighting.

The local population in Congo, and in particular those in North and South Kivu provinces have borne the brunt of a conflict characterised by murder, rape and displacement.

The metals mined in eastern Congo enter global markets and make their way into products such as mobile phones, cars, aeroplanes and jewellery. It is difficult for consumers to know if their favourite products contain minerals that have funded violence overseas.

Recent international efforts to tackle the trade in conflict minerals have focused on requiring companies sourcing from Congo to do checks on their supply chains – known as due diligence – to make sure they are not supporting abusive armed groups through their purchases.

https://www.globalwitness.org/en-gb/campaigns/conflict-minerals/conflict-minerals-eastern-congo/

Skills practice exercises

Activity 4

Consider Document 2.

1. What issues does the cartoon raise?

2. Is this only a personal perspective? Give your reasons.

Activity 5

Refer to Document 1.

1. What international conflict issues does the article raise?

2. What national conflict issues does the article raise?

3. What is your opinion on the presence of British troops in Syria despite a democratic vote against sending troops to Syria?

Activity 6

1. Outline the causes and consequences that led to civil war in Liberia. Use a diagram or flow chart to help you. [9]

2. You need to establish how bad the humanitarian crisis is in Liberia.

   a) How would you gather evidence? [3]

   b) What problems would you expect to have in gathering this evidence? [3]

3. A refugee from Liberia tells you: "The only way to help Liberia is by supporting the Liberian Liberation Army (CLA). The CLA will bring peace and unity to the people, and we need guns and tanks and nuclear missiles to achieve this peace. I know, I've been there."

   a) Do you think this refugee would provide reliable knowledge claims? Explain your answer.

   b) How logical is this refugee's reasoning?

Activity 7

Refer to Document 4

1. Summarise Document 4 in your own words. You can use diagrams to help you. Think about:

   - Key issues
   - Consequences
   - Different perspectives
   - Possible courses of action

2. Is it harder to avoid buying products with tantalum in them than products with diamonds in them?

   a) Research different products using these raw materials

   b) Justify your answer with reference to the evidence.

Activity 8

1. What are the conflict and peace issues most likely to affect these individuals? Think about the differences between similar people in LEDCs and MEDCs.

   - A politician in Ethiopia
   - School student
   - Syrian child
   - Toddler in Glasgow
   - Business leader in Washington DC

2. Think about the different cultural perspectives these people have. What are the needs, expectations, beliefs and desires that make their perspectives different?

3. To what extent are conflict and peace personal, local/national or global concerns?

Activity 9

1. What are the most important problems in your area related to conflict and peace?

   a) What do you already think? Are you prepared to change your mind?

   b) What search terms will you use?

   c) What key words and phrases will you skim read for?

   d) Remember to think about which problems are most important, and why.

2. Choose a city or country in a very different part of the world. What are their most important problems related to conflict and peace?

3. What are the similarities and differences in the conflict and peace problems experienced by your area and the area you have studied?

4. In what ways do these two areas have different perspectives on conflict and peace?

5. What is the most interesting issue you have considered so far? Do you think that this issue is suitable for a team project?

6. Add your own questions to help you plan a line of inquiry.

> Use quick internet searches if necessary to help you.

Language

MEDC stands for more economically developed country.

LEDC stands for less economically developed country.

Can you think of other sorts of development apart from economic development?

Activity 10

- There is a conflict in a neighbouring country. It is based on religion and ethnic identity.

- There is a conflict in a country which is economically important for your country.

1. What are the likely consequences in each of these conflicts if your country intervenes?

2. What are the likely consequences in each of these conflicts if your country does not intervene?

3. What different cultural perspectives would you expect in each case?

Activity 11

1. a) Think of different cultural perspectives in your local area on a particular conflict. Compare the values and attitudes that underlie these perspectives.

   b) Research cultural perspectives on this conflict in a very different country, for example Saudi Arabia, China, Zimbabwe, Argentina, Germany, etc.

> How might a fight at school be in some ways similar to a war?

Reflection

1. Have you changed your opinions about conflict and peace issues generally?

2. Is there a particular debate about conflict and peace in your local area? Do you see the issues differently now? If so, how? Why?

3. Use diagrams and mind maps to help you reflect on the issue.

Reflection

1. After you have carried out your project, answer these questions:

   a) How well did your team work together?

   b) What problems did you have? How did you solve these problems?

   c) How will you avoid these problems next time?

   d) How effective was your outcome?

   e) How effective was your individual contribution?

Ideas for discussion, debate and practice

- What is conflict?

- What is peace?

- Is there a right and wrong in most conflicts?

- Conflict drives progress. Peace leads to stagnation. Do you agree?

- In conflict situations, how important is it to see the other perspective/viewpoint?

- Is it better to negotiate a compromise peacefully or to keep going until you get everything you want? Think about this on a personal, local/national and global scale. Is there a difference between fighting with your brother over the best toy and fighting with your neighbouring state over the best resources?

- What is the best way to deal with conflict on personal, local/national and global scales?

- What is the best way to prevent conflict on personal, local/national and global scales?

  - Choose a particular conflict. Examine the causes and consequences of the conflict and suggest how peace could be achieved in this conflict.

  - How effective is the UN as a peacekeeper?

Discussion

You have to advise your government on the appropriate action for your country to take regarding Liberia.

Options for your country include (but are not limited to):

- Fund one group so that there is one victor who can form an unchallenged government.

- Support UN peacekeeping troops.

- Send your own army.

- Work with local economic and religious organisations.

- Provide a "neutral space" for negotiation to achieve an agreed peace.

- Work with local organisations to provide therapy, education and support for economic growth.

- Provide humanitarian aid.

Carry out the debate. Write up your preferred proposal.

Is your outcome SMART? Remember to consider different cultural perspectives during your research.

Produce a short documentary video about the experiences and consequences of a particular conflict.

Suggestions for aims and outcomes

Work with a local youth group to reduce conflicts and fights in your area.

Work with a refugee group. Find a practical way of providing help.

2 Disease and health

Some of the key issues include:

- Effects of poor health
- Preventable disease
- Preventative health care
- Access to health care
- Funding health care
- Whose responsibility is health?
- Equality
- Health and economic development
- Health effects of lifestyle choices

Do some of these comments and questions raise more than one issue?

Activity 1

1. Match the comments and questions below to the issues above.

   a) "Statistics of the Ministry of Health (MoH) indicate that under-five mortality rate declines from 58‰ in 2001, to 27.5‰ in 2005 and 25.0‰ by 2009, which achieved the target set for 2001–2010 period. According to the Millennium Development Goal, by 2015, this indicator will be reduced to 19.3‰. If this trend continues to 2015, Vietnam will certainly achieve the Millennium Development Goal (MDG)."

   b) "People who smoke and drink, and overeat and don't exercise, should not get free health care on the National Health Service. We all have a responsibility to make healthy choices."

   c) "Investments in roads can improve access to health services; inflation targets can constrain health spending; and civil service reform can create opportunities - or limits – to hiring more health workers."

   d) "People who refuse to get their children vaccinated for measles are irresponsible. Measles kills."

   e) "It is unfair that rich people have better access to health care than poorer people. We used to be quite well off, but my father got cancer and couldn't work. We also had big medical bills, so now we are really struggling. My mother has to work and look after my sister, and I had to leave school to get a job so that we could eat."

   f) "Why should the government pay for my medication? It's my health."

2. Do any of these comments come from particular cultural perspectives?

3. Choose an issue, comment or question that interests you and discuss it with a partner.

   a) Think about the possible different cultural perspectives on this issue.

   b) Research the issue and identify different cultural perspectives.

Activity 2

1. Use dictionaries and online resources to find definitions of the following words and phrases.

If English is not your first language, avoid using online translation tools. They are often not very good! Your language skills will develop better if you use dictionaries.

Words and phrases	Definition
a) Preventative health care	
b) Measles	
c) National Health Service	
d) Vaccination	
e) Lifestyle choice	
f) Malaria	
g) Acute respiratory infection	
h) Health insurance	
i) Medical ethics	

Activity 3

1. Make cards with the words from Activity 2. Make separate cards with the definitions you have found. Play these games to help you remember the words.

   a) Turn all the cards face down so that you cannot see them. Mix them up so that you don't know which card is where. Turn over two cards at a time. If you have a word and its definition, you keep the pair. The player with the most pairs wins.

   b) Mix all the definition cards up and put them in one pile. Take a card from the pile. Read the definition and give the word it defines.

   c) Mix all the word cards up and put them in one pile. Take a card from the pile. Read the word and give its definition.

Stimulus material

Document 1

Antonia: Around 75% of deaths among people aged 10–24 in the US are caused by unintentional injuries or violence. More than half of child deaths in developing countries in 2001 were caused by acute respiratory infections, measles, diarrhoea, malaria, and HIV/AIDS. Added to this, in 2001 99% of child deaths were in developing countries. It doesn't really matter if these young people are dying from preventable accidents or preventable diseases – it's just wrong.

Julian: Here in Australia the major causes of ill health include heart disease and strokes, and these are caused mainly by poor lifestyle – bad diets, smoking and not enough exercise.

Qing Yu: We've been having a debate in the UK about cigarette packaging. The evidence shows that young people are less likely to smoke if cigarettes come in plain packets. But the government has decided not to pass a law enforcing plain packets. Interestingly, one of the Prime Minister's advisers also works for two major cigarette firms. We don't have corruption in Britain – just "hidden persuasion."

Document 2

World Fit for Children, PROTECTING CHILDREN AND THEIR DIGNITY

Message from the Children's Forum, delivered to the UN General Assembly Special Session on Children by child delegates, Gabriela Azurduy Arrieta, 13, from Bolivia and Audrey Cheynut, 17, from Monaco on 8 May 2002.

We are the world's children.
We are the victims of exploitation and abuse.
We are street children.
We are the children of war.
We are the victims and orphans of HIV/AIDS.
We are denied good-quality education and health care.
We are victims of political, economic, cultural, religious and environmental discrimination.
We are children whose voices are not being heard: it is time we are taken into account.

We want a world fit for children, because a world fit for us is a world fit for everyone.

In this world,

We see respect for the rights of the child:

- governments and adults having a real and effective commitment to the principle of children's rights and applying the Convention on the Rights of the Child to all children,

- safe, secure and healthy environments for children in families, communities, and nations.

We see the provision of health care:

- affordable and accessible life-saving drugs and treatment for all children,

- strong and accountable partnerships established among all to promote better health for children.

We see the eradication of HIV/AIDS:

- educational systems that include HIV prevention programs,

- free testing and counselling centres,

- information about HIV/AIDS freely available to the public,

- orphans of AIDS and children living with HIV/AIDS cared for and enjoying the same opportunities as all other children.

http://www.unicef.org/malaysia/campaigns_wffc.html

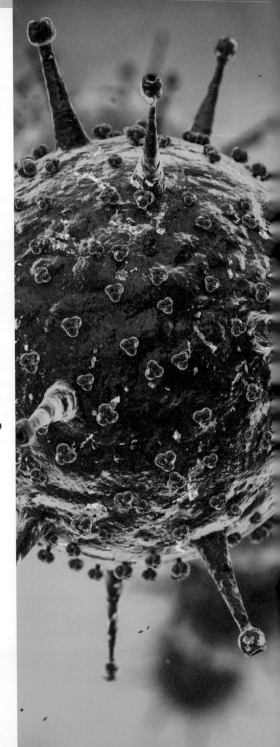

Document 3

Should health care be free?

 A: Health care is a basic human right, and should therefore be free to all citizens. No one should have to choose between food and their medication, or heat and going to the doctor. In addition, no one should face bankruptcy because of an illness or accident. Everyone should have access to healthcare.

 B: Free health care, yes, and so if you are for free health care, you are for abortion. If you want to add more taxes to the ballot, paying for your health care, firemen, law enforcement services, and so much more, let's do it! You all think you do not pay for other services, but you do; however, this service will make the economy more depressed than it is now, adding more fees by governments to the employer and so forth. HUGE companies need to pay for health care, especially when their CEO's make $5 million plus a year – they need to pay for health care.

 C: No, health care should not be free. Nothing in life is "free." Health care services that a person doesn't pay for might seem "free" to that person, but it is being paid for by someone else. Any good or service that a person receives should be paid for, and the person should know how much it costs. People are completely out of touch with the true and exorbitant cost of healthcare. It's like we're demanding the government provides us with free diamonds.

 D: I don't want the government deciding whether I get to live or die. And that's what free health care means. Also, why should idiots who contribute to their own illness and injury get free health care? Don't smoke, don't go skiing, don't drive like a maniac. Simple.

> What different cultural perspectives can you identify in these comments? What are the attitudes and values underlying these perspectives?

Skills practice exercises

Activity 4

Refer to Document 2.

1. Do you think that this is a reasonable list of aims?

2. This document was produced in 2002. How relevant do you think it is now? Why?

3. To what extent do the actions of adults affect the health and well-being of children? Consider personal, local/national and global perspectives.

Activity 5

Consider Document 3.

1. Are any of these opinions from a reliable source? Justify your answer.

2. Does B predict likely consequences? Otherwise, is the reasoning good? Explain your answer.

3. Do you think C's reasoning is good? Give your reasons.

4. Whose view do you most agree with? Refer to the reasoning and use your own opinions.

Activity

Refer to Document 1 on page 97.

1. Identify two facts and an opinion given by Antonia. Explain your answer.

2. Antonia compares statistics for 10–24 year olds and children. Is this acceptable? Explain your answer.

3. Can you check Antonia's facts? Can you find more recent figures?

4. Julian says, "Here in Australia the major causes of ill health include heart disease and strokes, and these are caused mainly by poor lifestyle – bad diets, smoking and not enough exercise." Is this a fact or opinion? Explain your answer.

5. "Young people are less likely to smoke if cigarettes come in plain packets." How would you check this claim to see if it is a fact?

6. "We don't have corruption in Britain – just 'hidden persuasion.'" Is this a fact or opinion? Explain your answer.

> Remember, facts can be verified and opinions cannot.

> Think about your search terms. If your first search doesn't work, what other search terms could you try?

Activity 7

1. What are the most important problems in your area related to disease and health?

    a) What do you already think? Are you prepared to change your mind?

    b) What search terms will you use?

    c) What key words and phrases will you skim read for?

    d) Remember to think about which problems are most important, and why.

2. Choose a city or country in a very different part of the world. What are their most important problems related to disease and health?

3. What are the similarities and differences in the health problems experienced by your area and the area you have studied?

4. In what ways do these two areas have different perspectives on health and disease?

> For example, in the UK there is a National Health Service, and people expect to pay higher taxes to get free health care. In the USA, on the other hand, health care is paid for by individuals or by health insurance, and many people dislike the idea of tax funded health care.

5. What is the most interesting health issue you have considered so far? Do you think that this issue is suitable for a team project?

6. Add your own questions to help you plan a line of inquiry.

Activity 8

1. What are the health issues most likely to affect these individuals? Think about the differences between similar people in developed and undeveloped countries.

   - Labourer who has migrated to Hanoi, Vietnam to find work.
   - School student in Beijing, China.
   - Pregnant woman in Kampala, Uganda.
   - Toddler in Glasgow, UK.
   - Business leader in Washington, DC, USA.

   Use quick internet searches if necessary to help you.

2. Think about the different cultural perspectives these people have. What are the needs, expectations, beliefs and desires that make their perspectives different?

3. To what extent are disease and health personal, local/national or global concerns?

Activity 9

1. **a)** What are the likely consequences of allowing people to choose their lifestyle freely with no government interventions?

   b) What are the likely consequences of the government trying to change people's lifestyle choices? Does it vary depending on which country you think about?

Activity 10

1. **a)** Think of different cultural perspectives in your local area on an issue within Disease and Health. Compare the attitudes and values that underlie these perspectives.

   b) Research cultural perspectives on this issue in a very different country, for example Saudi Arabia, China, Zimbabwe, Argentina, Germany, etc.

Activity 11

1. a) Have you changed your opinions about disease and health issues generally?

   b) Is there a particular health debate in your local area? Do you see the issues differently now? If so, how? Why?

   c) Use diagrams and mind maps to help you to reflect on the issue for your research report.

Reflection

1. After you have carried out your project, answer these questions:

   a) How well did your team work together?

   b) What problems did you have? How did you solve these problems?

   c) How will you avoid these problems next time?

   d) How effective was your outcome?

   e) How effective was your individual contribution?

Ideas for discussion, debate and practice

Read the following article. Did the hospital make the right choice? Discuss the issues.

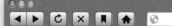

An 86-year-old patient with vast influence in the community wanted a surgery for incurable cancer that would not be fully covered by Medicare [health insurance], and "the healthcare providers registered their concerns about risks and futility of surgery but acceded to family wishes because the old gentleman was influential, well known, and well respected in the community; there was no desire to antagonize either the patient or his family". The same hospital denied the child of a less influential family vaccination because they were unable to pay for it.

http://journalofethics.ama-assn.org/2011/05/jdsc1-1105.html

Medical dilemmas

1. There is a natural disaster, and the hospital generators fail. Which patients should be helped first in the rescue? Give your reasons.

2. After an earthquake, a doctor sees an unconscious young man. The doctor needs to amputate the man's leg to save his life. But the young man cannot consent because he is unconscious. Should the doctor amputate without consent?

3. A teenager (14) wants to see the doctor without a parent present. What should the doctor do?

4. Should it be legal to buy and sell organs for transplant?

Perhaps one of these online health-related games will give you a project idea.

http://www.ready.gov/kids/games/data/dm-english/wildfire.html

http://www.nlm.nih.gov/medlineplus/games.html

Discussion

1. How effectively is my country dealing with health issues? What else should the government do?

2. Should governments put more emphasis on maintaining good health rather than curing disease?

3. What is the best action to take to ensure that people make healthy lifestyle choices?

4. What is the best action to take to ensure that everyone has at least some access to healthcare?

5. How can we persuade more people to donate blood?

6. What health issues does migration raise? Think about different kinds of migrants – migrants from rural areas to cities within one country, from LEDCs to MEDCs, refugees, students, medical professionals, high-income workers.

Your outcome must be active – it cannot be an essay – and it must involve team work and cross-cultural perspectives.

Produce a video campaign to raise awareness of health issues for students in two different countries.

Suggestions for aims and outcomes

What actions need to be taken in (country/city of your choice) to improve healthcare? Put together a proposal to persuade the city leaders to take action.

Design your own healthcare system. You could use a computer game or paper for your design. Justify your choices and present your design to an audience, showing how your system deals with different cultural perspectives.

Design and conduct a medical ethics survey. Present the results, showing different cultural perspectives.

Remember to consider different cultural perspectives during your research.

3 Human rights

Some of the key issues include:

- **Individual rights vs. social stability**
- **Civil rights vs. national security**
- **Freedom to vs. freedom from**
- **Where do human rights come from?**
- **Human rights and neocolonialism**
- **How universal are human rights?**
- **Limits on human rights**

Do some of these comments and questions raise more than one issue?

Activity 1

1. Match the comments and questions below to the issues listed above.

    a) "For too long, the Burkinabé authorities have neglected the rights of women and girls. Redressing this wrong and lifting the barriers faced by women and girls must be a central aim of any election candidate's campaign."

    b) "The Egyptian government has issued a new draft for a counterterrorism law. It has been widely circulated by the local press, while President Abdel Fatah El-Sisi has vowed to achieve "rapid justice against terrorism." Said Boumedouha, deputy director of the Middle East and North Africa Programme at Amnesty International, said: 'The proposed counterterrorism law vastly expands the Egyptian authorities' powers and threatens the most fundamental rights to freedom of expression, peaceful assembly and association.'"

    c) "A pledge to challenge the authority of the European Court by abolishing the Human Rights Act (HRA) and replacing it with a "British" Bill of Rights, had been widely expected to be included in last week's Queen's Speech. Although plans to scrap the HRA were put on hold, the Justice Secretary has told advisers he remains determined to break the formal link between British courts and Strasbourg."

    d) "Human rights are rights inherent to all human beings, regardless of race, sex, nationality, ethnicity, language, religion, or any other status."

    e) "I don't really get human rights. Where do they come from? How can we have human rights if we live in a country that doesn't recognise them as legal rights?"

2. Do any of these comments come from particular cultural perspectives?

3. Choose an issue, comment or question that interests you and discuss it with a partner.

    a) Think about the possible different cultural perspectives on this issue.

    b) Research the issue and identify different cultural perspectives.

Activity 2

1. What do you understand by the words and phrases below?

2. Use dictionaries and online resources to find definitions of the words and phrases in the table. Concentrate on different ways in which these words can be understood – don't stop at the first dictionary definition.

If English is not your first language, avoid using online translation tools. They are often not very good! Your language skills will develop better if you use dictionaries.

Words and phrases	Definition
a) Human rights	
b) Legal rights	
c) Natural rights	
d) Freedom to	
e) Freedom from	
f) Civil rights	
g) Universal	
h) National security	

Activity 3

1. Complete the mind map below. Add as many ideas, events, thoughts and feelings that you associate with human rights as you can think of. Use online resources and dictionaries as necessary. Some initial ideas have been suggested below.

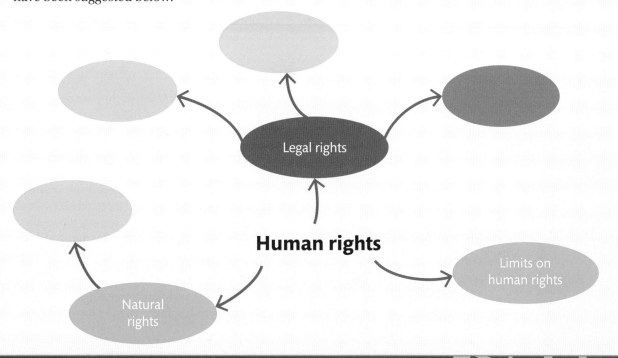

Stimulus material

Document 1

Extracts from the Universal Declaration of Human Rights

Article 3

Everyone has the right to life, liberty and security of person.

Article 4

No one shall be held in slavery or servitude; slavery and the slave trade shall be prohibited in all their forms.

Article 5

No one shall be subjected to torture or to cruel, inhuman or degrading treatment or punishment.

Article 7

All are equal before the law and are entitled without any discrimination to equal protection of the law. All are entitled to equal protection against any discrimination in violation of this Declaration and against any incitement to such discrimination.

Source: http://www.un.org/en/documents/udhr/

Document 2

Should criminals have rights?

@governmentminister

No, criminals should not have rights. By committing crimes, criminals have waived their human rights. They do not deserve to have rights. It is of utmost importance that we should protect the public. What about the rights of someone's son who was killed by a criminal?

@member ofthepublic

When do we define someone as a criminal and remove their rights? When they are caught breaking the speed limit? When they are a Member of Parliament who makes corrupt use of government money for their own purposes or to line their own pockets? When they share the same name as someone who *might* be a terrorist?

@victim

Criminals have far too many rights and they don't deserve them because they don't care about other people's rights. They get more rights than the victims. The police go out and try to protect us and catch criminals and then the criminals go free but they're better off in prison anyway where they get everything they want provided for them, not like us who have to keep working for our food.

@law professor

You don't have human rights because you deserve them. You have them because you are human. So of course criminals have human rights. But society can place limits on those rights – for example on someone's liberty – in order to protect the rights of others. But a crime must be proven. We are innocent until proven guilty.

Human rights excuse for neo-colonialism

(China Daily)
Updated: 2011-04-21 07.56

What different cultural perspectives can you identify in these documents? What attitudes and values underlie them?

Editor's note: The human rights issue is being used by a handful of countries as a pretext and tool to pursue selfish interests, demonize the image of other countries and intervene in their internal affairs, a Beijing Daily commentary said on April 15. The following are excerpts:

The US State Department published on April 8 an annual report on other countries' human rights, lashing out at human rights conditions in more than 190 countries and regions. As expected, the unpopular report has once again evoked unanimous rebuttals and criticism from the targeted countries, including China.

The next day a spokesperson for China's Foreign Ministry warned the United States not to behave as a self-proclaimed human rights judge and said it should reflect on its own human rights conditions. The Information Office of China's State Council also published a white paper two days later on US human rights practices in 2010, urging Washington to face up to its own human rights issues.

The US has published annual reports on human rights practices in other countries since 1977 and has been accustomed to, and is intent on, behaving as a "judge". However, Washington has received a cold shoulder from countries worldwide, because of its own human rights violations and its double standard on human rights issues.

The US has never hesitated to point the finger at other countries' human rights and to advocate that "human rights are superior to sovereignty" when it serves its own interests. But the US has refused to sign some of the major United Nations human rights covenants. On March 18, the UN Human Rights Council made 228 proposals for the US to improve its own human rights conditions, including urging Washington to ratify some key international human rights treaties, improving the rights for minorities and reducing racial discrimination. However, the US refused most of these proposals on the grounds that its human rights allow no intervention from the outside.

The double standard embraced by the US testify to the fact that human rights are being used by some countries as a tool to interfere with others' internal affairs and the idea that "human rights stand higher than sovereignty" has become a political slogan for some to justify their hegemonic activities.

Until the outbreak of World War II, Western countries were still enmeshed [involved] in their history of colonialism, racial discrimination and outside aggression. The widespread national liberation and democratic movements across the world following the end of World War II quickly resulted in the collapse of the West's long-held moral excuses that were used to justify their past crimes and "use of force" and it turned to concepts, such as "humanitarian intervention" and "human rights are superior to sovereignty", as the main means to regain their lost moral dominance and maintain their dwindling domain of influence throughout the world.

By using abstract terms and their own criteria to define the concept of human rights, Western countries have attempted to completely separate human rights from sovereignty and then cause conflicts in specific countries and regions from which they can benefit and achieve their own political purposes.

Human rights in individual countries can only be realized and protected in a sovereign country, when there are still strong and weak countries and when hegemonic activities and power politics still prevail.

A country belongs to all its people and the country's sovereignty is the concentrated embodiment of its collective human rights. The existence of sovereign nations constitutes the foundation of the current international society and under this precondition human rights conditions worldwide have made continuous advancements.

In the absence of sovereignty, a country will have no ability and means to protect the human rights of its people. From Kosovo to Iraq, Afghanistan and Libya, under the pretext of "human rights being superior to sovereignty", Western countries have chosen to use guns and bombs against the governments of these countries to realize their own ulterior motives. But the use of force has failed to bring the people in these countries improved human rights, on the contrary it has plunged them deep into humanitarian disasters and cost many their lives.

Protecting human rights is a universal pursuit of people of all countries across the world. But if this issue is rigged by a handful of countries as the excuse to interfere with other countries' internal affairs, the human rights of these countries and their people are ignored.

Military interventions under the guise of moral slogans are in essence a kind of neo-colonialism.

Document 4

Eritrea leads the way in Africa on issues ranging from the prevention and treatment of malaria, HIV/AIDS and other preventable diseases, to access to clean drinking water, literacy promotion, and countless other issues. But none of this is deemed worthy by the UN for inclusion in a report about "human rights."

This is of course not to suggest that Eritrea, like every other country in the so called "developing" and "developed" worlds, is without problems, as that would be simply false. Rather, it is to note that a truly objective report that actually sought a substantive analysis of human rights in Eritrea, rather than a politically motivated propaganda campaign, would have revealed a country busy transforming itself and its people, leaving behind the decades of colonial oppression and subjugation, beating an independent path for itself.

First appeared: http://journal-neo.org/2015/06/17/eritrea-human-rights-and-neocolonial-propaganda/

Skills practice exercises

Activity 4

Refer to Document 1 and use the internet to read the full list of rights.

1. Do you agree that everyone should have all of these rights all of the time? Give your reasons.

2. Which rights, if any, do you think should be limited sometimes? Give your reasons.

3. Which groups of people, if any, do you think should have limited rights? Give your reasons.

4. How would you feel if these rights did not apply to you for some reason?

Activity 5

Refer to Document 4

1. Can you find any evidence to support the claims made in Document 4?

2. What search terms will you use?

3. How will you make sure you find a balanced view?

> Remember that "I agree" is different from "this is effective reasoning".

Activity 6

Refer to Document 2

1. Whose opinions do you most agree with?

2. What beliefs and experiences do you think have influenced their perspectives?

3. Whose reasoning is the most effective? Consider
   - their use of evidence
   - how logical they are.

Activity 7

Refer to Document 3

1. Summarise the key issues in this document. Use diagrams to help you.

2. How do you respond to the ideas in this document? Does it support your views or challenge them?

3. Discuss the issues.

> Use quick internet searches if you need help.

Activity 8

1. What are the human rights issues most likely to affect the following individuals? Think about the differences between similar people in LEDCs and MEDCs.

   - Detainee in Guantanamo Bay
   - Human rights activist in prison
   - Amnesty international worker
   - Murderer in prison
   - Person deciding which jewellery/trainers/computer to buy

2. Think about the different cultural perspectives these people have. What are the needs, expectations, beliefs and desires that make their perspectives different?

3. To what extent are human rights personal, local/national or global concerns?

Activity 9

1. What are the most important problems in your area related to human rights?

   a) What do you already think? Are you prepared to change your mind?

   b) What search terms will you use?

   c) What key words and phrases will you skim read for?

   d) Remember to think about which problems are most important, and why.

2. Choose a city or country in a very different part of the world. What are their most important problems related to human rights?

3. What are the similarities and differences in the human rights problems experienced by your area and the area you have studied?

4. In what ways do these two areas have different perspectives on human rights?

5. What is the most interesting human rights issue you have considered so far? Do you think that this issue is suitable for a team project?

6. Add your own questions to help you plan a line of inquiry.

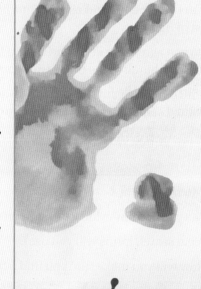

Activity 10

1. **a)** What are the likely consequences of allowing human rights with no restrictions?

   b) What are the likely consequences of the government putting severe restrictions on human rights? Does it vary depending on which rights or which country you think about?

   c) What are the consequences of Western governments and NGOs encouraging other countries to accept human rights?

   d) Examine the values and attitudes which underlie different cultural perspectives on human rights.

Reflection

- Have you changed your opinions about human rights issues generally?

- Is there a particular human rights debate in your local area? Do you see the issues differently now? If so, how and why?

- Use diagrams and mind maps to help you to reflect on the issue.

Activity 11

1. After you have carried out your project, answer these questions.

   a) How well did your team work together?

   b) What problems did you have? How did you solve these problems?

   c) How will you avoid these problems next time?

   d) How effective was your outcome?

   e) How effective was your individual contribution?

Ideas for discussion, debate and practice

1. If you could only have one right, which one would you choose?

2. What sort of limits should we put on human rights?

3. Where is the boundary between freedom and security?

4. Should we restrict family size to combat over population?

5. Should we detain terrorist suspects without charge?

6. Are Western governments hypocritical for insisting that other countries improve their human rights record when theirs are not perfect?

7. Is it ever acceptable to torture someone? Give your reasons.

Research

Investigate the Stamford Prison experiment. What does that tell us? Do we really have good judgement about when it's acceptable to deprive someone of their human rights?

Remember to consider different cultural perspectives during your research.

Set up a democratic student council to evaluate and safeguard human rights within school. Present your progress to the school board.

Suggestions for aims and outcomes

Identify a human rights problem or abuse in your local area. Produce a realistic plan of action for tacking this problem, and present the plan to your local authorities.

Produce a video documentary about human rights issues.

4 Language and communication

Some of the key issues include:

- **Should there be one world language?**
- **Language and identity**
- **Access to language of science**
- **English vs. local languages**
- **Language and culture**

- **Access to internet language**
- **English vs. Chinese**
- **Gendered language**
- **Globalisation vs. localisation**
- **Communication and conflict**
- **Language and thought**
- **Changing language**

Do some of these comments and questions raise more than one issues?

Hello!

Activity 1

1. Match the comments and questions below to the issues in the diagram above.

   a) Why should I have to learn a foreign language? Everyone speaks English anyway.

   b) Do people from around the world end up attending to, understanding, and remembering their experiences differently simply because they speak different languages? This is a profound question in the study of mind, with important implications for politics, law and religion. Until now, there has been relatively little study into this question, however new research is showing that language has an enormous influence on how we perceive the world.

   c) In addition to space and time, languages also shape how we understand causality.

   For example, English likes to describe events in terms of agents doing things. English speakers tend to say things like "John broke the vase" even for accidents. Speakers of Spanish or Japanese would be more likely to say "the vase broke itself." Such differences between languages have profound consequences for how their speakers understand events, construct notions of causality and agency, what they remember as eyewitnesses and how much they blame and punish others.

   d) History shows us that a language becomes a global language mainly due to the political power of its native speakers, and the economic power with which it is able to maintain and expand its position. A global language can allow for easier communication and trade.

2. Do any of these comments come from particular cultural perspectives?

3. Choose an issue, comment or question that interests you and discuss it with a partner.

a) Think about the possible different cultural perspectives on this issue.

b) Research the issue and identify different cultural perspectives.

Key vocabulary and language exercises

Activity 2

1. Identify three important differences between the way English works and the way another language works. How do they affect the ways in which speakers understand and shape the world?

2. Make a note of key vocabulary and definitions.

Activity 3

1. Complete the mind map below. Add as many ideas, events, thoughts and feelings that you associate with language and communication as you can think of. Use online resources and dictionaries as necessary, for example: http://www.ecosystem.org/types-of-ecosystems. Some initial ideas have been suggested below.

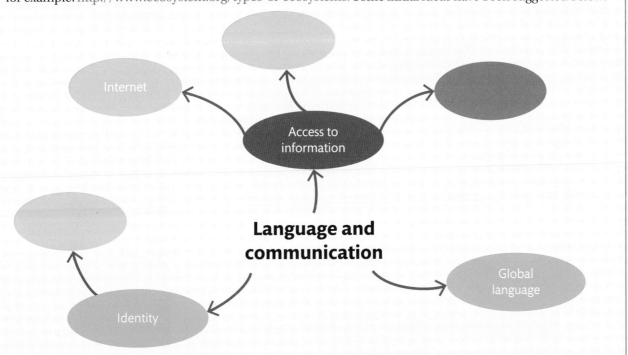

Stimulus material

Document 1

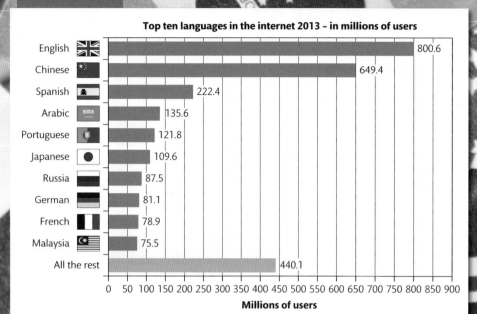

Top ten languages in the internet 2013 – in millions of users

Language	Millions of users
English	800.6
Chinese	649.4
Spanish	222.4
Arabic	135.6
Portuguese	121.8
Japanese	109.6
Russia	87.5
German	81.1
French	78.9
Malaysia	75.5
All the rest	440.1

Source: Internet World stats- www.internetworldstats.com/stats7.htm
Estimated Internet users are 2,802,478,934 in December 31, 2013

Document 2

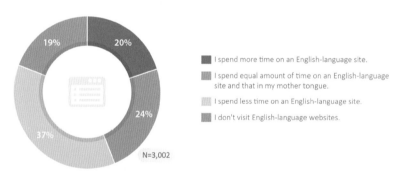

How would you compare the time you spend on English-languages sites vs. ones in your own language?

20%
19%
24%
37%

N=3,002

- I spend more time on an English-language site.
- I spend equal amount of time on an English-language site and that in my mother tongue.
- I spend less time on an English-language site.
- I don't visit English-language websites.

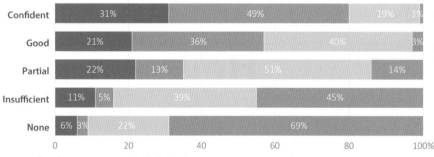

Confident	31%	49%	19% 1%
Good	21%	36%	40% 3%
Partial	22%	13%	51% 14%
Insufficient	11% 5%	39%	45%
None	6% 3% 22%	69%	

Consumers Spend More Time on Sites in Their Own Language
Source: Common Sense Advisory, Inc., "Can't Read, Won't Buy," 2014

Document 3

"Son, we're learning how to speak teenage."

Activity 4

Look at the statistics in Documents 1 and 2.

1. "All companies should have English and Chinese versions of their website."

   Do the statistics give you good reason to accept this claim? Justify your answer.

2. What information do you need to help you explain the statistics in Document 1? How would this information help to explain the statistics?

3. How exactly would you find this information?

Activity 5

1. Explain the issues the cartoon in Document 3 raises with regards to language. Consider different cultural perspectives, for example, how do the parents and teenager have different cultural perspectives?

Document 4

In my work on gender equality I focus on words that students consider just fine: male (so-called) generics. Some of these words refer to persons occupying a position: postman, chairman, freshman, congressman, fireman. Other words refer to the entire universe of human beings: "mankind" or "he." Then we've got manpower, manmade lakes and "Oh, man, where did I leave my keys?" There's "manning" the tables in a country where children learn that "all men are created equal." The worst, from my observations, is the popular expression "you guys." Please don't tell me it's a regional term. I've heard it in the Triangle, New York, Chicago, San Francisco and Montreal. I've seen it in print in national magazines, newsletters and books. And even if it were regional, that doesn't make it right. I'll bet we can all think of a lot of practices in our home regions that we'd like to get rid of.

I sound defensive. I know. But that's because I've so often heard (and not only from students) ... *What's the big deal?*

One consequence of male-based generics is that they reinforce the system in which "man" in the abstract and men in the flesh are privileged over women. But the words we use can also reinforce current realities when they are sexist (or racist). Words are tools of thought. We can use words to maintain the status quo or to think in new ways – which in turn creates the possibility of a new reality. It makes a difference if I think of myself as a "girl" or a "woman"; it makes a difference if we talk about "Negroes" or "African-Americans." Do we want a truly inclusive language or one that just pretends?

In 1986 Douglas Hofstadter, a philosopher, wrote a parody of sexist language by making an analogy with race. His article ("A Person Paper on Purity in Language") creates an imaginary world in which generics are based on race rather than gender. In that world, people would use "fresh *white*," "chair *white*" and yes, "you *whiteys*." People of color would hear "all whites are created equal" – and be expected to feel included. Substituting "white" for "man" makes it easy to see why using "man" for all human beings is wrong. Yet, women are expected to feel flattered by "freshman," "chairman" and "you guys."

And can you think of one, just one, example of a female-based generic? Try using "freshwoman" with a group of male students or calling your male boss "chairwoman." Then again, don't. There could be serious consequences for referring to a man as a "woman" – a term that still means "lesser" in our society. If not, why do men get so upset at the idea of being called women?

Sherryl Kleinman teaches in the Department of Sociology at the University of North Carolina

http://www.alternet.org/story/48856/why_sexist_language_matters

Skills practice exercises

teşekkür ederim

Activity 6

Refer to Document 4.

1. Summarise the key points made in the article.

2. Is Sherryl Kleinman a reliable source of information on gender equality and language? Justify your answer.

3. Is this article mostly fact or opinion? Justify your answer.

4. How effective is Kleinman's reasoning in Document 4?

   In your answer you should consider:

   - The causes and consequences she suggests.
   - Whether you agree with any values she expresses.
   - Any other relevant issues.

Activity 7

1. What are the language and communication issues most likely to affect the following individuals? Think about the differences between similar people in LEDCs and MEDCs.

   - A migrant from Syria to Germany.
   - School student in Beijing.
   - Physics student from Ghana who finds English challenging.
   - Business leader in Brazil.
   - Business leader in Washington D.C.

   If necessary, use quick internet searches to help you

2. Think about the different cultural perspectives these people have. What are the needs, expectations, beliefs and desires that make their perspectives different?

3. To what extent are language and communication personal, local/national or global concerns?

Activity 8

1. What are the most important problems in your area related to language and communication?

   a) What do you already think? Are you prepared to change your mind?

   b) What search terms will you use?

   c) What key words and phrases will you skim read for?

   d) Remember to think about which problems are most important, and why.

2. Choose a city or country in a very different part of the world. What are their most important problems related to language and communication?

3. What are the similarities and differences in the language and communication problems experienced by your area and the area you have studied?

4. In what ways do these two areas have different perspectives on language and communication?

5. What is the most interesting issue you have considered so far? Do you think that this issue is suitable for a team project?

6. Add your own questions to help you plan a line of inquiry.

> "How effective is the reasoning?" is another way of asking, "Is the reasoning good quality?" or "Does the reasoning work well?"

Activity 9

1. a) Think of different cultural perspectives on an issue relating to language and communication in your local area. Compare the attitudes and values that underlie these perspectives.

   b) Research cultural perspectives on this issue in a very different country, for example Saudi Arabia, China, Zimbabwe, Argentina, Germany, etc.

Activity 10

1. After you have carried out your project, answer these questions:

   a) How well did your team work together?

   b) What problems did you have? How did you solve these problems?

   c) How will you avoid these problems next time?

   d) How effective was your outcome?

   e) How effective was your individual contribution?

Reflection

- Have you changed your opinions about language and communication issues generally?

- Is there a particular language and communication debate in your local area? Do you see the issues differently now? If so, how? Why?

- Use diagrams and mind maps to help you to reflect on the issue.

Ideas for discussion, debate and practice

- Should everyone speak more than one language?

- What is language?

- How important is it to have one standard from a language?

- Should literature, music and films be in English to gain a world audience, or in a national language to strengthen local culture?

- Do you think that lack of communication is the cause of most conflicts?

- Should language adapt to reflect cultural changes or be kept the same to preserve culture?

- How does your language affect your thoughts and belief?

- Is your language a part of your identity?

- Should there be one world language? If so, which one?

- If you are bilingual, do you think and behave differently in different languages? For example, some bilingual Chinese/English speakers say they find it easier to question authority in English than in Chinese, and have more outgoing personalities when they are speaking English. What do you think?

Produce a video campaign to raise awareness of language and communication issues for students in two different countries.

What actions need to be taken in [country/ city of your choice] to improve language learning? Put together a proposal to persuade the city leaders to take action.

Suggestions for aims and outcomes

Is your outcome SMART?

Design and conduct a survey about language use/learning. Present the results, showing different cultural perspectives.

Remember to consider different cultural perspectives during your research.

5 Poverty and inequality

Some of the key issues include:

- **Absolute and relative poverty**
- **Equality**
- **Health and economic development**

- **Equal opportunities**
- **Effects of poverty on health**
- **Minimum wage**
- **Consequences of inequality**

> Do some of these comments and questions raise more than one issue?

Activity 1

1. Match the comments and questions below to the issues in the diagram above.

   a) I don't want to be rich. But I do want to be paid a fair wage for a fair day's work.

   b) The OECD examines the trends and patterns in inequality and poverty for OECD and emerging countries. Its work analyses the multiple causes linked to growing inequalities, such as globalisation, technological change and changes in redistribution and policy fashion. It also assesses the effectiveness of social and labour market policies in tackling poverty and high inequalities.

   c) The "greedy bankers" are in no way blameless for the global credit crisis that led to our recession. To proportion all of our blame towards them, however, would not only be inaccurate but lose sight of what caused the problem. Solely blaming Investment Banks would be like shouting at the clouds because it's raining.

   d) Today it is widely held that one cannot consider only the economic part of poverty. Poverty is also social, political and cultural. Moreover, it is considered to undermine human rights. The Millennium Development Goals are an agenda for reducing poverty, its causes and manifestations.

   e) Money can't buy you happiness. But it can buy really good health care. And I'd be a lot happier if we could afford the treatment my mum needs.

2. Do any of these comments come from particular cultural perspectives?

3. Choose an issue, comment or question that interests you and discuss it with a partner.

   a) Think about the possible different cultural perspectives on this issue.

   b) Research the issue and identify different cultural perspectives.

Key vocabulary and language exercises

Activity 2

1. Use dictionaries and online resources to find definitions of these words and phrases:

> If English is not your first language, avoid using online translation tools. They are often not very good! Your language skills will develop better if you use dictionaries.

Words and phrases	Definition
a) Absolute poverty	
b) Relative poverty	
c) Inequality	
d) Millennium Development Goals	
e) Global credit crisis	
f) Economic development	
g) Social poverty	
h) Cultural poverty	

Activity 3

1. Complete the mind map below. Add as many ideas, events, thoughts and feelings that you associate with poverty and inequality as you can think of. Use online resources and dictionaries as necessary. Some initial ideas have been suggested.

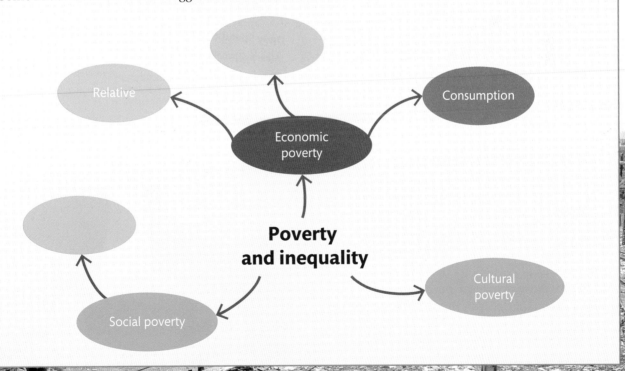

Stimulus material

Document 1

A well-known restaurant has partnered with Visa to make a website dedicated to showing its employees how to properly budget their meager salaries. However, what it actually does is illustrate the fact that it is nearly impossible to get by on minimum wage, as shown in this "example" budget chart:

That is actually what you would make if you were working *full-time* at the restaurant. 1,105 [US] dollars a month.

Now let's say that the "second" job that they budget in here is also minimum wage. The [US] national minimum wage is $7.25. That translates to **74 hours** a week. That's almost a whole other full time job.

And what do you get for working 74 hours a week? Well, you don't get heat, clearly. Also noticeably absent in this budget? Food. And gas. There is really no such thing as health insurance for $20 a month.

Right now, we have people in our government saying that we shouldn't even have a minimum wage. That employers should be free to pay people whatever they can get someone to agree to work for. If they can get someone to work for $3 an hour, then it should be allowed.

There are people who comfort themselves by telling themselves that poor people are only poor because poor people are *lazy*. Pretty sure someone who works 74 hours a week isn't lazy.

You may think that most of these minimum wage earners are teenagers. Well, 87.9% of minimum wage earners are over the age of 20. 28% of those people are parents trying to raise a kid on this budget. That is not a good thing for our future and it is not a good thing for our economy. In order for the economy to thrive, people have to be able to buy things.

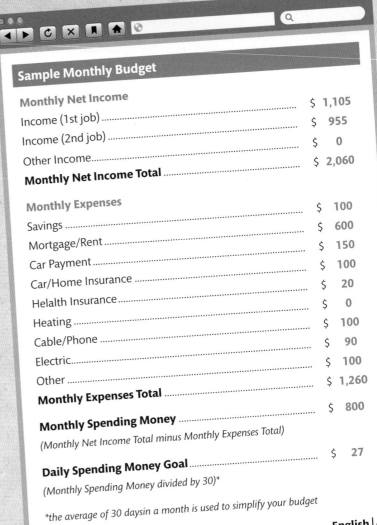

Sample Monthly Budget

Monthly Net Income	
Income (1st job)	$ 1,105
Income (2nd job)	$ 955
Other Income	$ 0
Monthly Net Income Total	$ 2,060

Monthly Expenses	
Savings	$ 100
Mortgage/Rent	$ 600
Car Payment	$ 150
Car/Home Insurance	$ 100
Helalth Insurance	$ 20
Heating	$ 0
Cable/Phone	$ 100
Electric	$ 90
Other	$ 100
Monthly Expenses Total	$ 1,260

Monthly Spending Money .... $ 800
(Monthly Net Income Total minus Monthly Expenses Total)

Daily Spending Money Goal .... $ 27
(Monthly Spending Money divided by 30)*

*the average of 30 daysin a month is used to simplify your budget

English | 4

Document 2

 A: There are people out there earning less than $1 a day, and we are arguing about $7.25 an hour? These people live in the richest nation in the world. They should get their acts together.

 B: The minimum wage needs to be removed as it has been one of the leading causes of unemployment in this country. Wages like all prices need to be set by the market otherwise there will be negative consequences. The primary minimum wage earners had been teenagers and minorities who were training for full time positions eventually. Raising the minimum wage caused companies to do without these employees. As a result we have a growing percentage of the population that does not have the basic skills needed for higher level jobs and is unemployable at the current artificially high market wages. The last minimum wage hike in 2007 began the loss of employment that led to the last recession. Let's help out the young and poor by repealing the minimum wage.

 C: Can you provide citations for any of these flawed and incorrect statements?

 D: Minimum wage increases are good for business. You need to pay your employees enough to buy the products you make. If people have more money, they spend more in local shops, restaurants, etc. and you can raise prices without major opposition.

Document 3

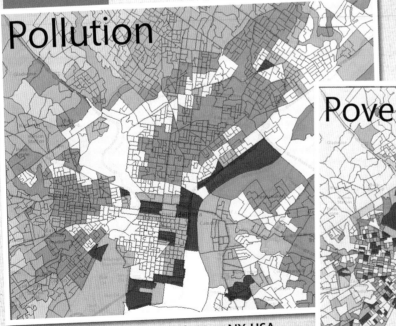

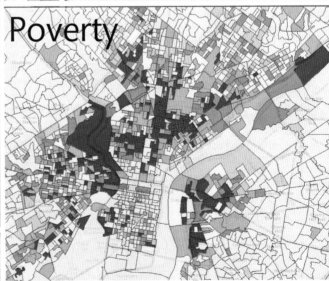

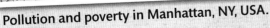

Pollution and poverty in Manhattan, NY, USA.

Document 4

Skills practice exercises

Activity 4

Refer to Document 2

1. "The national minimum wage is $7.25 [in the US in 2013]." What is the national minimum wage in the US now?

2. What is the national minimum wage in your, or another, country?

3. "There really is no such thing as health insurance for $20 a month." Is this a fact or an opinion? Explain your answer.

4. How would you check what health insurance in the US costs?

5. "Someone who works 74 hours a week isn't lazy." Is this fact or opinion? Explain your answer.

> Remember, facts can be verified and opinions cannot.

6. "87.9% of minimum wage earners (in the US) are over the age of 20." Can you cross check this fact? Is the figure the same now as in 2013 when the article was written?

> Think about your search terms. If your first search doesn't work, what other search terms could you try?

Activity 5

Refer to Document 2.

1. "If they can get someone to work for $3 an hour, then it should be allowed." Is this opinion or prediction? Justify your answer.

2. Do you agree?

3. What are the likely consequences for the children of parents who earn the minimum wage?

4. What are the likely consequences for businesses if the minimum wage is significantly raised?

5. Are any of these comments a good source of information and expert opinions on issues relating to the minimum wage?

6. Does B suggest likely causes and consequences?

7. Do you think D's reasoning is good?

8. Whose view are you most in agreement with? Refer to the reasoning and use your own opinions.

Activity 6

Refer to Document 3.

1. What do the images tell you about the relationship between poverty and pollution in Manhattan, USA?

2. Do you think this relationship holds true in other cities around the world?

3. How will you find out?

4. Do you think that poverty causes pollution or that pollution causes poverty? Use internet and other resources to find evidence.

Activity 7

Refer to Document 4.

1. What issues are raised by the cartoon strip in Document 4?

2. What different cultural perspectives can you think of on these issues?

Activity 8

1. What are the problems associated with poverty and inequality for the following people?

   a) Labourer who has migrated to the city to find work.

   b) School student from a disadvantaged background.

   c) Young migrant mother with two children and asthma.

   d) Builder with a bad back.

   e) Sales person whose employer has shut down. Lives in a declining town near elderly mother.

2. Think about the different cultural perspectives these people have. What are the needs, expectations, beliefs and desires that make their perspectives different?

3. To what extent are poverty and inequality personal, local/national or global concerns?

Activity 9

1. What are the most important problems in your area related to poverty and inequality?

   a) What do you already think? Are you prepared to change your mind?

   b) What search terms will you use?

   c) What key words and phrases will you skim read for?

   d) Remember to think about which problems are most important, and why.

2. Choose a city or country in a very different part of the world. What are their most important problems related to poverty and inequality?

3. What are the similarities and differences in the poverty and inequality problems experienced by these two areas?

4. What is the most interesting issue you have considered so far?

   a) Can you think of an active outcome for a team project related to this issue?

   b) Is this outcome SMART?

5. Add your own questions to help you plan your own line of inquiry to answer your own question. Use diagrams to help you.

Activity 10

1. a) Think of different cultural perspectives in your local area on an issue relating to poverty and inequality. Compare the attitudes and values that underlie them.

   b) Research cultural perspectives on this issue in a very different country, for example Saudi Arabia, China, Zimbabwe, Argentina, Germany, etc.

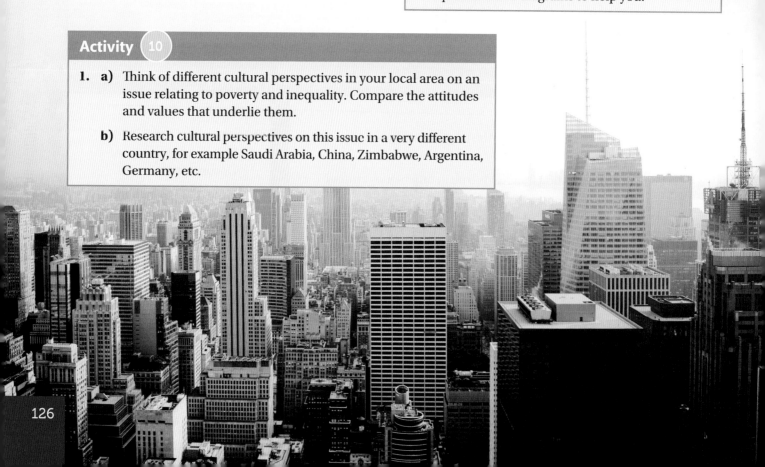

Reflection

After you have carried out your project, answer these questions:

1. How well did your team work together?

2. What problems did you have? How did you solve these problems?

3. How will you avoid these problems next time?

4. How effective was your outcome?

5. How effective was your individual contribution?

Ideas for discussion, debate and practice

1. To be part of the privileged few, all you have to do is successfully throw a ball of paper into the bin. Everyone in the class should attempt this. What issues of equality does this raise?

2. "My family isn't rich in terms of money. But we are rich in love, we support each other, and we are well educated and culturally rich – we take part in local arts festivals and are members of the local amateur dramatic society. This is much better than having lots of money and no taste."

   a) Do you agree?

   b) Is it mere snobbery to be scornful of other people's taste? Or is there a real issue with people who are economically rich but culturally poor? What actions – if any – should be taken about this?

Remember to consider different cultural perspectives during your research.

Produce a video campaign to raise awareness of a problem associated with poverty or inequality.

What actions need to be taken in [city of your choice] to reduce poverty and inequality? Put together a proposal to persuade the city leaders to take action.

Suggestions for aims and outcomes

Engage in a charity project in your city relating to poverty and inequality. Prepare a presentation to the school board showing the affects you have had.

Produce a comic strip or comedy sketch illustrating an issue relating to poverty or inequality.

6 Sport and recreation

Some of the key issues include:

- International cooperation/ competition
- Effects of, e.g. the Olympics
- Supporting youth development
- Sport and national pride
- Corruption in world sporting bodies
- Benefits of hobbies
- Free time and leisure activities
- Sport and health
- Sport/hobbies and community
- Doping in sport

Do some of these comments and questions raise more than one issue?

Activity 1

1. Match the comments and questions below to the issues in the diagram above.

   a) It is impossible these days to win international sporting competitions without using performance enhancing drugs and technologies.

   b) Fifa, football's governing body, is being investigated by US and Swiss authorities over claims of corruption. Fourteen people, including senior officials, are accused of accepting bribes and kickbacks estimated at more than $150m (£97m) over a 24-year period.

   c) Schools are no longer encouraging competitive sport. This is killing elite national sports so that we are no longer top international players.

   d) We are told that international sporting competitions increase international cooperation and understanding. But they actually seem to increase unthinking national support and drunken brawls between rival national teams.

   e) It's more important to have a sport or hobby that you enjoy than it is to be the best at something. Sports and hobbies can improve our mental and physical health.

   f) National televisions stations should show a better range of sports. This would show young people a greater variety of opportunities, and make it more likely that they can find the sport that is right of them.

2. Do any of these comments come from particular cultural perspectives?

3. Choose an issue, comment or question that interests you and discuss it with a partner.

   a) Think about the possible different cultural perspectives on this issue.

   b) Research the issue and identify different cultural perspectives.

Key vocabulary and language exercises

Activity 2

1. Use dictionaries and online resources to help you answer the questions below.

   a) What is the difference between sport, recreation and hobbies?

   b) What are the differences between drug use and enhancement?

   c) What different meanings can you think of for competition?

   d) What is the difference between national pride and patriotism?

> If English is not your first language, avoid using online translation tools. They are often not very good! Your language skills will develop better if you use dictionaries.

Activity 3

1. Use internet resources to help you complete the mind map with sporting issues.

2. Produce another mind map showing language and concepts relating to other forms of recreation.

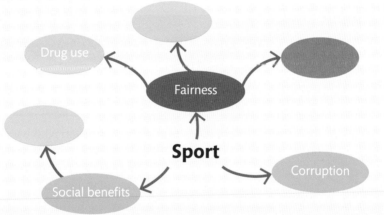

Drug use — Fairness — Corruption — Social benefits — **Sport**

Stimulus material

Document 1

FAIR PLAY — FIFA — BUSINESS — CORRUPTION SCANDALS — PARESH

Document 2

Keira: In my opinion, everyone should have to learn and practise a martial art, a form of dance, and cookery. These are really fundamental aspects of human nature. So, if we introduce this as a policy, there will be far fewer problems with dissatisfied, unhappy people. And therefore we'll have fewer issues with gangs, street violence and crime. It will also make us more equal.

Hassan: It's wrong that they make children do sport at school. It's so embarrassing and humiliating for people like me. I just can't do sport. I like walking and cycling, and this keeps me healthy. But why would I want to kick a ball into a net anyway?

Bina: For me, the problem with school sport is that it's all about competition, and being the best. It's supposed to feed into national sport. But only a small proportion of young people become elite athletes in national teams. So the rest of us get bored and give up. Really though, sport and exercise should be for everyone. We all need to be fit.

Discussion

Do you agree with Keira? What are your reasons?

What different cultural perspectives can you identify in the documents? What attitudes and values underlie them?

Document 3

Time to get the basics right

IF Malaysia wants to have a good future in sports, there has to be more emphasis on athletics. There are no two ways about it.

Malaysia's recent showing at the Singapore SEA Games in athletics was disappointing, as we only won three gold, two silver and nine bronze medals altogether. This is the lowest ever haul in the history of the games.

We finished sixth overall in athletics. Thailand finished top with 17 gold medals, followed by Vietnam with 11 gold and Indonesia with seven gold medals. Even Singapore and Philippines finished ahead of us. In terms of the number of overall medals in athletics, we finished fifth.

How have we failed in this aspect?

Athletics is the simplest form of sports as there is not much equipment needed – making its cost low.

Unless you are Usain Bolt or someone like that, athletics might not be the "sexiest" of sports. But it is the most competed in sport at the world level and there must be more concerted efforts to improve on it.

Back in the '70s, Malaysia was one of the leading powerhouses in Asian athletics with the likes of Tan Sri Dr M. Jegathesan who won three gold medals at the 1966 Bangkok Asian Games. His time of 20.92sec in the 200m semifinals of the 1968 Mexico Olympics still stands till today. That's 45 years!

We certainly lag behind Thailand and Vietnam in the region and nowhere close to the likes of Japan and China at the Asian level.

Yes, we won gold medals in many other competitions in the recent SEA Games, but athletics, alongside gymnastics, is the foundation for all sports. It is where one learns to be flexible.

This flexibility is important when it comes to any other sport be it basketball, hockey, badminton or football.

In short, to be a good sportsperson, you have to be athletic. Yes you can start playing football at a young age but athletics helps out very much in the development of sportsmen.

We have to get the basics right again.

Source: http://www.thestar.com.my/Opinion/Online-Exclusive/Bend-It-Like-Bedi/Profile/Articles/2015/07/05/Time-to-get-the-basics-right/

Skills practice exercises

Activity 4

Refer to Document 1.

1. What issues are raised by this cartoon?

2. What different perspectives can you think of on these issues?

3. What is your opinion on these issues?

4. Can you find more information? What search terms will you use?

Activity 5

Refer to Document 2.

1. Keira says, "These are really fundamental aspects of human nature." Is this a fact or opinion? Explain your answer.

2. Identify one prediction and that Keira makes. Explain your answers.

3. Identify one value judgement that Hassan makes.

4. Identify one fact and one opinion in Bina's words. Explain your answers.

5. What might be the consequences if we did not have school sport?

6. What might be the consequences if schools concentrated on fun exercise instead of competitive sport?

7. Which is better, in your opinion? Competition or exercise just for fun? Give reasons for your answer.

8. From a national perspective, is it more important to find elite athletes for national teams or to encourage everyone to be fit and healthy? Give reasons for your answer.

Activity 6

Refer to Document 3.

1. Summarise the key points in the document using your own clear English.

2. Do you agree with the author's views?

Activity 7

1. What kind of information do you need to answer each of the following questions?

   - What proportion of women play a sport?

   - Will Uruguay win the World Cup?

   - Who should fund national sports development programmes?

   - What is the average age at which girls stop doing sport?

   - Why do young people sometimes become violent in their leisure time?

2. Do quick internet searches to find information, ideas and opinions.

Activity 8

1. What are the sports and recreation issues most likely to affect these individuals? Think about the differences between similar people in LEDCs and MEDCs.

   - Working parent.

   - School students in Beijing, Washington, DC, Dubai.

   - Fourteen-year-old girl who wants to be an elite gymnast.

   - Politician.

   - Elite athlete in a sport where betting is important.

   Use quick internet searches if necessary to help you.

2. Think about the different cultural perspectives these people have. What are the needs, expectations, beliefs and desires that make their perspectives different?

3. To what extent are sport and recreation personal, local/national or global concerns?

Activity 9

1. What are the most important problems in your area related to sport and recreation?

   a) What do you already think? Are you prepared to change your mind?

   b) What search terms will you use?

   c) What key words and phrases will you skim-read for?

   d) Remember to think about which problems are most important, and why.

2. Choose a city or country in a very different part of the world. What are their most important problems related to sports and recreation?

3. What are the similarities and differences in the sports and recreation problems experienced by your area and the one you have studied?

4. In what ways do these two areas have different perspectives on sports and recreation?

5. What is the most interesting sports and recreation issue you have considered so far? Do you think that this issue is suitable for a team project?

6. Add your own questions to help you plan a line of inquiry.

Activity 10

1. What are the likely consequences of encouraging activity for fun?

2. What are the likely consequences of the government trying to change people's attitudes to sport and recreation? Does it vary depending on which country you think about?

3. What different cultural perspectives relating to attitudes and values underlie them?

Activity 11

1. a) Think of different cultural perspectives in your local area on an issue relating to sport and recreation. Compare the attitudes and values that underlie this perspective.

   b) Research cultural perspectives on this issue in a very different country, for example Saudi Arabia, China, Zimbabwe, Argentina, Germany, etc.

Reflection

- Have you changed your opinions about sport and recreation issues generally?

- Is there a particular sport and recreation debate in your local area? Do you see the issues differently now? If so, how? Why?

- Use diagrams and mind maps to help you to reflect on the issue.

Reflection

After you have carried out your project, answer these questions:

1. **a)** How well did your team work together?

   b) What problems did you have? How did you solve these problems?

   c) How will you avoid these problems next time?

   d) How effective was your outcome?

   e) How effective was your individual contribution?

Ideas for discussion, debate and practice

1. Which is more important and why:

   a) Health and fitness or competitive success? Does it make a difference if you're young or old?

   b) Enjoyment or competitive success?

   c) National teams or local sporting communities?

2. How far should parents and coaches push talented young sportspeople? Explain your opinion.

3. It doesn't matter what hobby you have, so long as you have one. Do you agree? Explain your opinion.

4. It doesn't matter whether sport is fair – it just needs to be exciting. Do you agree? Explain your opinion.

5. How can we prevent problems of violence at international sporting events?

6. What are the best solutions to the problems of unfairness in sport?

7. How can we encourage more young women to take up a sport?

8. How do you prevent young people becoming violent in their leisure time?

Remember to consider different cultural perspectives when you are doing your research.

Make a photo display of different national sports and recreations. Discuss what your national sports and recreations mean to you, and how you think they affect the national character.

Design a public information advertisement (poster or film) explaining the value of regular exercise and recreation.

Design and produce an artistic or craft product which reflects local issues. Produce a business plan to market and sell the product.

Suggestions for aims and outcomes

Design a craft project to help disadvantaged communities.

Engage in a local charity which uses sporting projects to improve local communities. Report back to the school board on the effectiveness of your action.

7 Tradition, culture and identity

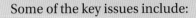

Some of the key issues include:

- Global vs. local culture and tradition
- Everyday culture
- Relationship between knowledge and culture
- Is tradition outmoded?
- Technology and culture
- Migration, culture and identity

- Intangible cultural heritage
- Changing culture and identity
- National identity
- Art and culture
- Relationship between tradition, culture, identity
- Global identity

Do some of these comments and questions raise more than one issue?

Activity 1

1. Match the comments and questions below to the issues in the diagram above.

   a) Our cultures and traditions are part of the way in which we see reality. They shape our world, and they determine how we act in the world.

   b) The cultural values of a country influence its national psychology and identity. Citizens' values and public opinions are conveyed to state leaders through the media and other information channels, both directly and indirectly influencing decisions on foreign policy. The traditional cultural values that influence the psyche of the Chinese people are harmony, benevolence, righteousness, courtesy, wisdom, honesty, loyalty, and filial piety [respect for your father].

   c) Intangible cultural heritage does not only represent inherited traditions from the past but also contemporary rural and urban practices in which diverse cultural groups take part.

   d) The people who control knowledge in society also control power.

   e) When peoples lose this untouchable, fragile fragment of their culture (oral stories, traditional music etc.) – as it daily happens to aboriginal societies all around the world – they lose their reason for living, their past and their future.

2. Do any of these comments come from particular cultural perspectives?

3. Choose an issue, comment or question that interests you and discuss it with a partner.

   a) Think about the possible different cultural perspectives on this issue.

   b) Research the issue and identify different cultural perspectives.

Key vocabulary and language exercises

Activity 2

1. What do you understand by the words and phrases below?

2. Use dictionaries and online resources to find definitions of these words and phrases. Concentrate on different ways in which these words can be understood – don't stop at the first dictionary definition.

> If English is not your first language, avoid using online translation tools. They are often not very good! Your language skills will develop better if you use dictionaries.

Words and phrases	Definition
a) Intangible cultural heritage	
b) Culture	
c) Identity	
d) National identity	
e) Global identity	
f) Tradition	
g) Reality	
h) Art	

Activity 3

1. Complete the mind map below. Add as many ideas, events, thoughts and feelings that you associate with poverty and inequality as you can think of. Use online resources and dictionaries as necessary. Some initial ideas have been suggested.

Art and culture

Tradition, culture, identity

International culture

Religious identity?

135

Stimulus material

Document 1

"I dreamt last night that a lecture about the decline of culture in the early twenty-first century topped the viewing figures on the internet.'

"Preservation of one's own culture does not require contempt or disrespect for other cultures."
– Cesar Chavez

"No two languages are ever sufficiently similar to be considered as representing the same social reality. The worlds in which different societies live are distinct worlds, not merely the same world with different labels attached."
– Amy Tan

"We are in the process of creating what deserves to be called the idiot culture. Not an idiot sub-culture, which every society has bubbling beneath the surface and which can provide harmless fun; but the culture itself. For the first time, the weird and the stupid and the coarse are becoming our cultural norm, even our cultural ideal."
– Carl Bernstein

Document 2

For many people, television is a major source of news, information and entertainment and it strongly influences their sense of local and national identity. A local content measure reflects the extent to which we see our culture reflected through this medium.

Current level and trends

In 2009, local content on six national free-to-air television channels made up 39 percent of the prime-time schedule.

International comparisons are difficult due to the inconsistencies in measurement approaches by different countries. However, in 1999, local content accounted for 24 percent of total transmission time in New Zealand, a smaller proportion than that in 10 other surveyed countries.

Note this is a measure of total air-time programming rather than prime-time programming, which is the measure this indicator is based on.

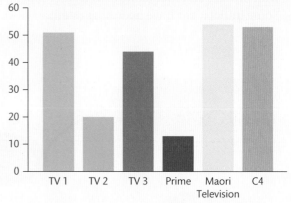

The percentage of local content in prime-time transmission hours in 2009 differs across the channels

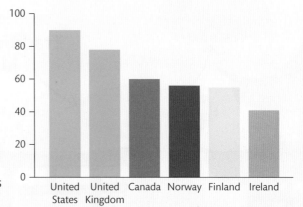

Document 3

@anti_globalisation

We have to fight globalisation or it will bring about the end of everything we value. It's destroying our local cultural identities and making us all the same. We all watch American TV, eat burgers and buy our clothes at the same chain stores. You can walk through Shanghai, New York, London or Delhi and not know which city or even which continent you're on. The only differences are fakes of local traditions put there for tourists.

@global_girl

Like shopping and tourist districts are culture. Perhaps if @anti_globalisation ever got beyond the tourist districts, he would notice the real cities with their own distinct identities?

@lovemynationbecauseimtoldto

What is cultural identity anyway? Isn't this just another western idea that we all have to accept? Governments and the media put a lot of effort into creating national identities and they tell us we have to accept them or be "unpatriotic". But actually, in lots of these nations, there are traditionally multiple, shifting cultural groups. There isn't one, national, traditional identity that never changed until globalisation. These are just social constructs. And they're breaking down in many places – look at Wales and Scotland breaking away from England, or civil war in Syria, or ... you could name anywhere in the world and find national identities breaking down because they were never real.

@global_girl

Well, @lovemynationbecauseimtoldto has one good point. Identity isn't a fixed thing. I'm Chinese when I'm with my mother's parents, but Indian when I'm with my father's parents, and Australian when I'm with my friends . All these things are who I am, but none of them is all of me.

> What cultural perspective can you identify in the documents? What attitudes and values underlie them?

Skills practice exercises

Activity 4

Refer to Document 1.

1. Identify and explain two different understandings of culture seen in Document 1.

2. Do you think that culture is mostly a personal, local/ national or global issue? Justify your answer.

Activity 5

Refer to Document 2.

1. Document 2 states that, "A local content measure reflects the extent to which we see our culture reflected through [TV]". What do you need to know about the types of programme shown on New Zealand TV to decide whether it really is showing local culture?

2. According to Document 2, in 1999, television in the UK (BBC only) showed 78% local content. What else do you need to know to decide whether television in the UK strongly reflects local culture?

3. Is a social report produced by the New Zealand government a reliable source of information? Justify your answer.

4. Why might it be problematic to compare total air time programming with prime time programming? Justify your answer.

Activity 6

Refer to Document 3.

1. Whose reasoning is most effective?

    Consider

    - the reliability of any knowledge claims they make
    - how logical their reasoning is
    - how well they answer each other's points
    - whether you agree with any values they express
    - any other relevant points.

    > "How effective is the reasoning?" is another way of asking, "Is the reasoning good quality?" or "Does the reasoning work well?"

Activity 7

1. What tradition, culture and identity issues are most likely to affect these individuals? Think about the differences between similar people in LEDCs and MEDCs.

    - Labourer who has migrated to Hanoi to find work.
    - American student who wants to do an internship in China.
    - Film maker in Kampala.
    - Toddler in Glasgow.
    - The last speaker of a minority language.

    If necessary, use quick internet searches to help you.

2. Think about the different cultural perspectives these people have. What are the needs, expectations, beliefs and desires that make their perspectives different?

3. To what extent are tradition, culture and identity personal, local/national or global concerns?

Activity 8

1. What are the most important problems in your area related to tradition, culture and identity?

    a) What do you already think? Are you prepared to change your mind?

    b) What search terms will you use?

    c) What key words and phrases will you skim-read for?

    d) Remember to think about which problems are most important, and why.

    e) Are they really local problems or are they part of a global trend?

2. Choose a city or country in a very different part of the world. What are their most important problems related to tradition, culture and identity?

3. What are the similarities and differences in the problems experienced by your area and the area you have studied?

4. In what ways do these two areas have different perspectives on tradition, culture and identity?

5. What is the most interesting issue you have considered so far? Do you think that this issue is suitable for a team project?

6. Add your own questions to help you plan a line of inquiry.

Activity 9

1. a) What are the likely consequences of allowing globalisation to alter tradition, culture and identity without government intervention?

    b) What are the likely consequences of the government trying to reinforce local traditions, culture and identity?

    c) What different cultural perspectives on globalisation and local tradition can you think of?

Reflection

1. a) Have you changed your opinions about tradition, culture and identity issues generally?

    b) Is there a particular health debate in your local area? Do you see the issues differently now? If so, how? Why?

    c) Use diagrams and mind maps to help you to reflect on the issue.

2. After you have carried out your project, answer these questions.

    a) How well did your team work together?

    b) What problems did you have? How did you solve these problems?

    c) How will you avoid these problems next time?

    d) How effective was your outcome?

    e) How effective was your individual contribution?

Ideas for discussion, debate and practice

Imagine you have to represent your national and local cultures to friends from abroad. How can we develop a valuable national identity whilst also respecting the cultural identities of immigrants?

- How important are tradition and culture to our identity in modern society?

- In your opinion, what are the most important aspects of culture – art, sport, architecture, traditions, language, religion, festivals, attitudes and beliefs, food, shopping, fashion?

- How important are traditions?

- Are traditions just for older people? Should young people develop new ways?

- Are the traditions and culture of your region an important part of your identity? For example, think of a major festival in your country. What would it be like not to celebrate that festival?

- How would you feel about living in a country where your traditions and culture were not important?

- How important is it to understand our own traditions?

- How important is it to understand other people's traditions?

- Culture is a way of imagining a life different than your own – for example, thinking of the lives of the people who worshipped in an old church or temple, or seeing the lives of the people in a painting. Do you agree with this statement?

- What is a national identity? How does your national identity relate to your personal identity?

- Could we imagine a global identity? What do you think we would need to change for us to see ourselves as citizens of the world?

Produce a display comparing different local and national traditions and how these affect your identity.

Remember to consider different cultural perspectives when you are researching.

Organise an event celebrating different traditions and cultures. Produce information leaflets for visitors to increase their understanding.

Suggestions for aims and outcomes

Produce a video documentary showing migrants' experiences in adapting to different cultures and traditions.

Plan and carry out a three–five day programme of events for visitors to your school or local area. This programme should give your friends the best possible understanding of your culture. Provide a plan and an information leaflet.

8 Water, food and agriculture

Some of the key issues include:

- Water as a human right
- Price of water
- Farming and market forces
- National security
- Equality
- Access to water
- Water use
- Farming as a way of life
- Fairness

- Access to clean water
- Drought, flooding and food
- Self sufficiency
- Sustainable farming
- Conflict over water
- Sources of water
- Affordable food
- Farming and the environment

> Do some of these comments and questions raise more than one issue?

Activity 1

1. Match the comments and questions below to the issues in the diagram above.

   a) Our country has to import a lot of food. This is dangerous – what if we go to war?

   b) "So this 380 liters of water [Brabeck's estimation of the excess water Americans use]; I don't think is a human right. This should have a price. Why? Because if you do not put the price, we would not make the investments which are necessary in order to use the most precious of the resources that we have in a more responsible manner."

   c) Sustainable farming is good for both the farmer and the environment. The farmer profits from increased productivity on his land, and the environment benefits from a reduction in greenhouse gases and energy demands, as well as an improvement in soil and water quality.

   d) The food price spike of 2008 was a warning of what is to come. Staple food prices rocketed – wheat up 130%; sorghum rose by 87% and rice 74% – and caused riots in 36 countries. The government of Haiti was toppled as people took to the streets.

   e) I want to be able to give my daughter clean water to drink. I want her to have access to a private toilet with clean water to wash in. And I want her to be able to spend time studying instead of fetching water. But I can't give her any of these things.

2. Do any of these comments come from particular cultural perspectives?

3. Choose an issue, comment or question that interests you and discuss it with a partner.

   a) Think about the possible different cultural perspectives on this issue.

   b) Research the issue and identify different cultural perspectives.

Key vocabulary and language exercises

Activity 2

1. Use dictionaries and online resources to find definitions of the words and phrases below.

> If English is not your first language, avoid using online translation tools. They are often not very good! Your language skills will develop better if you use dictionaries.

Words and phrases	Definition
a) Self-sufficiency	
b) National security	
c) Drought	
d) Flooding	
e) Sustainable farming	
f) Market forces	
g) Price discrimination	
h) Pipeline	

Activity 3

1. Make cards with the words from Activity 2. Make separate cards with the definitions you have found. Play these games to help you remember the words

   a) Turn all the cards face down so that you cannot see them. Mix them up so that you don't know which card is where. Turn over two cards at a time. If you have both a word and its definition, you keep the pair. The player with the most pairs wins.

   b) Mix all the definition cards up and put them in one pile. Take a card from the pile. Read the definition and state the word that it defines.

   c) Mix all the word cards up and put them in one pile. Take a card from the pile. Read the word and give its definition.

   d) Add words from your research and include them in the game.

Stimulus material

Document 1

California water regulators flexed their muscles by ordering a group of farmers to stop pumping from a branch of the San Joaquin River amid an escalating battle over how much power the state has to protect waterways that are drying up in the drought. As usual, governments do what they want with one almond farmer raging *"I've made investments as a farmer based on the rule of law... Now, somebody's changing the law that we depend on."* This is not about to get any better as NBC News reports, this drought is of historic proportions - **the worst in over 100 years**.

The current drought has averaged a reading of -3.67 over the last three years, **nearly twice as bad as the second-driest stretch since 1900**, which occurred in 1959.

http://www.zerohedge.com/news/2015-07-17/california-water-wars-escalate-state-changes-law-orders-farmers-stop-pumping

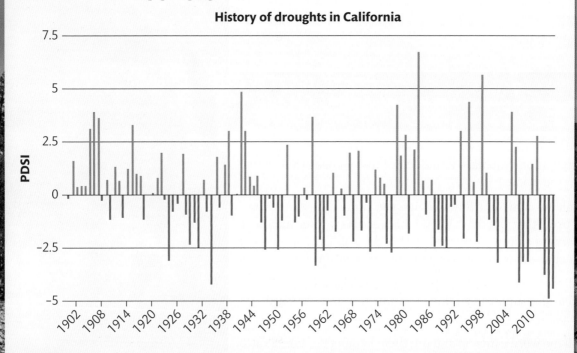

History of droughts in California

Document 2

One method of price discrimination is to offer the poor a specially tailored price quality mix. For example, poor people who can afford to buy water at times—but not regularly—can do so by the bucket. Or the poor can be served by simpler pipelines. In other ways, too, the poor can be offered flexible service that is better than what they had before, yet not exactly what the rich receive. (Water that is not fully treated can still serve many common uses, such as flushing toilets. Poor people can make their water potable [safe to drink] by boiling it.)

http://www.urbanknowledge.org/ur/docs/UR_Flagship_Full%20Report.pdf

What different cultural perspectives can you identify in the documents? What attitudes and values underlie them?

Comments

A: This is just another instance of discrimination against poor people – treating them like they're not fully human. If we can't provide proper services for everyone in society, we have no hope of achieving a society in which every child has the opportunity to succeed.

B: Some clean water is clearly better than no clean water. What worries me is that poor people – especially those who are desperate and/or poorly educated – will end up drinking the not fully treated water and becoming ill, which will make it harder for them to earn money, and could put pressure on health care systems (if they exist).

C: Nobody should have to buy water. It's ok to have luxuries available to the rich but not the poor, but clean water is not a luxury.

Document 3

The American bottled water craze began in the late 1970s, partly as a way for people to present a healthful image that ran counter to the three-martini business lunch, which was increasingly seen as a serious social problem. In the 1980s, bottled water's marketing centered on images of fit young people sweating at the gym. Madonna popularized Evian by drinking it onstage at her concerts. "It was a status symbol," says Ed Slade, who became Evian's vice president of marketing in 1990. "If you were cool, you were drinking bottled water."

A sense of social justice is another factor that inspires many who want to see the bottled water fad become passé. The act of spending top dollar for a product you can get almost free, while 1 billion people in the world have no dependable source of safe drinking water, seems to many the height of arrogant, conspicuous consumption.

The island of Fiji makes a good case in point. Fiji has a modern bottling plant that produces over 1 million bottles a day of Fiji® artesian water, one of the hottest brands of bottled water on the U.S. market today. Yet, more than half the people in Fiji don't have clean reliable drinking water. Charles Fishman writes that "it is easier for the typical American in Beverly Hills or Baltimore to get a drink of safe, pure, refreshing Fiji water than it is for most people in Fiji."

http://www.terrificscience.org/downloads/health_science/waterethicsFINAL.pdf

Document 4

The government needs to seriously consider its policies on farming and agriculture. Consumers are demanding ever cheaper meat and milk, and supermarkets are providing these products at less than the cost of producing them. Our farmers cannot compete so they are going out of business and we are eating imported meat and drinking imported milk. The consequences for farmers are bad enough – but if the government does not give thought to our food security, the nation could be in a disastrous position, especially if war comes.

Comments

@whodofthoughtit?

It's only right that meat and milk are affordable. Otherwise poor people would have nothing to eat and we'd be a poor country like Africa! Farmers should stop complaining and get on with their jobs, they're lucky to have jobs at all, or they should chose to do something else if they don't like it.

@Sweetpea

We should take the plight of farmers more seriously. My friend's stepdad's old school friend John is a farmer, and his life is really hard. There is no money to be made and he's struggling. But he says he can't just choose another job. Farming is in his blood, and the land is part of him. And anyway, what else can he do?

Skills practice exercises

Activity 4

Refer to Document 1.

1. Describe the trend of rainfall and drought in California over the last 100 years.

2. How reasonable is it for the government to limit farmers' water in times of drought? Consider different perspectives.

3. What are the likely consequences of limiting farmers' access to water

   a) for the farmer

   b) for the consumer

   c) for the state

   d) for other water users?

4. Find out more about the drought in California, its consequences and actions that are being taken.

5. Research a drought in a different part of the world. Compare government and individual actions with those in California.

Activity 5

Refer to Document 2.

1. Is http://www.urbanknowledge.org/ur/docs/UR_Flagship_Full%20Report.pdf a good source of information and expert opinions on issues relating to urbanisation?

2. Do you think A's reasoning is good? Give your reasons.

3. Does B predict likely consequences?

4. How far do you agree with C? Refer to the reasoning and use your own opinions.

Activity 6

Refer to Document 3.

1. Summarise the key issues in Document 3.

2. Research different opinions on bottled water.

3. What is your opinion about bottled water?

Activity 7

Refer to Document 4.

1. Do you think this is a serious newspaper or a sensationalist newspaper? What are your reasons?

2. Do you think it is reasonable to suggest that getting much of our food from abroad will lead to bad consequences? Give your reasons.

3. In your opinion, is @whodofthoughtit a reliable source? Give your reasons.

4. Does @whodofthoughtit suggest likely consequences? Explain your answer.

5. Is @whodofthoughtit's reasoning good quality? Explain your answer.

6. @Sweetpea refers to her "friend's stepdad's old school friend John." Is this a reliable source?

7. Is @Sweetpea providing reasons to support an opinion or proposal?

145

Activity 8

1. What are the personal, local/national and global issues and cultural perspectives that arise from the following?

   a) Farmers in my country aren't making money, so they are giving up on farming.

   b) It hasn't rained for 18 months in parts of Australia.

   c) A hurricane is forecast for Ohio.

   d) Storms and flooding are forecast in Bangladesh.

   e) Food shortages are leading to riots around the world.

   > Remember that other people have personal and local perspectives too.

2. To what extent are disease and health personal, local/national or global concerns?

Activity 9

1. What are the most important problems in your area related to water, food and agriculture?

   a) What do you already think? Are you prepared to change your mind?

   b) What search terms will you use?

   c) What key words and phrases will you skim-read for?

   d) Remember to think about which problems are most important, and why.

2. Choose a city or country in a very different part of the world. What are their most important problems related to water, food and agriculture?

3. What are the similarities and differences in the water, food and agriculture problems experienced by your area and the area you have studied?

4. In what ways do these two areas have different perspectives on water, food and agriculture?

5. What is the most interesting issue you have considered so far? Do you think that this issue is suitable for a team project?

6. Add your own questions to help you plan a line of inquiry.

Activity 10

1. **a)** Think of different cultural perspectives in your local area on an issue relating to water, food and agriculture. Compare the attitudes and values that underlie them.

   b) Research different cultural perspectives on this issue in a very different country, for example Saudi Arabia, China, Zimbabwe, Argentina, Germany, etc.

Activity 11

1. Have you changed your opinions about water, food and agriculture issues generally?

2. Is there a particular water, food or agriculture debate in your local area? Do you see the issues differently now? If so, how? Why?

3. How does your personal perspective link with different national and global perspectives?

4. Is your personal perspective well thought through? What evidence and reasons can you give to support your perspective?

Reflection

1. Have you thought about water, food and agriculture in any new ways? If so, what and why?

2. Have you changed your mind about anything? Give your reasons.

3. What is the most important issue you have considered while preparing for your research report?

4. Think of other questions to help you reflect on the issues and perspectives. Think of possible answers to these questions.

5. After you have carried out your project, answer these questions:

   a) How well did your team work together?

   b) What problems did you have? How did you solve these problems?

   c) How will you avoid these problems next time?

   d) How effective was your outcome?

   e) How effective was your individual contribution?

Ideas for discussion, debate and practice

- How can we deal with the humanitarian effects of drought and flooding?

- How can we prevent conflict over water in dry areas?

- Do you think that milk and meat should be cheap, even if farmers struggle to make a living?

- How can my country ensure its food security?

- How far do you think our upbringing and job (for example, farming) becomes a part of who we are?

Make a photo display of different problems associated with food or water. Explain the causes and consequences of these problems (using diagrams or a short talk).

Suggestions for aims and outcomes

Design a set of cartoons that illustrate the personal, local/national and global problems related to food and water. Use these cartoons in a display, or to make mugs or T-shirts to sell at a school event.

Produce a video documentary about a particular water conflict/issue in food or agriculture.

Individual report

Section C

How will I be assessed?

You will research a global aspect of one of the eight topics in this Section and produce an Individual Report of 1500–2000 words. This will be continuous writing with no video or sound files.

This is worth 60 marks. These marks are mostly for your ability to research, analyse and evaluate information and ideas, but there are marks for how well you communicate and reflect.

After choosing an aspect of one of the topics, you will:

1. Think of your own question (with the help of your teacher).

2. Use this question as the title of your report.

3. Research a wide range of information.

4. Identify and think about key issues.

5. Consider local, national and global perspectives.

6. Identify and consider the causes and effects of the issues.

7. Propose a relevant course of action.

8. Evaluate sources of information.

9. Discuss how your research has affected your personal perspective.

10. Do all of the work yourself without copying.

The following section provides one possible way of approaching the topics, however many different approaches may be taken.

1 Belief systems

Some key issues include:

- Religious belief
- Power of belief
- Role of evidence in belief
- Scientific belief
- Tolerance of others' beliefs
- Do we know what we believe?
- Why do we find others' beliefs threatening?
- Superstition
- Can a belief be wrong?
- Why do we believe what we believe?

> Do some of these comments and questions raise more than one issue?

Activity 1

1. Match the comments and questions below to the issues listed above.

   a) In the UK, it is unlawful to discriminate against workers because of their religion or belief or lack of.

   b) "Faith is the great cop-out, the great excuse to evade the need to think and evaluate evidence. Faith is belief in spite of, even perhaps because of, the lack of evidence."

   – Richard Dawkins

   c) "There are two ways to be fooled. One is to believe what isn't true; the other is to refuse to believe what is true."

   – Kierkegaard

   d) The World Values Survey has over the years demonstrated that people's beliefs play a key role in economic development, the emergence and flourishing of democratic institutions, the rise of gender equality, and the extent to which societies have effective government.

   e) How can you think that? You're wrong.

2. Identify at least one comment or question which comes from a

   a) personal perspective

   b) national perspective

   c) global perspective.

3. Choose an issue, comment or question that interests you and discuss it with a partner.

   a) Think about personal, local/national and global perspectives on this issue. For example, think about the perspectives of a worker, a company boss, a head of government, an international charity worker, and so on.

   b) What information do you need to help you discuss this?

Key vocabulary and language exercises

Activity 2

1. What is the difference between belief, faith, superstition and knowledge? Use dictionaries and online resources to help you.

2. What is the difference between tolerance of other views and an unacceptable fall in moral standards?

Activity 3

1. Use the words on the right to fill in the gaps

Most of us want the freedom to believe whatever we want. But there must be some restrictions. If we believe in religious freedom for ourselves, we must _____ other people's religious views. This includes the idea that we should not _____ against other people on the basis of their beliefs, for example when choosing employees.

When should our beliefs be restricted by the facts? Religious belief is characterised by _____, so religious believers sometimes hold their beliefs despite the _____. _____, on the other hand, tend to believe only what can be supported by facts and evidence. It is important to be able to _____ clearly between beliefs which need _____ and those which do not. For instance, it would not make sense at all to believe that the sky is green.

distinguish

discriminate

faith

scientists

proof

tolerate

facts

Stimulus material

Document 1

The Placebo Effect is well known in medicine. A patient is told that they are given medication, but they are actually given a pill with no medical benefits. The patient gets better because they believe they are being healed.

In a recent study, different groups were given different information about the effects of an energy drink on mental performance. They were asked to drink and then attempt a word test. The results were as follows:

Group	Information given about the drink	Score
Control group	No information given	7 words
Group 1	The drink provides a slight improvement to mental performance.	5–6 words
Group 2	The drink provides a slight improvement, and was bought at a discount for $0.89	4 words
Group 3	The drink provides a significant improvement to mental performance.	8–9 words
Group 4	The drink provides a significant improvement to mental performance and was bought at the full price of $1.89.	10+ words

Document 3

How far should we tolerate other people's beliefs? The answer here is not simple. Our behaviour depends on our beliefs. This goes right from cleaning our teeth because we believe that will keep them healthy, through looking after family members because we believe it is right to do so, to our beliefs about religion. And our beliefs affect the way we react to other people.

This means that beliefs are not entirely private. For example, if someone is preaching hatred and violence against other people, this is a public matter. Their beliefs affect me if it leads to violence in my neighbourhood. So I have the right to object to their beliefs.

But where do we draw the line between tolerance and intolerance? For me, we shouldn't tolerate beliefs that cause harm. Beliefs can cause harm by promoting or justifying harm towards others, or even just by stopping people thinking about the world with an open mind.

@deepthinker

This is fine, but you're confusing belief and action. It's the action of preaching hatred and violence that causes harm.

@Suki

This is all very well, but can we agree on harm? Let's say my beliefs about motherhood lead me to report a mother for leaving her tiny children alone while she goes out. The children are taken from the mother. Have my beliefs led me to do good or harm?

@thatsallthereis

You all are wishy-washy liberals. The facts are simple: either we tolerate all beliefs, or we tolerate none. Then we would descend into a tyranny of the mind, where there can be no freedom. This would lead to the loss of all that we believe in, all political advances, scientific progress and technological breakthroughs.

Document 4

British public wrong about nearly everything

A new survey for the Royal Statistical Society and King's College London shows public opinion is repeatedly off the mark on issues including crime, benefit fraud and immigration.

The research, carried out by Ipsos Mori from a phone survey of 1,015 people aged 16 to 75, lists ten misconceptions held by the British public. Among the biggest misconceptions are:

- Benefit fraud: the public think that £24 of every £100 of benefits is fraudulently claimed. Official estimates are that just 70 pence in every £100 is fraudulent - so the public conception is out by a factor of 34.

- Immigration: some 31 per cent of the population is thought to consist of recent immigrants, when the figure is actually 13 per cent. Even including illegal immigrants, the figure is only about 15 per cent. On the issue of ethnicity, black and Asian people are thought to make up 30 per cent of the population, when the figure is closer to 11 per cent.

- Crime: some 58 per cent of people do not believe crime is falling, when the Crime Survey for England and Wales shows that incidents of crime were 19 per cent lower in 2012 than in 2006/07 and 53 per cent lower than in 1995. Some 51 per cent think violent crime is rising, when it has fallen from almost 2.5 million incidents in 2006/07 to under 2 million in 2012.

- Teen pregnancy is thought to be 25 times higher than the official estimates: 15 per cent of girls under 16 are thought to become pregnant every year, when official figures say the amount is closer to 0.6 per cent.

Among the other surprising figures are that 26 per cent of people think foreign aid is in the top three items the Government spends money on (it actually makes up just 1.1 per cent of expenditure), and that 29 per cent of people think more is spent on Jobseekers' Allowance than pensions.

In fact we spend 15 times more on pensions – £4.9 billion on JSA vs £74.2 billion on pensions.

http://www.independent.co.uk/news/uk/home-news/british-public-wrong-about-nearly-everything-survey-shows-8697821.html

Skills practice exercises

Activity 4

1. Document 4 shows that the British public holds some important beliefs which are not supported by evidence.

   a) Give two examples of wrong beliefs that the British public hold.

   b) Show how these beliefs are wrong.

2. What are the likely consequences of the British public holding factually wrong beliefs?

3. What actions could/should the British government take to correct people's beliefs?

4. Give examples of beliefs that a government should not try to correct, and explain why.

Activity 5

1. Look at Document 1. Why might there be a conflict between intellectual integrity and belief? Explain your answer.

2. Is belief just a personal issue? Briefly justify your answer with reference to national and global perspectives.

Activity 6

Refer to Document 2.

1. Explain how beliefs about the energy drink affected people's performance in the word test.

2. Look at the study in Document 2. What additional information is needed in order to decide whether the drink itself has an effect on mental performance? How would this information help?

Activity 7

Refer to Document 3.

1. In Document 3, @Suki asks, "Have my beliefs led me to do good or harm?" What additional information is required in order to answer this question? How would this information help you to decide whether @Suki's beliefs led her to do good or harm?

2. a) "Our behaviour depends on our beliefs."

   Is this a fact or an opinion? Justify your answer.

   b) "We shouldn't tolerate beliefs that cause harm."

   Is this one or more of: fact/opinion/value judgement/prediction? Justify your answer.

3. Is cleaning our teeth a good example of how beliefs affect our behaviour? Explain your answer.

4. How reasonable is @deepthinker's response to the article? Justify your answer.

5. How effective is the reasoning provided by @thatsallthereis? Justify your answer.

Activity 8

1. What are the belief issues most likely to affect these individuals? Think about the differences between similar people in LEDCs and MEDCs.

   - A migrant from Syria to Germany.
   - A female head of state.
   - A woman who wants to wear a hijab in Paris.
   - A woman who does not want to wear a hijab or a niqab in Riyadh.
   - A physics professor who believes in God.

   Use quick internet searches to help.

Activity 9

1. What are the most important problems in your area related to belief?

   a) What do you already think? Are you prepared to change your mind?

   b) What search terms will you use?

   c) What key words and phrases will you skim-read for?

   d) Remember to think about which problems are most important, and why.

2. Choose a city or country in a very different part of the world. What are their most important problems related to belief?

3. What are the similarities and differences in the issues regarding belief experienced by your area and the area you have studied?

4. In what ways do these two areas have different perspectives on belief?

5. What is the most interesting belief issue you have considered so far? Do you think that this issue is suitable for an Individual Report?

6. Add your own questions to help you plan a line of inquiry.

> How would you decide whether a belief caused harm?

Activity 10

1. What are the likely consequences of allowing people to choose their beliefs freely with no restrictions at all?

2. If a person migrates to another country, should they change their beliefs to fit into that country?

   a) Do you think that you could change your beliefs if you lived in another country? Or are you convinced that your way of thinking is right?

   b) *How* could a person change their beliefs?

3. What would the likely consequences be if migrants did change their beliefs

   a) for the migrants themselves

   b) for the migrants' families

   c) for the host nation?

Ideas for discussion, debate and practice

- How far should we tolerate other people's beliefs?

- To what extent can we decide what we believe?

- Do we have subconscious beliefs that might surprise or even horrify us? If so, how can we combat these beliefs?

- Does it matter if different people believe different things?

- Are some beliefs wrong and others right? Or are they just opinions or perspectives?

- Are there any beliefs that other people hold that really upset you? What are your reasons?

- What links can you see between beliefs, conflict, language and culture?

Given the rise of terrorism driven by different belief systems, how justified are governments in restricting civil liberties?

Suggestions for research

Belief can change the world. How can individuals, nations and global communities ensure that this change is positive?

What actions can individuals take to support freedom of belief, when many governments would like to restrict it?

Biodiversity and ecosystem loss

2

Some key issues include:

- Role and value of biodiversity
- Effects of human activity on ecosystems
- Relationship between economics and environmental concerns
- Value of different ecosystems

- Lifestyle changes we need to make
- Ecosystems and poverty
- Effect of human activity on biodiversity
- Human consequences of ecosystem loss

Do some of these comments and questions raise more than one issue?

Activity 1

1. Match the comments and questions below to the issues in the diagram above.

   a) We depend on freshwater ecosystems for our drinking water. We need to protect these ecosystems for our own interests, as well as in the interests of biodiversity.

   b) In Bangladesh and India, for example, logging of trees and forests means that the floods during the monsoon seasons can be very deadly.

   c) I agree that we need to protect ecosystems, but the only way that I can send my children to school is by working for a logging company.

   d) Social costs to some segments of society can also be high. Take for example the various indigenous Indians of Latin America.

   Throughout the region, as aspects of corporate globalization spread, there is growing conflict between land and resources of the indigenous communities, and those required to meet globalization related needs.

   e) Local biodiversity markets could play a positive role in tropical conservation strategies.

   f) It looks as if the most effective way to protect biodiversity and fragile ecosystems is to give them an economic value in the global economy.

2. Identify at least one comment or question which comes from a

   a) personal perspective

   b) national perspective

   c) global perspective

Discussion

1. Choose an issue, comment or question that interests you and discuss it with a partner.

   a) Think about personal, local/national and global perspectives on this issue. For example, think about the perspectives of a worker, a company boss, a head of government, an international charity worker, and so on.

   b) What information do you need to help you discuss this?

Key vocabulary and language exercises

Activity 2

1. Use dictionaries and online resources to find definitions of the words and phrases in the table.

> If English is not your first language, avoid using online translation tools. They are often not very good! Your language skills will develop better if you use dictionaries.

Words and phrases	Definition
a) Biodiversity	
b) Ecosystem	
c) Mangroves	
d) Habitat loss	
e) Deforestation	
f) Reforestation	
g) Conservation	
h) Financial incentives	

Activity 3

1. Use internet resources to help you complete the mind map with different types of ecosystems. Add as many types as you can find. For example:
   http://www.ecosystem.org/types-of-ecosystems

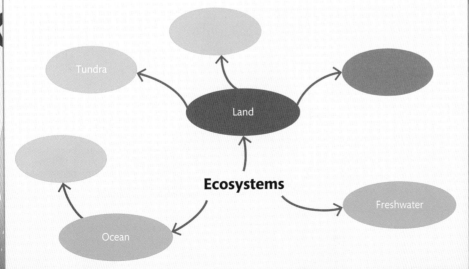

> When you search for internet resources on ecosystems, you will find materials produced by very young children at school. Do you think these are good resources for you to rely on? Give your reasons.

Stimulus material

Document 1

Sri Lanka has recently launched a mangrove protection scheme, becoming the first nation in the world to engage in a country-wide initiative such as this. The scheme includes replanting projects, job training, and microloans of $50 to $2000 in exchange for protecting the local mangrove forests.

The local population are also educated on the importance of the trees for the ecosystem – in particular, the healthy population of fish which is sustained by the mangrove forests, providing the livelihood of self-sustaining fishing communities for generations.

The program is provided by Sudeesa, a national organization, together with the Sri Lankan government and the US environmental conservation group Seacology. Over five years and at cost of $3.4 million, the initiative aims to protect 21,800 acres of mangroves forests and replant 9600 acres that have been felled.

Mangroves are salt-tolerant trees and can therefore grow in harsh coastal conditions. The stilted root systems form a breeding ground for fish and other marine wildlife, as well as protect against coastal erosion, high tides and storms. A study conducted by the International Union for Conservation of Nature showed that the Sri Lankan mangrove forests significantly reduced the impact of the devastating tsunami in 2004.

Mangroves have also been shown to store greater quantities of carbon, and for much long periods of time, than other types of forests. The trees accumulate the carbon in the top layer of soil, where there is a lack of oxygen. As such, there is an absence of organisms which would usually decompose organic material.

Document 2

Turtle terror!
Why Hong Kong should embrace its wild side

Hong Kong's country parks are home to a vast array of animals but any encounter with them is more likely to cause panic than invoke wonder. Stuart Heaver reveals why we shouldn't be afraid to embrace our wild side.

A crab-eating mongoose.

Some 2,000 years ago, Hong Kong was part of a great tropical broad-leaf forest that was home to elephants, tigers, red dogs and a huge variety of tropical species.

With about 40 per cent of our territory designated as country park, and with many of our threatened species protected by government ordinance, it might be assumed that Hongkongers would be very comfortable with their wild side. The reality, of course, is more complicated.

While many of us are aware of the hazards presented by snakes and poisonous centipedes, few are familiar with the 50 or so species of wild mammal that call Hong Kong home. According to Agriculture, Fisheries and Conservation Department (AFCD) surveys, eight types of mammal are ranked as species of conservation concern in Hong Kong: five species of bat as well as the crab-eating mongoose, the Chinese pangolin and the Eurasian otter.

Despite what ecologists call "massive human impacts" and habitat destruction, the crab-eating mongoose, which was thought to be extinct in the 1960s, is making a comeback and the small Asian mongoose and the yellow-bellied weasel have been recorded locally for the first time, perhaps having fled habitats in Guangdong province. Hong Kong can also boast that the East Asian porcupine, Muntjac (barking deer), masked palm civet, small Indian civet, rhesus macaque, Chinese ferret badger and leopard cat are all relatively abundant, along with a colourful host of amphibians, birds, reptiles and invertebrates.

Hong Kong native the pangolin, believed to be the most trafficked mammal in the world, is prized for its meat and scales.

Sadly, though, few Hongkongers appear to attach much value to this wonderful range of wild fauna and, for most urban dwellers, the concept of biodiversity is more likely to cause panic than fascination. Last month, when a wild boar strayed from its rural habitat into a Chai Wan shopping mall, it caused public mayhem, followed by a police stand-off more reminiscent of a terrorist attack than a wildlife rescue. Last summer, when a small harmless shark was spotted by a member of the public off Lamma Island, helicopters were scrambled and armed officers on police boats rushed to the scene, ready to shoot on sight. During the infamous 2001 Kowloon monkey chase, a four-year-old male rhesus macaque went on the run in downtown Tsim Sha Tsui. Media reported that it took police and AFCD officers more than two days to track down the crafty primate, which even caught the Star Ferry to evade its pursuers.

Most residents of the metropolis appear to be distinctly uncomfortable with native wildlife and, according to one occasional *Post Magazine* contributor and respected conservationist who has worked in Hong Kong for more than 25 years, there has been an effort over the past two millennia to eliminate it.

The first settlers "had a great love of chopping down forests and vegetation to reduce the threat of wild animals", says Dr Martin Williams, who does not think the colonial British were much better in terms of respect for wildlife.

"The massive reforestation undertaken by the British was an engineering project to secure decent freshwater supplies, not a conservation project. The British were more than happy to shoot tigers and just about any other animal if they got half a chance," he says.

"Sadly, there is very little knowledge and affection for our indigenous species..." he says, although "the protection of wild animals did increase with the introduction of the country parks, in the 1970s, and local demand for wildlife as a source of food has reduced with increased affluence and education".

http://www.scmp.com/magazines/post-magazine/article/1831646/
turtle-terror-why-hong-kong-must-embrace-its-wild-side

Document 3

Adam: Politicians never think their decisions through or consider the consequences. My uncle was telling me about how they used DDT on mosquitoes to stop malaria, but just killed all the birds and we've still got malaria anyway. And they use pesticides that kill bees, so now there are no bees to pollinate our food crops. Thirty percent of our food needs to be pollinated, so this is going to be a total disaster. There are already enough hungry people.

Dinesh: Some people say we should make a set of rules about how our biodiversity – "genetic resources" – can be used. This is a terrible idea. It will result in a price tag on biodiversity. Another consequence is that we'll only conserve the things we understand the value of. It will be a way of rich countries gaining commercial benefit while poor countries are exploited.

Skills practice exercises

Activity 4

Refer to Document 1.

1. According to the article, what benefits do mangroves offer humans?

2. What are the environmental benefits of mangroves?

3. Find out more about:

   a) Sudeesa

   b) Seacology

4. Research the Sri Lankan mangrove protection scheme mentioned in the article.

5. Do you think that this protection scheme is likely to be effective? What are your reasons?

Activity 6

Refer to Document 3.

1. What do you need to know about Adam's uncle to know whether he is a reliable source of information?

2. How reliable do you think Adam and Dinesh are as sources of information? What do you need to know about them?

3. How reasonable are the causes and consequences suggested by Adam? Can you spot any exaggeration?

4. How reasonable are the consequences suggested by Dinesh? Can you think of any plausible alternatives?

5. Is Adam's reasoning good quality? Does he give reasons? Does he become emotional?

6. Is Dinesh's reasoning good quality? Does he give reasons? Does he become emotional?

   a) Are good reasons and evidence given to support the author's views?

   b) Are emotions being used instead of reasons?

   c) Are opinions being used instead of facts?

Remember that other people have personal and local perspectives too.

Activity 5

Refer to Document 2.

1. Summarise the main points by thinking about

   • key issues for biodiversity in Hong Kong

   • main threats

   • main successes

   • main possible courses of action.

Remember that you do not need to read and understand every word. Learning what not to read is an important skill!

Remember to skim-read and look for key words.

You may find it useful to draw a diagram or mind map.

Activity 7

What are the personal, local/national and global consequences, issues and perspectives that arise from the following?

a) Why do we need to keep mangroves around Mumbai? Surely there is a cleaner, more modern solution.

b) Approximately 297 million farmland birds were wiped out of existence across Europe in the past 30 years.

c) All the different species on earth depend on each other.

d) Around the world, 3000 listed companies were responsible for over $2 trillion in environmental costs that have to be borne by society and social costs in 2009 alone.

e) Inland wetlands cover at least 9.5 million km^2 (i.e. about 6.5% of the Earth's land surface).

Use quick internet searches to help you.

Activity 8

1. What are the most important ecosystems in your area?

2. Why are these ecosystems important for humans?

3. Why are these ecosystems important for the environment?

> If you do not know the answers to these questions, do some research!

4. What are the most important problems in your area related to ecosystem loss and/or biodiversity?

   a) What do you already think? Are you prepared to change your mind?

   b) What search terms will you use?

   c) What key words and phrases will you skim-read for?

   d) Remember to think about which problems are most important, and why.

5. Choose a city or country in a very different part of the world. What are their most important problems related to ecosystem loss and/or biodiversity?

6. What are the similarities and differences in the problems experienced by your area and the area you have studied?

7. What possible solutions are these areas considering to their problems?

8. In what ways do these two areas have different perspectives on ecosystems and/or biodiversity?

9. What is the most interesting issue you have considered so far? Do you think that this issue is suitable for an Individual Report?

10. Add your own questions to help you plan a line of inquiry.

Activity 9

1. Look at the sources you have found so far.

   a) Are they reliable? If not, what will you do?

   > If your source is not reliable, look for a more reliable source.

   b) Is the reasoning good quality? How will this affect the way you use the ideas, information and perspectives in your work?

   c) Are the causes and consequences likely? If not, what will you do?

   d) Are there alternative possible consequences? If so, how will this affect the way you use these ideas in your work?

   > If the reasoning is poor or the consequences unlikely, look for better quality sources of ideas, information and perspectives. Don't quote material that you have identified as illogical or poor quality.

Reflection

1. a) Have you thought about biodiversity and ecosystems in any new ways? If so, how and why?

   b) Have you changed your mind about anything? Give your reasons.

   c) Do you think that animals are as important as humans? Give your reasons

   d) Are there any ecosystems – such as coastal systems, forests etc. that are important in your life? What value do they have for you?

   e) What is the most important issue you have considered while preparing for your research report?

   f) Think of other questions to help you to reflect on the issues and perspectives. Think of some possible answers to these questions.

   g) How does your personal perspective link with different national and global perspectives?

   h) Is your personal perspective well thought through? What evidence and reasons can you give to support your perspective?

Ideas for discussion, debate and practice

Ecosystem game

Divide the class into groups of five. Each group represents a planet with competing ecosystems – you represent one of those ecosystems and your job is to save it!

- You must persuade the others in your group (planet) that your ecosystem is so valuable that it must be kept.

- After each round, everyone votes on which ecosystems to save. One ecosystem must leave the "planet". This represents ecosystem loss.

Investment game

Your group has $20 million to invest. You want to make money from your investment. You would also like to protect a vulnerable ecosystem in your area. What is your best option?

Options include:

- Investing in a multi-national corporation (MNC) that claims to be eco-friendly.

- Giving the money to a charity.

- Investing in a micro-finance project similar to the Sri Lankan mangrove protection scheme.

- Can you think of other options?

Option	Details	Make money?	Protect ecosystem?	Other?
Eco-friendly MNC				
Charity				
Micro-finance				

Do some research! Find real information to help you make a decision.

How can we protect vulnerable ecosystems?

Can economic solutions to ecosystem loss really work?

Suggestions for research

How can we deal with the problems of decreasing biodiversity?

Compare ecosystem issues in two areas. Which area has the more effective solutions?

3 Changing communities

Some key issues include:

- Social mobility
- Urbanisation
- Demographics
- Shrinking cities
- De-industrialisation
- Loneliness and social problems
- Community response to climate change
- Online communities
- Religion and community

> Do some of these comments and question raise more than one issue?

Activity 1

1. Match the comments and questions below to the issues listed above.

   a) Tokyo has become a highly efficient global megacity in the last four decades – but despite its enviable integrated public transport system and the forthcoming Olympics in 2020, the city is likely to lose 400,000 people over the next 15 years as a result of low-birth rates and a slowing national economy.

   b) For every 12 net new jobs that have been created in cities and towns in southern England since 2004 only one has been generated in towns in the rest of Britain, according to a report by a thinktank that has compared urban areas across the country.

   c) "Previously, at the village meeting only the leaders would meet and make the decisions without asking the households. I would keep silent," Mrs. Vu Thi Hanh explains. "The community-based approach changed the way to make the decisions in our village and the people also changed their way to leaders. Now we are confident enough to make sure that any decisions being made benefit the whole community."

   d) My grandmother talks about going to dances in the village hall with local friends. She didn't have any friends from more than ten miles away. A lot of my social life is online, and my friends live around the world.

   e) In recent decades, religion has had considerable impact upon politics in many regions of the world. The belief that societies would invariably secularize as they modernize has not been well founded.

2. Identify at least one comment or question which comes from a

   a) personal perspective

   b) national perspective

   c) global perspective

Discussion

1. Choose an issue, comment or question that interests you and discuss it with a partner.

   a) Think about the personal, local/national and global perspectives of this issue. For example, think about the perspectives of a worker, a company boss, a head of government, an international charity worker, and so on.

   b) What information do you need to help you discuss this?

Key vocabulary and language exercises

Activity 2

1. Use dictionaries and online resources to find definitions of the words and phrases in the table.

> If English is not your first language, avoid using online translation tools. They are often not very good! Your language skills will develop better if you use dictionaries.

Words and phrases	Definition
a) Urbanisation	
b) De-industrialisation	
c) Secularisation	
d) Demographics	
e) Modernisation	
f) Social enterprise	
g) Social isolation	
h) Rural	

Activity 3

1. Make cards with the words from Activity 2. Make separate cards with the definitions you have found. Play games to help you remember the words.

    a) Turn all the cards face down so that you cannot see them. Mix them up so that you don't know which card is where. Turn over two cards at a time. If you have a word and its definition, you keep the pair. The player with the most pairs wins.

    b) Mix all the definition cards up and put them in one pile. Take a card from the pile. Read the definition and give the word it defines.

    c) Mix all the word cards up and put them in one pile. Take a card from the pile. Read the word and give its definition.

    d) Add more words as you do your research. Include them in the games.

Document 1

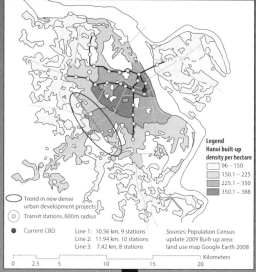

Legend
Hanoi built-up density per hectare
- 96 – 150
- 150.1 – 225
- 225.1 – 350
- 350.1 – 388

⬯ Trend in new dense urban development projects
◉ Transit stations, 600 m radius
● Current CBD

Line 1: 10.56 km, 9 stations
Line 2: 11.94 km, 10 stations
Line 3: 7.42 km, 8 stations

Sources: Population Census update 2009 Built-up area: land use map Google Earth 2008

Kilometers
0   2.5   5   10   15   20

Document 2

 Javier: We have to take action to prevent so many people from moving into cities. Urbanisation is causing terrible overcrowding in slums, insanitary conditions and illness, and it's putting unmanageable pressure on cities' resources.

 Ngoc: We can't prevent urbanisation. It's happening so we have to deal with it. If governments and city leaders make good decisions, urbanisation will be a good thing. For example, my city, Hanoi, has grown, but we don't have large slums, because the government made strict rules about land use.

 Kefilwe: If you look at world statistics, the more urbanised nations have higher life expectancy and literacy rates. Innovation thrives in cities, and 80% of world Gross Domestic Product (GDP) is generated in cities. So Ngoc is right. But here in South Africa, the government decided to build two million homes on cheap land outside cities – and didn't provide transport links. So it takes three hours to get to work.

Document 3

How to shrink a city

Many cities are losing inhabitants. Better to manage decline than try to stop it

May 30th, 2015

ONE of the biggest challenges for the world this century is how to accommodate the hundreds of millions of people who will flock to cities, especially in emerging economies. Coping with this human torrent will be fearsomely difficult—but at least the problem is widely acknowledged. That is not true of another pressing urban dilemma: what to do with cities that are losing people.

They are hardly unusual. Almost one in ten American cities is shrinking. So are more than a third of German ones—and the number is growing. Although Japan's biggest cities are thriving, large numbers of its smaller ones are collapsing. Several South Korean cities have begun to decline—a trend that will speed up unless couples can somehow be persuaded to have more babies. Next will come China, where the force of rapid urbanisation will eventually be overwhelmed by the greater power of demographic contraction. China's total urban population is expected to peak by mid-century; older industrial boom towns are already on a downward slope.

An abandoned street containing a rotting nursery or primary school is a sad sight. And declining cities have more than visual problems. Disused buildings deter investors and attract criminals; superfluous infrastructure is costly to maintain; ambitious workers may refuse to move to places where the potential clientele is shrinking. Where cities are economically self-sufficient, a smaller working population means a fragile base on which to balance hefty pension obligations. That is why Detroit went bust.

So it is unsurprising that governments often try to shore up their crumbling smaller cities. Japan recently announced tax cuts for firms that are willing to move their headquarters out of thriving Tokyo. Office parks, art museums and tram lines have been built in troubled American and European cities, on the assumption that if you build it, people will come.

For the most part, they will not. Worse, the attempt to draw workers back to shrinking cities is misconceived. People move from smaller to larger cities in countries like Germany and Japan because the biggest conurbations have stronger economies, with a greater variety of better-paying jobs. The technological revolution, which was once expected to overturn the tyranny of distance, has in fact encouraged workers to cluster together and share clever ideas. Britain's productivity is pitiful these days but it is almost one-third higher in London than elsewhere.

Policies meant to counteract the dominance of big cities are not just doomed to fail but can actually be counter-productive. The most successful metropolises should be encouraged to expand by stripping away planning restrictions. If housing were more plentiful in the bigger conurbations it would be cheaper, and the residents of declining cities, who often have little housing equity, would find it easier to move to them. Rent controls and rules that give local people priority in public housing should go, too: they harm the poor by locking them into unproductive places.

A new kind of garden city

Even so, many people will stay stuck in shrinking cities, which will grow steadily older. Better transport links to big cities will help some. But a great many cannot be revived. In such cases the best policy is to acquire empty offices and homes, knock them down and return the land to nature—something that has worked in the east German city of Dessau-Rosslau and in Pittsburgh in America. That will require money and new habits of mind. Planners are expert at making cities work better as they grow. Keeping them healthy as they shrink is just as noble.

http://www.economist.com/news/leaders/21652343-many-cities-are-losing-inhabitants-better-manage-decline-try-stop-it-how-shrink

Document 4

Three ways communities are changing for the better

Communities are home to many problems including loneliness, isolation of the elderly, spending cuts to services to name a few. But having worked with thousands of groups across the UK over the last four years, here at Stickyboard we have seen some great local projects tackling and overcoming these challenges with the aid of technology.

We'd like to share some of these projects, and explain how we see the majority of social challenges being tackled through three mechanisms:

- The mobilisation of local and social entrepreneurship,
- Building on what's already there, and
- Bridging gaps between neighbours.

http://www.socialenterprise.org.uk/news/three-ways-communities-are-changing-for-the-better

Skills practice exercises

Activity 4

Refer to Document 1.

1. Look at the image of Hanoi. What are the likely consequences of dense urban development projects (such as businesses and homes) in an area that is not served by the new train system?

2. In some cities, central slums are being cleared. What are the likely consequences for slum dwellers, other residents, local businesses, commuters?

> Think about your search terms. If your first search doesn't work, what other search terms could you try?

Activity 5

Refer to Document 2.

1. Javier says, "We have to take action to prevent so many people from moving into cities." Is this a fact or an opinion? Explain your answer.

2. "It's putting unmanageable pressure on cities' resources." Is this fact or exaggeration? Explain your answer.

3. How would you check what effects urbanisation is having on your city/local area? See how much information you can find in ten minutes.

4. Find and write down one opinion and one prediction that Ngoc makes.

5. How would you check whether Hanoi really has grown without forming large slums? See how much information you can find in ten minutes.

6. "More urbanised nations have higher life expectancy and literacy rates." How would you check this claim to see if it is a fact?

7. "Ngoc is right." Is this a fact or opinion? Explain your answer.

8. "It takes three hours to go to work." Is this a fact or exaggeration? How would you check?

> Remember, facts can be verified and opinions cannot.

Activity 6

1. Summarise the article in Document 3.

   a) Use diagrams to help you.

   b) Think about key issues.

   c) Think about causes, consequences and possible solutions.

   d) Think about different perspectives.

2. Use your own ideas, research and Document 3 to help you. Think about possible courses of action to deal with shrinking cities for

   a) individuals

   b) city authorities

   c) national governments

   d) international agencies such as NGOs.

Activity 7

1. Identify three community problems from Document 4.

2. Identify three mechanisms for dealing with social challenges, from Document 4.

3. What do you understand by these mechanisms? Discuss this in groups.

4. Go to the website
   http://www.socialenterprise.org.uk/news/three-ways-communities-are-changing-for-the-better

   a) Find examples of projects that are effectively helping to change communities.

   b) How effective do you think they are?

   c) Find out about Stickyboard's crowd funding campaign.

5. Research social enterprise projects in your area – are they changing communities in positive ways?

Activity 8

1. What are the challenges and benefits of rapid urbanisation to each of the following individuals?

   a) Labourer who has migrated to the city to find work.

   b) School student.

   c) Owner of a new computer business.

   d) Commuter.

   e) City leader.

2. What are the challenges and benefits of shrinking cities to each of these individuals?

   a) A young person who wants to look after older family members and also have a career.

   b) A government policymaker

   c) Someone who wants to set up a business

3. Think about the different perspectives these people have. What are the needs, expectations, beliefs and desires that make their perspectives different?

4. To what extent is urbanisation a personal, local/national or global concern?

Use quick internet searches to help you.

Activity 9

1. What are the most important problems in your area related to changing communities?

   a) What do you already think? Are you prepared to change your mind?

   b) What search terms will you use?

   c) What key words and phrases will you skim-read for?

   d) Remember to think about which problems are most important, and why.

2. Choose a city or country in a very different part of the world. What are their most important problems related to changing communities?

3. What are the similarities and differences in the changing community problems experienced by your area and the area you have studied?

4. In what ways do these two areas have different perspectives on changing communities?

5. What is the most interesting issue you have considered on the topic of changing communities so far? Do you think that this issue is suitable for an Individual Report?

6. Add your own questions to help you plan a line of inquiry.

Activity 10

1. How likely are these consequences? Discuss and explain your answers.

   a) If the government provides cheap but unreliable electricity to everyone:

   b) If the government provides reliable electricity to businesses:

Consequence	Serious exaggeration / highly unlikely	Quite likely	Very likely
The economy will grow			
People will work from home instead of migrating to the city			
There will be problems financing the electricity long term			
There will be frequent power cuts			
Quality of life will be dramatically improved			

> Remember to think about exaggeration, oversimplification and ignoring other possibilities.

Reflection

- Have you changed your opinions about urbanisation generally?

- Do you see any changing communities issues differently now? If so, how and why?

- Use diagrams and mind maps to help you to reflect on the issue for your research report.

Reflection

1. Look at your research materials again and think about whether any predicted consequences are likely and realistic. Think about the following.

   a) Are the predicted consequences exaggerated?

   b) Are the consequences oversimplified?

   c) Are there other possibilities which are ignored?

2. What are you going to do if your research materials predict unlikely consequences?

Ideas for discussion, debate and practice

Work in groups.

Use a city building game or app to build cities. Each group should have different criteria for city development.

Compare the cities you have built. How much difference did the different criteria make?

Free city building games include:

http://www.planitgreenlive.com/en/build-your-own-city

http://www.risingcities.co.uk/

How effectively is my country meeting the challenges of rapid urbanisation? What else should the government do?

Some old cities are shrinking. What is the best way to deal with the challenges that this brings?

Suggestions for research

How can we ensure that rapid urbanisation does not lead to an increase in urban poverty?

How effective is social enterprise as a tool for changing communities/ addressing social problems in communities?

How can coastal communities work together to meet the challenges of rising sea levels?

4 Digital world

Some key issues include:

- Effects of computer use on our brains
- Privacy
- International connectedness
- Digital surveillance
- Digital enhancements

- Fairness
- Effects on trade
- Access to broadband/computers
- Use of our data
- Effects on culture

> Do some of these comments and questions raise more than one issue?

Activity 1

1. Match the comments and questions below to the issues in the diagram above.

   a) Life has become more complex but we hardly ever notice it because technology has made complexity simpler than ever. Psychologists explain this in terms of two distinct aspects of human intellect, namely fluid and crystallized intelligence.

   b) I want to get a chip implanted in my brain that will connect to the internet and tell me where all the best restaurants are.

   c) In China, where automatic surveillance is common, people sometimes write messages on paper, then send photographs of those messages over the Internet. It won't help at all against targeted surveillance, but it's much harder for automatic systems to monitor.

   d) Almost four in five people around the world believe that access to the internet is a fundamental right, according to a poll for the BBC World Service.

   e) In 1998, Walt Disney World Resort opened DisneyQuest, a five-story indoor interactive theme park in Florida, USA. At the time it was a ground-breaking step in virtual reality,

   however the company has recently announced plans to close the attraction after 18 years of operation. With the advent of smartphones and video games, it seems DisneyQuest has quickly become outdated.

   f) I get a bit bored with looking at pictures of cats doing silly things and other people's babies, but social media is a great way of keeping in touch with friends and colleagues around the world.

2. Identify at least one comment or question which comes from a

   a) personal perspective

   b) national perspective

   c) global perspective

3. Choose an issue, comment or question that interests you and discuss it with a partner.

   a) Think about personal, local/national and global perspectives on this issue. For example, think about the perspectives of a worker, a company boss, a head of government, an international charity worker, and so on.

   b) What information do you need to help you discuss this?

Key vocabulary and language exercises

Activity 2

1. We talk about digital technology and the digital world. What does digital actually mean? Use dictionaries and online resources to help you find out.

2. Read through the stimulus material quickly. Identify ten words that seem important but you aren't sure what they mean. Use dictionaries and online resources to help you find out.

Stimulus material

Document 1

Broadband Affordability

Cost of broadband subscription as a percentage of average yearly income

>100	Madagascar, Zimbabwe, Afghanistan, Guinea-Bissau
50–100	Mali, Nigeria, Ethiopia, Iraq, Tanzania
25–50	Sudan, Mauritania, Cambodia, Ghana, Ivory Coast
10–25	Bolivia, Namibia, Angola, Pakistan, Nepal
2.5–10	China, Mongolia, India, Mexico
1–2.5	Russia, Brazil, Australia, Spain, Germany
<1	UK, France, Italy, USA, Canada, Japan

Cost of one month of broadband subscription in 2011 (US$)

>100	Namibia, Iraq, Guinea-Bissau, Tajikistan
50–100	Australia, Mali, Angola, Botswana
40–50	Libya, Germany, Ivory Coast, New Zealand
30–40	Canada, Sweden, Finland, Spain, Madagascar
20–30	UK, Kazakhstan, Saudi Arabia, Sudan, Argentina
10–20	China, Russia, Brazil, Peru, USA
<10	India, Mongolia, Ukraine, Romania, Nepal

Data from World Bank: data.worldbank.org

Document 2

What your social media likes say about you – and what other people do with them

There are more than 1 billion active users on Facebook and over half a billion active users on Twitter. Every one of these users creates a profile with information about themselves, and regularly posts information about what they like, where they are and what they are doing.

We are collectively creating vast quantities of data – demographic data, data about our behaviour and data about our preferences. Social media data mining is the new big thing for scientists – they can learn tremendous amounts about us. By tracking patterns of behaviour amongst millions of people, scientists can predict people's political beliefs, their gender and sexuality, whether they abuse substances, what their health is like and so on. For example, researchers from HP Labs tracked 2.9 million tweets looking for mentions of new films, and found that they could accurately predict how successful a film would be.

But what many people do not understand is that the information they put on social media sites is public information – whatever privacy settings you choose. Companies can approach social media sites with lists of email addresses, and get adverts targeted at those users. They can ask social media sites to target adverts at people *like* those on their email lists, and the social media sites will use likes, dislikes and other information that people post to help companies to target their adverts. More and more, companies are using social media and the information we post to create demand for their products.

Often, it is not even the obvious things that allow behaviour and events in our lives to be predicted. One company sent coupons for baby clothes to a fifteen year old girl – weeks before she even told her parents that she was pregnant, and certainly before she posted this online. But companies can generate a pregnancy score, based on whether a woman is taking more vitamins than normal, buying a bag big enough for baby gear, etc. This is based on data from millions of pregnant women following certain patterns. So when an individual starts to follow that pattern, it is highly likely that she, too, is pregnant.

Increasingly, all this information we willingly put online is being used to make money. You may think that it's fair enough for companies to advertise to us – without online advertising, we would have to pay for content on the internet, and most of us like to believe that we can control the impulse to buy in response to these adverts. But what if someone started selling information about us to possible employers? Telling Josh's boss that, based on his Facebook profile, he does not work well in teams and is actually often on the beach when he claims to be sick? Or telling Suki's employer that she has a compulsive shopping habit?

It seems as if we should have some control over the data that we put online. But we don't. Social media sites make our information available to businesses, who can do whatever they want with it. So, should governments pass laws to change this? This seems like a good idea. However, not all governments will want to pass this kind of law – many governments, even in democratic countries, put the interests of businesses before the interests of individuals.

Some scientists propose an alternative to passing laws. They recommend that warnings are given when people like or share a post. These warnings would tell them the uses that their data could be put to. They argue that this would create empowered and educated social media users. What do you think – could this work?

Document 3

U.S. military researchers have had great success using "transcranial direct current stimulation" (tDCS) — in which they let electrical current flow through your brain. tDCS can more than double the rate at which people learn a wide range of tasks, such as object recognition, math skills, and marksmanship.

Is brain boosting fair? Will it create a social divide, where the rich can afford to be smarter and everyone else will be left behind? Will Tiger Moms force their lazy kids to strap on a zappity helmet during piano practice?

After trying it myself, I have different questions. To make you understand, I am going to tell you how it felt. To start with, I found the marksmanship task difficult, and I became obsessed with my failure. But with the electrodes on, my constant self-criticism virtually disappeared and I was able to complete the marksmanship task.

If you told me tDCS would allow someone to study twice as fast for the bar exam, I might be worried because I have visions of rich daddies paying for Junior's thinking cap. But now think of a different application — could school-age girls use the zappy cap while studying math to drown out the voices that tell them they can't do math because they're girls?

And then, finally, the main question: What role do doubt and fear play in our lives if their eradication actually causes so many improvements? Do we make more ethical decisions when we listen to our inner voices of self-doubt or when we're freed from them? If we all wore these caps, would the world be a better place?

Skills practice exercises

Activity 3

1. Which of the following best describes the trends you can see in the graphics in Document 1?

   a) Broadband prices are falling everywhere but are still expensive in some places.

   b) Broadband prices are falling almost everywhere but are still expensive everywhere.

   c) Broadband prices are falling almost everywhere but there in an enormous difference in the relative cost of broadband between countries.

2. Are the following statements true or false?

   a) In 2011, broadband cost more in the UK than in China, but was more affordable.

   b) Australia had relatively low broadband costs in 2011, but broadband was still relatively expensive.

3. Why do you think it matters how affordable broadband is?

4. Can you find any more recent data on the price and affordability of broadband for your own country?

Activity 4

Refer to Document 2.

1. What key issues does this raise?

2. How do you feel about social media sites analysing your interactions and making predictions about you? Why do you feel like this?

3. Do you think that we should put pressure on governments to pass laws to protect us from people using our online data? Why or why not?

4. Social media sites are international. What problems does that raise for law makers around the world?

5. Do you agree with the author when she says that people would change what they put on social media if risk warnings came up?

Activity 5

Refer to Document 3.

1. Using the document, your own knowledge and internet resources

   a) make a list of the ways that digital technology can be used to enhance humans

   b) give three reasons for using technological enhancements

   c) give three reasons against using technological enhancements.

2. Is technological enhancement mostly a personal, local/national or global issue?

3. Sally Adee, the author of Document 3, asks, "Do we make more ethical decisions when we listen to our inner voices of self-doubt or when we're freed from them?"

   Suggest an experiment that would help you to find out the answer to this question. What problems would you expect to encounter?

Activity 6

1. What are the most important problems in your area related to the digital world?

   a) What do you already think? Are you prepared to change your mind?

   b) What search terms will you use?

   c) What key words and phrases will you skim-read for?

   d) Remember to think about which problems are most important, and why.

2. Choose a city or country in a very different part of the world. What are their most important problems related to digital technologies?

3. What are the similarities and differences in the digital problems experienced by your area and the area you have studied?

4. In what ways do these two areas have different perspectives on the digital world?

5. What is the most interesting digital technology issue you have considered so far? Do you think that this issue is suitable for an Individual Report?

6. Add your own questions to help you plan a line of inquiry.

Activity 7

1. What are the likely consequences of allowing the internet to operate with no restrictions at all?

2. What are the likely consequences of governments putting restrictions on the internet?

3. Do you think that there should be any restrictions on social media?

4. Do you think there should be any restrictions on other parts of the internet?

5. What are the likely consequences of online bullying and trolling?

6. What actions could or should be taken against these?

7. What would the likely consequences be if the internet stopped working?

Reflection

1. Write in your reflective journal.

   a) Have you changed your opinions or formed new opinions?

   b) Do you think the digital world is generally good for people? Why or why not?

   c) How is your research progressing?

   d) What do you need to do to make progress?

Ideas for discussion, debate and practice

- "If people post personal information online, they must be happy for the government, companies and future employers to see it." What are your thoughts on this statement?

- Which is most important to economic development: communications technology (such as the internet), military technology, medical technology, engineering technology, other?

- What sort of ways can broadband internet access help improve a local economy?

- Can we, and should we, change the way technology emphasises divisions between rich and poor? If so, how?

- Who should invest in digital technology – governments, international organisations like the UN, multinational companies, individuals, other?

- Should digital technology be owned by companies or should everyone share the benefits?

- Are there some areas of life in which we should reject technological enhancement in order to increase fairness?

How can we provide high quality internet access to the majority?

Suggestions for research

How important is digital technology to economic and social progress?

5 Family

Some key issues include:

- Changing relationships within families
- Vulnerable children
- Effects of migration on families
- Family values
- Work-life balance in families
- Changing socio-economic roles of parents

- Effects of poverty on families
- Aging families
- One-child policy
- Role of corporations in family policy
- Young caregivers
- Role of state in supporting families
- Changing family structures

> Do some of these comments and questions raise more than one issue?

Activity 1

1. Match the comments and questions below to the issues in the diagram above.

   a) Businesses must have an awareness of family issues and priorities around the globe, because individual workers all have families – mothers, brothers, spouses, cousins, children, and so on. These individuals are international, and have different family priorities. International analysis can help businesses to broaden their understanding of what is possible in business-family relationships.

   b) When I was a child, I had my parents and my grandparents, but no great grandparents. Now I am old enough to be a grandmother, my daughter is old enough to have children, and my grandmothers are still alive, and hoping to see their great-great grandchildren.

   c) This paper discusses four current and main issues faced by family institutions in Malaysia... Contributing factors to problematic families are also identified such as economy, urbanisation, employment, communication and value change.

   d) Nickolaus Dent is 13 years old, yet he cooks every meal, does the laundry and cleans the house because his mother is very ill. "It does make it hard to pay attention in class," he said. "Helping her out is a bigger priority than going to school and getting [an] education, because I feel if I don't have her, I don't want to go to school. Whatever happens to her happens to me."

   e) When migrants leave to find work abroad, they often seek to improve the well-being of their family and provide better opportunities for their children over the long run. While migration may assist in achieving financial stability, research shows that the absence of a parent can be detrimental to a child's social and psychological development.

f) I would block off an hour lunch meeting with someone for business, so why not block off an hour dinner with my family at night?

2. Identify at least one comment or question which comes from a

a) personal perspective

b) national perspective

c) global perspective

3. Choose an issue, comment or question that interests you and discuss it with a partner.

a) Think about personal, local/national and global perspectives on this issue. For example, think about the perspectives of a worker, a company boss, a head of government, an international charity worker, and so on.

b) What information do you need to help you discuss this?

Key vocabulary and language exercises

Activity 2

1. Use dictionaries and online resources to find definitions of the words and phrases in the table.

> If English is not your first language, avoid using online translation tools. They are often not very good! Your language skills will develop better if you use dictionaries.

Words and phrases	Definition
a) Marriage	
b) Maternity leave	
c) Paternity leave	
d) Quality time	
e) Young caregiver	
f) Family priorities	
g) Family values	

Activity 3

1. Use internet resources to help you complete the mind map with different types of family issues. Add as many types as you can find.

> When you search for internet resources on family, you will find materials produced by very young children at school. Do you think these are good resources for you to rely on? What are your reasons?

Aging

Generational

Family issues

Work-related

Family structure

Stimulus material

"Son, I'd like us to spend more quality time together. Would you accept me as a Facebook friend and let me follow you on Twitter?"

Document 2

Planning a wedding in Malaysia?

Getting married in Malaysia is relatively simple. Under Malaysian law there are two officially recognised forms of marriage: Muslim and civil marriages. However, as Malaysia is a multi-racial country, many people, including Hindus, Buddhists, Sikhs choose traditional marriage ceremonies. These are not legally recognised under the Registration of Marriages Ordinance and Law Reform Act 1956, unless the marriage is first registered as a civil marriage with the Registration Department.

Under Islamic law in Malaysia, it is illegal for a non-Muslim to marry a Muslim.

Polygamy is legal in Malaysia, but it is no longer legal to enter a polygamous marriage under civil law. Polygamy is only practised by a minority of the population. A Malaysian Muslim man may marry up to four wives, if permitted to do so by a shariah court.

Document 3

Anya: My family are wonderful and annoying. They are always there when I need them, but they never let me do what I want. My parents are both teachers. I'm the oldest child, and I've got three little sisters and a little brother. All four of my grandparents live with us. My mother's mother and my father's mother don't like each other, so they are always arguing, about *everything*.

Kofi: I live with my Mum. It's just the two of us. Sometimes this is great, because we watch films together and cook together. I help with the household chores – it's only fair, I make a mess too. Sometimes though, I wish we had a bigger family. I think my mum will be lonely when I leave home.

Document 4

Paid paternity leave can help. Nearly half the world's countries now offer new fathers short periods at home; a growing number let mothers cede some maternity leave to their partners while they go back to work. Several European countries have started to reserve some of that leave for fathers to encourage them to make use of the opportunity: in Sweden couples get an "equality bonus" for splitting their time off more evenly.

Fathers and offspring benefit. When a woman hands her baby to the father and heads out of the door to work, he learns how to be a better parent. The hands-on habits he picks up persist: fathers who take even short paternity leave play a bigger role in child-rearing years later. An international study found that they were more likely to brush their toddlers' teeth, feed them and read to them. Babies whose fathers take paternity leave go on to do better in cognitive tests at school. Fathers are generally keen on their progeny, so some time to bond with them is a boon. Some men who thought that child care would not be much fun discover that they rather like it.

Bores, chores and bedtime stories: How parenting has changed in half a century.

Mothers are big winners, too. If both sexes are likely to take time off for child care, there is less temptation for employers to discriminate against women. Time-use studies show that even when both parents work the same amount, the mother usually does more child care and housework. More hands-on fathering should cut down on this "second shift", which is a big reason why many mothers work part-time or in jobs for which they are overqualified.

http://www.economist.com/news/leaders/21651215-both-parents-should-be-paid-spend-time-home-their-babies-more-hands-rock-cradle

Fewer chores, more bedtime stories
Average number of house per week spent on:

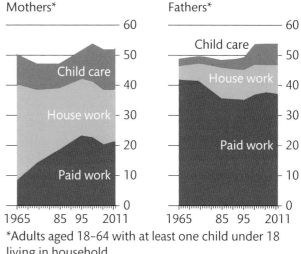

*Adults aged 18–64 with at least one child under 18 living in household

Document 5

@outraged traditionalist

This is feminist idiocy. This whole magazine is about childcare and feminism and money and glass ceilings and housework and gender politics. What is this nonsense? This is The Economist! These things have nothing to do with economics.

How did this woman get to be Editor when she clearly has no interest in economics. Why isn't she editing a woman's magazine which is obviously where she belongs.

@equality guru

Staying at home with their children does not make fathers better parents. Going to work in an office does not make a mother a worse parent. Men and women can both be breadwinners.

Men and women should have all the same opportunities – that is gender equality. This is true about parental leave just as much as it is true about opportunities for promotion.

Skills practice exercises

Activity 4

1. What family issues do the cartoons raise?

2. In each cartoon, how are the parent's and child's perspectives different?

3. Use your own opinions and research to answer this question: What are the advantages and disadvantages of parents and children being "friends" on social media?

Activity 5

Refer to Document 2.

1. How are marriage laws in Malaysia different from marriage laws in your country?

2. What do you think about these marriage laws?

3. Consider this statement:"People spend too much money on big weddings and they expect a fairy tale and think that love will conquer all. But they're going to end up married to a real person with real faults and smelly feet. They should focus on the years and years of hard work you need to put into making a marriage work, and not waste money on spectacular weddings."

   a) To what extent do you agree with this?

   b) How effective is the reasoning?

> If you are Malaysian, choose a different country to compare with – perhaps the USA, Rwanda, Pakistan, the UAE?

Activity 6

Refer to Document 3 on p.180.

1. Anya says, "they never let me do what I want." Is this a fact or opinion? Explain your answer.

2. Identify one fact, one opinion, one prediction and one value judgement in Kofi's words. Explain your answers.

3. What do you think are the causes of Anya's big family living together?

4. What do you think will be the consequences of Anya's big family living together?

5. What might be the consequences if your whole family lived together?

6. What do you think are the causes of Kofi's small family?

7. What do you think will be the consequences of Kofi's small family?

8. What might be the consequences if you lived alone with just one other family member?

9. Which is better, in your opinion? A big family or a small family? Give reasons for your answer.

10. From a national perspective, are big families or small families better? Give reasons for your answer.

Activity 7

Refer to Document 4.

1. Summarise this article. Focus on:

   a) Key issues

   b) Predicted consequences

2. Do you agree with the proposals in the Document? What are your reasons?

Activity 8

Refer to Document 5.

1. How effectively do these comments respond to Document 4? Think about:

   a) Do they give good reasons to

      i) support their own opinions

      ii) support/oppose the opinions in the Document?

   b) How logical are they?

   c) How relevant are they?

2. Write your own response to Document 4.

Activity 9

1. What are the family issues most likely to affect the following individuals? Think about the differences between similar people in LEDCs and MEDCs.

   - A woman who has migrated from Indonesia to the UEA to earn money for her children's education.

   - A child who grows up with her grandmother.

   - A Chinese national who is regional director of the African division of a multinational corporation.

   - A ten year old who cares for his sick mother.

   - A marriage counsellor.

Use quick internet searches to help you.

Activity 10

1. What are the most important problems in your area related to family?

   a) What do you already think? Are you prepared to change your mind?

   b) What search terms will you use?

   c) What key words and phrases will you skim-read for?

   d) Remember to think about which problems are most important, and why.

2. Choose a city or country in a very different part of the world. What are their most important problems related to family?

3. What are the similarities and differences in the family problems experienced by your area and the area you have studied?

4. In what ways do these two areas have different perspectives on family?

5. What is the most interesting family issue you have considered so far? Do you think that this issue is suitable for an Individual Report?

6. Add your own questions to help you plan a line of inquiry.

Activity 11

1. What are the likely consequences of allowing people to choose the kind of family they want with no restrictions at all?

2. What are the likely consequences of a state making decisions about family life?

3. The Singapore Maintenance of Parents Act provides for Singapore residents aged 60 and above, who are unable to support themselves on their own, to claim maintenance from their children who are capable of supporting them but are not doing so. What are the consequences of this act

   a) for the family as a whole

   b) for parents

   c) for children

   d) for the nation?

4. In many Western countries, senior citizens live alone or in old people's homes. What are the consequences of this

   a) for the family as a whole

   b) for parents

   c) for children

   d) for the nation?

5. Choose a family problem that interests you. What are the probable consequences of this

   a) for the family as a whole

   b) for parents

   c) for children

   d) for the nation?

> Remember to use research to help you.

Activity 12

Look at the sources you have found so far.

a) Are they reliable? If not, what will you do?

b) Is the reasoning good quality? How will this affect the way you use the ideas, information and perspectives in your work?

c) Are the causes and consequences likely? If not, what will you do?

d) Are there alternative possible consequences? If so, how will this affect the way you use these ideas in your work?

> If your source is not reliable, look for a more reliable source.

> If the reasoning is poor or the consequences unlikely, look for better quality sources of ideas, information and perspectives. Don't quote material that you have identified as illogical or poor quality.

Reflection

- Have you thought about families in any new ways? If so, how and why.

- Have you changed your mind about anything? Give your reasons.

Ideas for discussion, debate and practice

Make a marriage wall in the classroom.

- Find images of wedding ceremonies from around the world.

- Find wedding traditions and stories from different places.

- Talk to people who have been married for a very long time. Ask them to share stories.

- Talk to marriage counsellors. Ask them for tips about making a marriage work.

Debate. The most important family value is…

- Each group member choses, or is given, a value. They must argue why it is important.

- At the end of the debate, the class votes on which is the most important family value.

- Three class members should be "observers" – their role is to decide who has argued well.

Discussion. What role, if any, should the state/government play in family life? You could consider:

- Ensuring all children get an equal chance to succeed.

- Providing education.

- What sort of laws to make about family life.

- Supporting young caregivers.

- Other.

Discussion

1. Which is more important and why?

   a) Family support or independence? (Does it make a difference if you're young or old?)

   b) Love or money?

   c) Closeness or distance?

2. How far should parents push their children? Explain your opinion.

3. How much obedience should parents expect from their children? Explain your opinion.

4. How far should parents set goals for their children? How far should children be able to set their own life aims? Explain your opinion.

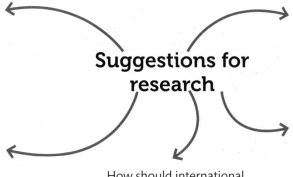

What are the best solutions to the problems of managing work and family life?

What are the main family challenges caused by migration? What actions can be taken to resolve these challenges?

Suggestions for research

How should families change to deal with the challenges of the twenty first century?

How should international businesses respond to the changing demands of families?

How should families, governments and NGOs respond to the issues of an aging world?

6 Humans and other species

Some key issues include:

- Human-animal interactions
- Humans and plants
- Species loss
- Evolution
- Stewardship
- Conservation
- Animal rights
- Differences between humans and animals
- Wild and domestic animals
- Ethical issues
- "Natural" and "right"

Do some of these comments and questions raise more than one issue?

Activity 1

1. Match the comments and questions below to the issues listed above.

   a) My dog is more important to me than most people are. Does that make me a bad person?

   b) Are we special? There's no agreement on whether humans are different from other animals. Are we simply the most intelligent of the animals or do we have a fundamentally different 'type' of existence?

   c) Can taking care of our planet reflect our faith? If you believe that God put man above all of the animals and that he gave us a beautiful planet to live on, the answer is probably yes. God calls us to be good stewards.

   d) The trade in wild animals is regulated by Cites, the Convention on International Trade in Endangered Species of Wild Fauna and Flora, which has procedures in place to protect rare species. The UAE is a signatory to the convention, which means rare animals may be traded only with the appropriate paperwork. Anyone convicted of smuggling endangered wildlife into the UAE can be jailed for up to six months and fined between Dh10,000 to Dh50,000.

   e) The belief that humans are in some way "above" plants and animals is a major cause of global species loss, as humans recklessly exploit world resources for our own benefit.

   f) Humans that leave the familiarity of Earth could morph into a separate species. "These people will become an offshoot of the human tree," Impey said in the interview. "They will probably evolve into something else."

2. Identify at least one comment or question which comes from a

   a) personal perspective

   b) national perspective

   c) global perspective.

3. Choose an issue, comment or question that interests you and discuss it with a partner.

   a) Think about personal, local/national and global perspectives on this issue. For example, think about the perspectives of a worker, a company boss, a head of government, an international charity worker, and so on.

   b) What information do you need to help you discuss this?

Key vocabulary and language exercises

Activity 2

1. What is the difference between:

   a) "It's natural" and "it's right"

   b) "We have the right to" and "it is right to"

   c) "Stewardship" and "domination"

   d) "Pet", "domestic animal", and "wild animal".

> Use dictionaries and online resources to help you find accurate definitions.

Activity 3

1. Use internet resources to help you complete the mind map with different types of human and other species issues. Add as many types as you can find. Some initial suggestions have been made.

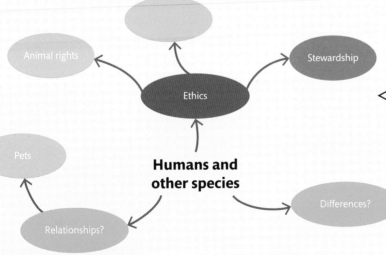

> When you search for internet resources on animals, you will find materials produced by very young children at school. Do you think these are good resources for you to rely on? What are your reasons?

Stimulus material

Humans and animals

A survey conducted on the relationship between the American public and animals.

Q: The main role of animals in society is as a source of food.

No   Yes

Pet owners

No   Yes

Non-pet owners

Q: What gives you the greatest sense of comfort?

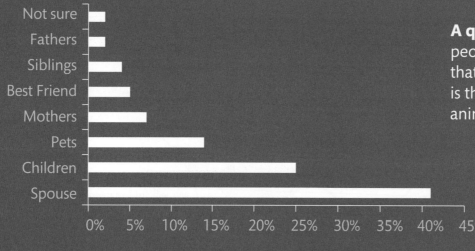

Not sure
Fathers
Siblings
Best Friend
Mothers
Pets
Children
Spouse

0% 5% 10% 15% 20% 25% 30% 35% 40% 45%

A quarter of people thought that companionship is the main role of animals in society.

Q: What is the role of the veterinarian in society?

The vast majority of people agree that the veterinarian has an extremely important role in the food industry – helping to raise healthy livestock.

Eight out of ten also agreed that the veterinarian has a vital position in protecting the public health through the prevention of diseases which originate or spread through animals.

Document 2

 Keith: We should all become vegetarians. If we did, there would be enough food for everyone. It takes 7kg of grain to produce 1kg of beef. It also takes thousands and thousands of litres of water. Also, it's wrong to eat beef. It's murder.

 Jacquie: People are so bad at using statistics. It takes 7kg of grain to produce 1kg of beef in intensive US farms. But around the world, most beef is grass fed, and the grass grows on land that isn't good enough for grain production. I wouldn't eat beef from cows that had been kept in poor conditions, but it's not wrong to eat meat – it's a natural part of who we are.

Document 3

Recent studies have made it clear that dolphins communicate with each other, but whether we can say they have their own 'language' is a controversial topic and raises many further questions about the nature of language and self-awareness.

Possible answers to some of these questions may profoundly influence the relationship between humans and animals. For example, recent studies have shown that animals display emotions such as empathy and grief, and many have complex systems of communication.

Denise Herzing has been studying dolphin communication in the wild for the past 30 years. She spends five months every summer living with a pod of Atlantic spotted dolphins, documenting their relationships. Herzing argues that individual dolphins have signature whistles, much as we have a naming system, and use buzzes and tickles to communicate with one another. Other studies have come to a similar conclusion, which then raises the question, if dolphins can communicate between themselves, what's to stop us communicating with them?

Listen to Herzing's TED talk, *Could we speak the language of dolphins?*, at the link below:

https://www.ted.com/talks/denise_herzing_could_we_speak_the_language_of_dolphins

Skills practice exercises

Activity 4

Refer to Document 1.

1. Look at the graphics. Identify three important roles that animals play in US society.

2. Do animals play similar roles in your society?

3. How important are pets in your society?

4. Do you think that it is reasonable to give a pet the same level of healthcare as a child or a grandparent?

5. How can you justify giving a pet a high level of healthcare (using evidence provided, whether or not you agree with it)?

Activity 5

Refer to Document 2.

1. Keith says, "We should all become vegetarians." Is this a fact or opinion? Explain your answer.

2. Identify one fact, one prediction and one value judgement that Keith uses. Explain your answers.

3. Jacquie says, "the grass grows on land that isn't good enough for grain production." Is this fact or opinion? Explain your answer.

4. What might be the personal consequences for you of not eating meat?

5. What might be the national and global consequences if no one ate meat?

6. "Large tracts of rainforest in South America are cut down to graze beef cattle and grow soya to feed crops."

   a) What consequences might this have? (Think about habitats, endangered species, etc.)

   b) How does this affect your opinion about eating beef?

Discussion

Is natural the same as right? Is unnatural the same as wrong? Discuss this.

Activity 6

Refer to Document 3.

1. What are the two most important questions raised by the author?

2. Why do you think these two are the most important?

3. Why does it matter if animals have language?

4. Do you think that intelligent animals can suffer more than less intelligent animals?

5. What are the consequences for humans if animals can suffer?

6. Use internet searches and other resources to find evidence of the following.

   a) Chimps using tools.

   b) Caledonian crows using tools.

   c) Evidence of animal empathy.

   d) Evidence of animal emotion.

   e) Evidence of animal concepts of fairness.

7. How do you react to this evidence? Does it challenge your ideas about humans and other species?

Activity 7

1. What kind of information do you need to answer each of these questions?

   a) What is habitat destruction?

   b) What proportion of people in your country are vegetarian?

   c) What would happen if we all stopped eating meat?

   d) Why should we respect the other creatures on this planet?

   e) How many different species live in Brunei's Sungai Ingei Conservation Forest?

   f) Why do Indonesian rainforests matter?

2. What search terms would help you to find information and ideas to answer these questions?

   a) What proportion of people in your country are vegetarian?

   b) What would happen if we all stopped eating meat?

   c) How many different species live in the Brunei's Sungai Ingei Conservation Forest region?

   d) Why do Indonesian rainforests matter?

Do you need to use the internet to answer all these questions? What other ways could you find out this information?

Activity 8

1. What are the most important problems in your area related to humans and other species?

   a) What do you already think? Are you prepared to change your mind?

   b) What search terms will you use?

   c) What key words and phrases will you skim-read for?

   d) Remember to think about which problems are most important, and why.

2. Choose a city or country in a very different part of the world. What are their most important problems related to humans and other species?

3. What are the similarities and differences in the issues related to humans and other species experienced by your area and the area you have studied?

4. In what ways do these two areas have different perspectives on humans and other animals?

5. What is the most interesting issue you have considered so far? Do you think that this issue is suitable for an Individual Report?

6. Add your own questions to help you plan a line of inquiry.

Activity 9

1. How likely are these consequences? Discuss and explain your answers.

   If we tighten regulations regarding keeping wild animals as pets:

Consequence	Serious exaggeration / highly unlikely	Quite likely	Very likely
The illegal market for wild animals will grow			
Fewer people will die when their pets attack them			
This will completely prevent transmission of serious diseases from exotic pets to people			
Some people may keep their exotic pets in better conditions			
People will realise that it is wrong to keep wild animals as pets			

2. Work in groups to create activities like this for your classmates.

Activity 10

Look at the sources you have found so far.

1. Are they reliable? If not, what will you do?

2. Is the reasoning good quality? How will this affect the way you use the ideas, information and perspectives in your work?

3. Are the causes and consequences likely? If not, what will you do?

4. Are there alternative possible consequences? If so, how will this affect the way you use these ideas in your work?

> If your source is not reliable, look for a more reliable source.

> If the reasoning is poor, or if the consequences are unlikely, search for better quality sources. Don't quote material that you have identified as illogical or poor quality.

Reflection

1. Do you think that animals are as important as humans? What are your reasons?

2. Have you thought about humans and other species in any new ways? If so, what and why?

3. Have you changed your mind about anything? What are your reasons?

Ideas for discussion, debate and practice

- Would the world be a better place if we reduced the number of humans?
- Is it selfish to protect endangered species for our own benefit?
- How much do endangered species matter to you/to the world?
- Is fur worse than leather?
- Is big game hunting beneficial overall?

Discussion

"Animal experiments are both cruel and wrong, and should be illegal." Discuss.

Discussion

Which is more important and why:

- Animal rights or benefits for humans? (Does it make a difference if you're young or old?)
- Good conditions for animals or cheap meat for humans?
- Economic development for humans or healthy natural habitats?

How can individuals and nations reduce their impact on habitat destruction?

How can we prevent poaching of endangered species?

Suggestions for research

How can we improve the ways in which we treat animals in our country?

To what extent is it ethically acceptable for us to use animals for our own purposes?

7 Sustainable living

Some key issues include:

- Using finite resources
- Whose responsibility is sustainability?
- Government legislation
- Reducing waste
- Lifestyle and status
- Sustainable development
- Individual and collective effort
- Changing attitudes

> Do some of these comments and questions raise more than one issue?

Activity 1

1. Match the comments and questions below to the issues in the diagram above.

   a) I want an Audi R8. Or maybe a Lotus. I want people to know how successful I am.

   b) We are using too many resources in this country. The Government should do something about it.

   c) "The problem is that people don't tend to want their attitudes changed and to attempt to do so smacks of paternalism and self-righteousness. The promotion of a commitment to sustainability as being a somehow 'enlightened' or 'higher' purpose has been a key barrier to these values making it into the mainstream."

   d) I think I should try to live more sustainably – I care about the planet, and I want it to still be there for my kids and my grandkids. But I don't want my kids to suffer now. I don't want the other kids at school calling my kids poor because we don't have all the stuff that everyone else has.

   e) We produce one-use plastic food containers. We are the biggest employer in this area, and we make sure that people round here can eat and pay their bills. Sustainability laws won't do any of us any good.

   f) Consumers are key to driving sustainable production and they play a central role in sustainable development. This report highlights OECD government initiatives to promote sustainable consumption, with an emphasis on individual policy tools and instruments and their effective combination. Here, the sustainability of consumption is considered in economic, environmental and social terms.

2. Identify at least one comment or question which comes from a

   a) personal perspective

   b) national perspective

   c) global perspective.

3. Choose an issue, comment or question that interests you and discuss it with a partner.

   a) Think about personal, local/national and global perspectives on this issue. For example, think about the perspectives of a worker, a company boss, a head of government, an international charity worker, and so on.

   b) What information do you need to help you discuss this?

Key vocabulary and language exercises

If English is not your first language, avoid using online translation tools. They are often not very good! Your language skills will develop better if you use dictionaries.

Activity 2

1. Use dictionaries and online resources to match the words on the right with the definitions in the table.

1	A lifestyle that uses as few resources as possible, and causes as little environmental damage as possible.	Sustainable living
2	Presence of harmful substances in the air, water or general environment.	Sustainable development
3	Using resources, goods and services.	Consumer
4	Generally used to refer to someone or something which aims to be sustainable or environmentally friendly.	Government initiative
5	A person who purchases goods or services.	
6	Growth and development which meets the needs of the present without using up all the resources that people will need in the future. Includes the idea that social, environmental and economic progress are all possible within the limits of earth's natural resources.	Consumption / Green
7	Converted from waste into a usable product.	Recycled
8	A course of action started by the government that begins a process of change.	Pollution

Activity 3

1. Make cards with the words from Activity 2. Make separate cards with the definitions you have found. Play games to help you remember the words.

   a) Turn all the cards face down so that you cannot see them. Mix them up so that you don't know which card is where. Turn over two cards at a time. If you have a word and its definition, you keep the pair. The player with the most pairs wins.

   b) Mix all the definition cards up and put them in one pile. Take a card from the pile. Read the definition and give the word it defines.

   c) Mix all the word cards up and put them in one pile. Take a card from the pile. Read the word and give its definition.

Stimulus material

This Dutch architect's big idea makes even our "greenest" cities look gray

What kinds of places do you think of when it comes to "green" cities?

If you're like me, you're probably imagining places with subways and solar panels, electric cars and urban farms. And you'd be right. Those things are important for a city to be considered "green."

A 2015 study of the nation's 150 largest cities by Nerd Wallet ranked eco-friendliness by looking at where people live, how they get around the city, where their energy comes from, and the quality of the air.

But what if I told you green cities could look like this:

This is OAS1S, the brain baby of Dutch architect Raimond de Hullu.

It's his template for building cities that are green in the truest sense of the word. In an interview with Fast Company, De Hullu explained his vision:

"We need a new building typology that goes beyond the usual technical sustainability. **We need a 100% green concept, not only technically but visually as well**, and which is desirable plus affordable at the same time."

De Hullu envisions buildings that take after trees, nature's original skyscrapers...

Image by OAS1S.

...and communities that blend with forests. He imagines neighborhoods **built entirely from recycled materials** that function completely off-grid with **solar energy and on-site water systems**.

And best of all, he wants OAS1S to be an affordable housing opportunity. For everyone. To achieve that, he wants these communities to be set up as land trusts. Under this model, a community nonprofit is formed to buy and own land, and the homes built on that land are owned by the occupants. According to the Democracy Collaborative:

"By separating the ownership of land and housing, **this innovative approach prevents market factors from causing prices to rise significantly**, and hence **guarantees that housing will remain affordable** for future generations."

OAS1S is still only a concept, but de Hullu is searching for a suitable place for a pilot community.

He hopes the first location can be in an established city, which would be great for visibility, especially if it proves an effective model. De Hullu wants the essence of the project to remain "**constructing a true balance between architecture and nature**." De Hullu's goal is simple: build communities that are good for people and good for the planet.

And the last thing, which I cannot stress enough, is that **we could live in tree houses!** How cool would that be?

http://www.upworthy.com/this-dutch-architects-big-idea-makes-even-our-greenest-cities-look-gray

Document 2

How do we achieve a sustainable lifestyle?

Although many of us have some idea of what sustainability means, how many of us have an idea of what this means in terms of our lifestyle and personal responsibilities? Where the progress of society towards a sustainable future may be viewed as inadequate, it may be easy for us to blame governments and corporations, but given that the activities of governments and organisations serve individuals, what can we as individuals do and influence? How can engineers empower and equip us to live sustainably from day to day and what might a sustainable lifestyle look like?

Sustainability is generally understood to mean something along the lines of not consuming resources faster than their production and not polluting the environment in an irreversible way. These resources may be environmental, economic or indeed societal. Many people believe they are living sustainably because they are doing better than others around them by for example separating their rubbish for recycling more than others or riding a bicycle to work rather than driving. How do we know though if we are doing enough? Even those who work professionally in the area of sustainability rarely have truly sustainable lifestyles themselves, even if they advocate them for others. Often people suggest that they are not prepared to live sustainably as individuals until there is a collective movement with those around them doing the same; otherwise there is a feeling of self-sacrifice with little notable impact whilst those around them continue to live in relative luxury. Furthermore responsibility is often transferred when it is said that we need the development of centralised systems before we can live a fully sustainable lifestyle. For example, it is often asked, "Why should we avoid using our car if the bus and railway systems are so inadequate?"

http://www.imeche.org/knowledge/industries/energy-environment-and-sustainability/news/Sustainable-Lifestyles

Document 3

Almost everyone is against a noisy Diwali; most of all the intellectuals... For them, the bursting of crackers during Diwali is evidence of our apathy towards the environment. Our lack of concern for pollution. Noise pollution. Air pollution. Water pollution. Blah blah blah. I am not denying that the bursting of crackers causes pollution, but to suggest that this single night of revelry is anti-environment and a major cause of pollution is blatantly unfair.

Blaming firecrackers for pollution is typical of our habit of misrepresenting the truth and directing the blame in the wrong direction. The real reasons for pollution are the CO_2 [sic] generating coal-power plants, effluent releasing industries and petrol and diesel guzzling two and four wheelers. Take these out and a bulk of our problems would be solved. But do we do enough to move towards a clean environment? Do we invest heavily in nuclear power plants and in electricity-driven trains? Not at all.

Worldwide, firecrackers are the preferred way to celebrate any happy occasion. When the Olympics start or end, there is a grand show of firecrackers. When we welcome the new year in, there is a pyrotechnics show organized in many major cities – from Sydney to Singapore to even London. If all this is fine in the far more environment-conscious world, then how come it's not fine in India?

http://blogs.timesofindia.indiatimes.com/the-real-truth/entry/in-support-of-a-noisy-polluting-diwali

Skills practice exercises

Activity 4

Refer to Document 1.

1. What do you think of Raimond de Hullu's vision of green cities?

2. Do you think this is a realistic vision?

3. Would you like to live in one? What are your reasons?

4. The author refers to a 2015 study by Nerd Wallet.

   a) Who or what is Nerd Wallet?

   b) What does this 2015 survey say about the greenest cities in the USA?

   c) Research how the greenest cities in your country compare to these USA cities. Think about your search terms.

Activity 5

Refer to Document 2.

1. Summarise the key questions/issues in this article in your own words. Use approximately 50 words.

> Use quick internet searches to help you.

Activity 6

Refer to Document 3.

1. This is an extract from a blog on the website of http://www.timesofindia.co.uk

   a) How is a blog on a newspaper website different from a personal blog?

   b) Is this a reliable source of information? Explain your answer.

2. The author discusses the causes of pollution. Does he suggest reasonable causes? Can you think of alternative causes that he does not mention? Explain your answer.

3. "Take these out and a bulk of our problems would be solved." Is this a likely consequence? Explain your answer.

4. Is this good quality reasoning?

   a) Are good reasons and evidence given to support the author's views?

   b) Is emotion being used instead of reasons?

   c) Are opinions being used instead of facts?

5. Should we take action on small sources of pollution even if we can't deal with big sources of pollution?

Activity 7

1. What are the personal, local/national and global consequences, issues and perspectives that arise from the following?

   a) "We're having a really cold summer. We could do with a bit of global warming."

   b) "My country is getting hotter and drier, mostly because of pollution made in other countries."

   c) "Rapid climate change means that ecosystems can't adapt naturally."

   d) "It doesn't matter if environmentally friendly living affects the economy now. Having a future is more important than being richer."

   e) "Polar bears are vicious predators that would eat us if they could. Let them die out."

Activity 8

1. What are the most important problems in your area related to sustainable living?

   a) What do you already think? Are you prepared to change your mind?

   b) What search terms will you use?

   c) What key words and phrases will you skim-read for?

   d) Remember to think about which problems are most important, and why.

2. Choose a city or country in a very different part of the world. What are the most important problems related to sustainable living in this area?

3. What are the similarities and differences in the sustainable living problems experienced by your area and the area you have studied?

4. How are the problems relating to sustainable living linked in the areas you have considered?

5. What is the most interesting sustainable living issue you have considered so far? Do you think that this issue is suitable for an Individual Report?

6. Add your own questions to help you plan a line of inquiry.

Activity 9

1. What are the likely consequences of continuing with our consumerist lifestyles with no restrictions at all?

2. What are the likely consequences of national governments trying to make us live more sustainably?

3. What are the likely consequences of global efforts (e.g. by charities such as Greenpeace) to make us live more sustainably?

Reflection

1. Write in your reflective journal:

    a) Have you changed your opinions or formed new ones?

    b) How do you feel about the problems of sustainable living?

    c) Can you see a positive future, in which people have found solutions?

    d) How do you see your role in a sustainable future?

Ideas for discussion, debate and practice

- You are going to try living in a more sustainable way – no cars, no central heating, no air conditioning, limited electricity, etc. Choose one electrical item that you want to keep using. Explain to the class why it is the most important. See if you can all agree.

- Catastrophe has come! The world can no longer sustain the demands we are placing on it. Your life is going to change beyond recognition. Write a letter or a story that explains the changes in your lifestyle to future generations.

- Plan a city that would allow people to live comfortably but sustainably. Would your city be like Raimond de Hullu's city or would it be very different?

What are the most important actions that individuals, governments and global organisations can take to ensure we live sustainably?

How can rich countries help less economically developed countries to develop in a cleaner, more sustainable way?

Suggestions for research

Is it reasonable for nations to keep using oil, even though the use of oil is unsustainable and is contributing to climate change?

A research question agreed with your teacher.

8 Trade and aid

Some key issues include:

- Social development
- Growth and progress
- Role of experts
- Neo-colonialism
- Economic development
- Food aid
- Role of individuals
- Exploitation of resources

- Human development
- Disaster relief
- Role of charities
- Free trade
- Inequality
- Development aid
- Role of businesses
- Protectionism

Do some of these comments and questions raise more than one issue?

Activity 1

1. Match the comments and questions below to the issues in the diagram above.

   a) "Do I buy these trainers because the company is giving people in Indonesia jobs they really need? Or do I refuse to buy them because the company employs children and runs sweat shops?"

   b) "They've all got mobile phones. Why should we give them aid?"

   c) "The EU wants its trade policy to support economic growth, social development, and environmental protection."

   d) "But many British charities have become hungry monsters, needing ever more of our money to feed their own ambitions. Many charities spend at least half their income on management, strategy development, campaigning and fundraising – not what most of us would consider 'good causes.'"

   e) "It is in our national interests to provide aid. If we can help to improve the quality of life in less economically developed countries, we will not have to deal with as many migrants."

   f) "Capitalist economic theory holds that free global trade is the most efficient way to foster growth, because each country specializes in producing the goods and services in which it has a comparative advantage. Yet, in practice, trade is inherently unequal and poor countries experience increasing unemployment, poverty, and income inequality."

   g) "International food aid is controversial; Donor countries fail to provide enough food for many hunger emergencies – often chronic hunger crises with little or no political or media attention. Food aid often arrives too late. Many of these challenges could be solved if donor countries' food aid policies would put the needs of the poor before their own."

2. Identify at least one comment or question which comes from a

    a) personal perspective

    b) national perspective

    c) global perspective.

3. Choose an issue, comment or question that interests you and discuss it with a partner.

    a) Think about personal, local/national and global perspectives on this issue. For example, think about the perspectives of a worker, a company boss, a head of government, an international charity worker, and so on.

    b) What information do you need to help you discuss this?

Key vocabulary and language exercises

Activity 2

1. Use dictionaries and online resources to find definitions of the words and phrases in the table.

> If English is not your first language, avoid using online translation tools. They are often not very good! Your language skills will develop better if you use dictionaries.

Words and phrases	Definition
a) Social development	
b) Economic development	
c) Human development	
d) Inequality	
e) Disaster relief	
f) Neo-colonialism	
g) Free trade	
h) Protectionism	

Activity 3

1. Use internet resources to help you develop the mind map with different issues relating to trade and aid. Add as many new categories as you can find. Some initial ideas have been suggested.

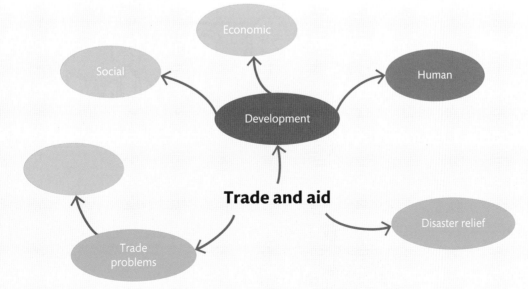

203

Stimulus material

Document 1

Document 2

Kofi Eliasa used to own a tomato farm, but now he breaks stones in a quarry for a living, earning less than a dollar a day to feed his family.

He is one of the many farmers in Ghana who have fallen victim to cheap European food imports that have flooded his country ever since the Ghanaian government was forced to open up its markets in return for loans and aid from the IMF and the World Bank.

The problem

It's all part of a wider global picture in which unfair trade rules designed largely by rich countries work against the interests of poor communities in developing countries.

While international trade is worth $10 million a minute, poor countries only account for 0.4% of this trade – half the share they had in 1980.

What we do

Here at Christian Aid, we believe that trade must be used to help bring an end to poverty – not deepen and prolong it.

Therefore, we are demanding that:

- The IMF and World Bank remove all economic policy conditions attached to their loans and debt-cancellation agreements.

- World Trade Organisation agreements support development rather than promote free trade for the sake of free trade.

http://www.christianaid.org.uk/whatwedo/issues/trade.aspx

Document 3

For just about every natural disaster there's a concert to raise money in aid of the victims. All well and good – disaster relief is important – but are these concerts really the way to raise money for people who have lost their homes, possessions and families in floods, earthquakes, tsunamis or hurricanes?

@musiclover

Disaster concerts are a great way to raise money quickly for a good cause. A celebrity could donate $1million dollars, but by organizing a concert they can raise so much more. And maybe we're selfish, but we get to feel good because we've done some good, as well as hearing some great music.

@cynicalrealist

Yeah, and how much of that money ends up as aid to people who need it? And how much in the artist's offshore bank account? Disaster concerts distract from real charity. First of all, it's just wrong to sing and dance and have fun when people are mourning their families, so really, it's all about us and our enjoyment, and not about the people we are supposed to be helping. And secondly, celebrities are not the right people to be leading charity campaigns. Non-governmental organisations and registered charities should be doing this.

@cherryblossom

@cynicalrealist attacking people who come out to support charity is a new low.

@peace not war

I would rather just give a donation to the Red Cross. At least with the RC, I am more comfortable that they are not in it for their own glorification.

Document 4

In recent years China's flourishing economic links with Africa have been threatened by instability and conflict. Chinese companies are increasingly encountering political and security risks. The country's diplomacy is adapting, no longer just promoting, economic interests but also protecting its trade and investment. The foreign ministry has, as a result, become more involved in mediating conflicts and assisting with peacekeeping and security. When conflict broke out in South Sudan last December, and hundreds of Chinese oil workers were evacuated, Zhong Jianhua, special envoy to Africa, was quick to support regional efforts to broker a ceasefire.

Debate within China, and criticism emanating from Africa, has also led Beijing to re-evaluate its development policies; it wants to avoid such incidents as last year's deportation of thousands of illegal Chinese miners in Ghana. Beijing is hoping, too, that enhancing the social aspects of its development policies will smooth the rough spots in its economic engagement; for example, it is increasing its support for education and joint research.

http://www.ft.com/cms/s/0/e05c6154-a90b-11e3-9b71-00144feab7de.html#axzz3gB5zpnKq

Skills practice exercises

Activity 4

Refer to Document 1.

1. Discuss the personal, local/national and global perspectives that arise from one of these cartoons. Make notes. You may use diagrams to help you.

2. Discuss the issues that arise from another cartoon. Make notes. You may use diagrams to help you.

3. Why did you choose the cartoons that you discussed? Why did you not choose the third cartoon? Have other groups discussed it? Have their discussions helped you?

Activity 5

Refer to Document 2.

1. This article says, "It's all part of a wider global picture in which unfair trade rules designed largely by rich countries work against the interests of poor communities in developing countries." Is this fact, opinion, prediction or value judgement? Explain your answer.

2. Is http://www.christianaid.org.uk/whatwedo/issues/trade.aspx a reliable source regarding trade and aid issues? Explain your answer.

> Go to the Christian Aid website and look at their "About us" page.

Activity 6

Refer to Document 3.

1. There has been a serious earthquake in your country. You have $500 to donate to the relief efforts. You are considering the following.

   a) Organising a disaster relief concert

   b) Donating to the Red Cross/Red Crescent.

   What do you need to know about each of these, and how will this help you decide how to donate your money?

2. a) Whose reasoning is better – @musiclover's or @cynicalrealist's?

In your answer you may consider some of the following.

- Are reasons given to support an opinion/conclusion/proposal?
- Is the reasoning logical?
- Does this use emotion to persuade me instead of reason?
- Are there gaps in the reasoning?
- Are the facts and evidence used well?

   b) How effectively does @cherryblossom answer @cynicalrealist?

Activity 7

Refer to Document 4.

1. Summarise this article. You may use diagrams to help you. Think about:

   a) Key problems

   b) Consequences

   c) Possible solutions

2. What different perspectives are there on China's involvement in Africa?

   a) What search terms will you use to help you research this?

   b) Think about perspectives linked to political power, e.g. America, Europe, Africa, China.

   c) Think about perspectives linked to economic interests.

   d) Think about perspectives linked to social development and charity.

Activity 8

1. What are the trade and aid issues most likely to affect these individuals? Think about the differences between similar people in LEDCs and MEDCs, for example

- an Oxfam volunteer
- a mother who can't feed her children
- a banker
- a farmer
- a woman who wants to set up a small business.

> Use quick internet searches to help you.

Activity 9

1. What are the most important problems in your area related to trade and aid?

   a) What do you already think? Are you prepared to change your mind?

   b) What search terms will you use?

   c) What key words and phrases will you skim-read for?

   d) Remember to think about which problems are most important, and why.

2. Choose a city or country in a very different part of the world. What are the most important problems related to trade and aid in this area?

3. What are the similarities and differences in the trade and aid issues experienced by your area and the area you have studied?

4. In what ways do these two areas have different perspectives on trade and aid?

5. What is the most interesting trade and aid issue you have considered so far? Do you think that this issue is suitable for an Individual Report?

6. Add your own questions to help you plan a line of inquiry.

Activity 10

1. How likely are these consequences? Discuss and explain your answers. What else do you need to know to make informed decisions?

   If our school raises $500 dollars for an education charity in Rwanda:

Consequence	Serious exaggeration / highly unlikely	Quite likely	Very likely
It will transform the lives of Rwandan children			
It will all be wasted on salaries for charity workers			
They will be able to build a new school in Rwanda			
The charity could buy some books and stationery for a local school			
It could contribute to a teacher's salary			

2. Work in groups to create activities like this for your classmates.

Activity (11)

1. Look at the sources you have found so far.

   a) Are they reliable? If not, what will you do?

   b) Is the reasoning good quality? How will this affect the way you use the ideas, information and perspectives in your work?

   c) Are the causes and consequences likely? If not, what will you do?

   d) Are there alternative possible consequences? If so, how will this affect the way you use these ideas in your work?

Reflection

- Have you thought about trade and aid in any new ways? If so, how and why?

- Have you changed your mind about anything? What are your reasons?

- How important do you think it is that all children have equal opportunities in life?

- What do you think is the best combination of trade and aid? What are your reasons?

Ideas for discussion, debate and practice

"Aid is like putting a sticking plaster on a badly broken leg. We need to treat the causes of poverty, inequality and injustice rather than the symptoms." Do you agree?

- How important is it for local people to be involved in decisions about their development?

- Should Western charities make decisions for people in less economically developed countries?

- Should multi-national corporations make all the decisions?

- How can local people be involved in decisions?

- What role does education play?

Debate

Your group has $500,000 to promote social development in Rwanda. How will you use this money? How will you ensure that it really does lead to development and is not wasted? You could consider:

- Microfinance projects for women to start up social enterprises
- Training one woman per village how to use the internet, and providing solar laptops
- Sponsoring children through their education
- Funding teachers for a school
- Donating the money to a health project

Can you find out how much $500,000 can buy and make a budget?

Make sure you research the likely consequences of each option.

How can we (individuals and states) best help those who are less fortunate than ourselves?

Suggestions for research

It is OK to trade with everyone, but we should only give aid to people who share our beliefs about the world. How far do you agree?

"We should concentrate trade and aid on our own country first and work with other countries only if we have resources to spare." How far do you agree with this statement?

Economic development is more important than human development.

Which is better for long-term development – trade or aid

- What are the consequences of different types of aid? Which is best?

Written examination

Section D

How will I be assessed?

The written examination paper will last for 1 hour and 15 minutes.

There will be 70 marks.

The written examination will deal with an issue relating to one or several of the written examination topics. You will be tested on how well you apply the Global Perspectives skills, rather than your knowledge.

It is worth thinking about issues within each topic so that you are familiar with the ideas and the language that you come across in the written examination. However, you should focus on applying your skills in a range of relevant contexts rather than on learning information. In the examination you must apply your skills – writing down everything you know will not be helpful at all.

You will be tested on your skills including your ability to:

- analyse information, causes, consequences, issues

- think about evidence, decide what you need to know and how to find this out

- evaluate sources and reasoning – think about who to trust, decide how well they are arguing

- develop a line of reasoning.

In the written examination you should expect to see:

- Source material. There will usually be several documents which present different perspectives on an issue. These documents will be linked to the topics in this section.

- Four main questions with sub questions.

The chapters provide some ideas, information and stimulus material as well as practice examination papers. If there are other relevant issues within these topic areas that interest you, you should feel free to research them and apply your skills in those contexts.

The following section provides one possible way of approaching the topics, however many different approaches may be taken.

Demographic change

1

Some key issues include:

- Aging population in developed countries
- More single people
- Demographics and health
- Demographics and development
- Increasing professional population

- Fewer children
- Relation between population and resources
- Population explosion in less developed countries
- Demographics and economic growth
- Effects of demographics on global trade

Do some of these comments and questions raise more than one issue?

Activity 1

1. Match the comments and questions below to the issues listed above.

   a) "Demography [the statistical study of populations] matters for sustainable development: Population dynamics affect the principle challenges that the world is confronting in the 21st century and therefore must be addressed in the post-2015 development agenda".

   b) "The government can provide incentives to make me leave the capital city and go back to the small town I grew up in. But I left because there was nothing happening and I hated it. I like living here, it's exciting."

   c) "Amna Fatani knows she wants a brilliant career and a life different from that of Saudi women of her mother's generation who married early, usually to a husband not of their own choosing. The 27-year-old, studying for her master's degree at Georgetown University in Washington and hoping to someday realize her ambitions, is part of a growing number of Saudi women choosing to remain single through their 20s and into their 30s as they pursue other ambitions."

   d) "Demographics are a useful business tool. Look at trends to spot business opportunities. Aging population? Invest in innovative aids for senior citizens. Baby boom with educated mothers? Invest in educational toys."

2. Identify at least one comment or question which comes from a

   a) personal perspective

   b) national perspective

   c) global perspective.

3. Choose an issue, comment or question that interests you and discuss it with a partner.

   a) Think about personal, local/national and global perspectives on this issue. For example, think about the perspectives of a worker, a company boss, a head of government, an international charity worker, and so on.

   b) What information do you need to help you discuss this?

Key vocabulary and language exercises

Activity 2

1. Use internet resources to help you complete the mind map with different words and ideas relating to demographic change. Use dictionaries and online resources to help you make lists of new vocabulary and technical terms.

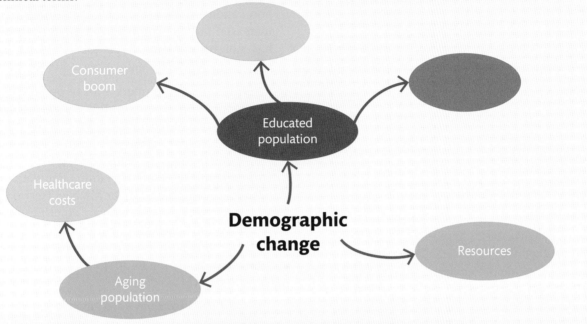

Activity 3

Complete the sentences below using the correct tense in each case.

1. If we invest in baby products now, _____ make lots of money.

2. If the government provided incentives for educated workers to move out of the capital, _____ develop thriving economic communities all around the country.

3. If I had stayed in the town where I was born _____ enjoy a fulfilling career in banking.

Stimulus material

Document 1

2015 challenges: demographic shifts

Rapid population growth in many developing countries is bringing challenges. What can NGOs do to minimise negative consequences?

UN predictions put the world population at 8 billion in 2025. That's an extra 5 billion people on the planet in less than a lifetime (the global population was 3 billion in 1960). The dramatic growth is driven by more people surviving beyond childhood and having children of their own, so it should be a cause for celebration of development, right?

Not everyone believes so, fearing that too many people will put unsustainable strain on resources. Humans are "a plague on the Earth", says David Attenborough, nature documentary-maker and patron of NGO Population Matters. "Either we limit our population growth or the natural world will do it for us. We keep putting on programmes about famine in Ethiopia. Too many people there. They can't support themselves." But is it fair to blame the poorest for straining natural resources? Or is it rather, as was Gandhi said, the world has enough for everyone's need, but not for everyone's greed?

Celebrity statistician Hans Rosling, whose popular YouTube videos have powerfully visualised the issue, argues that we do not need to panic about population growth. "The average number of children in the world is 2.4," he says. "The number of children below eight years of age in India has stopped growing. The number of children in the total world has stopped growing. Most of the fertility transition is done."

Promote family planning

The population of India, which is nearing 1.2 billion, has grown by that of the US since 1995... "Rapidly increasing population doesn't allow standard of living to go up in India," [Vivek Baid, founder of Mission for Population Control] says. "It doesn't allow better medical facilities for the poor. It doesn't allow better food standards." He berates the government and the main political parties for not prioritising family planning. "It should be top priority because only family planning can help to improve standards of living for the poor."

A recent report from the Copenhagen Consensus, a group of economists that is calling for fewer sustainable development goals, said that for every $1 spent on family planning, there is a return of $120.

Maaike van Min of Marie Stopes International... fears that unchecked population growth could "lead to a continued cycle of poverty and lack of opportunities: child mortality will stay high, education will remain low, literacy rates will remain low and therefore economic opportunities will also remain low."

The countries that do succeed in reducing fertility rates can benefit from a demographic dividend, where there are more people in work than children to support. "If you have very rapid decline in fertility, the younger population is no longer growing so fast and the economy gets a boost because the number of workers per child goes up and that gives you a period of rapid economic growth," says Bongaarts. "This is what happened in the east Asian 'tiger' countries like South Korea and Taiwan in the 70s. China and India are currently benefiting from a demographic dividend."

A consequence of falling child mortality but continuing high fertility is a "youth bulge" – a high population of young people. In Africa, because increased numbers of increasingly educated people has not been matched by jobs, this has led to significant youth unemployment.

A young population offers a lot of potential for the development of a country, but only if their talents are realised through investment. "We like to think it's great to have a lot of young people because that could be a potential resource for productive engagement," says United Nations Population Fund (UNFPA) economics adviser Michael Herrmann. "If all of these young people who are entering the labour market are productive it could give the economy a huge boost, but often there's a gap between what we expect young people to do and the investment that we're making."

The solution is to equip youth in sub-Saharan Africa with 21st-century skills, says Michael Boampong, founder of NGO Young People We Care, which is headquartered in Ghana. "Often you have a situation where you increase investment in education but when young people come out they are disconnected with what the industrial sector requires," he says. "We need to prepare them so they have the employable skills."

NGOs can help by providing education and training and more, because investment in "human capital" includes all aspects of development work, says Herrmann. "Investing in human capital starts with nutrition at the earliest childhood. It includes sexual and reproductive health." But this investment "is well beyond the capacities of the poorest countries ... It's a call for development aid."

A connection is often made between large numbers of unemployed young people and social unrest, even terrorism. But Herrmann says it's important not to overplay this. "It almost makes it sound as if young people are a danger in themselves," he says. "Evidence doesn't support that. If there are a lot of young people and we don't provide them with opportunities, you might have a backlash. But I wouldn't say that more young people equals inevitably social unrest."

Encourage long healthy lives

Another global demographic shift is ageing populations in developed countries such as Japan and Germany, and also in advanced developing countries. "In countries as diverse as Bangladesh, Cambodia, Mongolia and Vietnam, the population over age 60 will triple by 2050," William A Ryan wrote in an article for the UNFPA. "The growing health care and social support costs associated with ageing will pose tremendous challenges."

In response to these changing populations, NGOs need to focus on preventing non-communicable diseases (NCDs) in order to ensure older people are healthy. "It's not just about life expectancy, it's about healthy life expectancy," says Toby Porter, chief executive of HelpAge International. "At the moment most development health is orientated towards infectious disease control, which is important, but aging populations means higher rates of NCDs.

We need better regular monitoring of blood pressure. For example, undiagnosed hypertension is still responsible for more preventable deaths and avoidable disabilities than any other single cause around the world."

Herrmann says that society will need to respond to a higher population of older people by redesigning pension systems and making sure that they continue to be positively engaged in their communities. But he adds that we shouldn't lose sight of the fact that ageing populations are a cause for celebration. "Population ageing is a positive thing. It means we have had success in investing in people. It means development has taken place."

http://www.theguardian.com/global-development-professionals-network/2015/mar/16/2015-challenges-demographic-shifts-population-growth-youth-bulge-ageing

Activity 4

1. Use Document 1 to identify key demographic challenges relating to

    a) total world population

    b) youth population

    c) older population.

2. In your opinion, are these personal, national or global challenges?

3. Use Document 1 to identify possible solutions to each problem

    a) possible solutions for NGOs

    b) possible solutions for individuals

    c) possible solutions for national governments

4. Use the information in the document to draw a mind map of challenges and possible solutions.

5. Use the information in the document to draw diagrams of causes and consequences.

Ideas for discussion, debate and practice

- How should societies deal with the problems of older people?
- Will men soon be as involved in childcare as women are?
- Is a nuclear family better than an extended family?
- Who should look after older people?

Examination practice

Views on childhood vaccinations, by key demographics

% of U.S. adults who say parents should be able to decide not to vaccinate their children or that all children should be required to be vaccinated

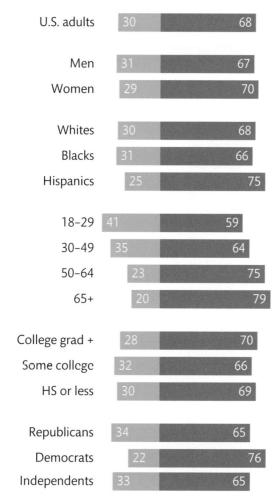

Views on evolution, by key demographics

% of U.S. adults who say humans and other living things have evolved over time or have existed in their present form from since the beginning of time

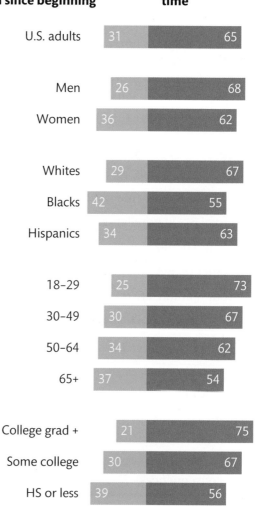

Survey of U.S. adults august 15–25, 2014. Q25. Those saying don't know are not shown. Whites and blacks include only non-hispanics; Hispanics are of any race.

Pew research center

Survey of U.S. adults august 15–25, 2014. Q16. Those saying don't know are not shown. Whites and blacks include only non-hispanics; Hispanics are of any race.

Pew research center

Source 2

LARAMIE, Wyo. — Residents of Wyoming often brag about its status as the nation's least populated state, boasting of its traffic-free highways and starry night sky — and taking pride in the fact that its cattle outnumber people by two to one.

Cattle, however, cannot open businesses or build homes, and so this spring, Wyoming embarked on a new quest: getting its young people back.

"We've got to make sure that we have the workers of tomorrow," the governor, Matt Mead, said in an interview. The state seeks to fill open jobs in fields including nursing and teaching, he said, and to bring in people who will expand its new sectors, like technology.

The state is dotted by shrinking agricultural communities where the median age is well above 40.

Extract from http://www.nytimes.com/2015/07/16/us/wyoming-long-on-pride-but-short-on-people-hopes-to-lure-some-back.html?ref=topics&_r=0

Source 3

Russia's population woes

The graph on the right shows that Russia's population has been declining for most of its post-Soviet history. The situation has been improving over the past decade, however analysts are worried that Russia's economic difficulties are causing the birth rate to decline once again. This coupled with a lack of immigration could spell trouble for the country.

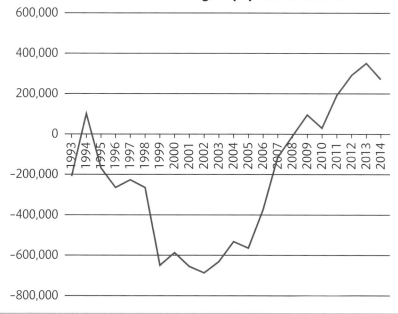

Russia annual change in population 1993–2014

Source 4

@Educated mother

We need more people to fuel economic growth. We need more people to look after the aging population. We can either persuade people to have more children, using tax incentives and government policy. Or we can invite more immigrants into the country.

@name

Well, people aren't going to have more children. Think about it - you're an educated, independent woman with two lovely children, a helpful husband and a job you love. You are socially and economically independent. You contribute to the economy in many ways. You pay tax, your work generates profits, and you have leisure time to take your kids to theme parks, to museums, to the theatre – thus aiding the social and economic development of the country. What could the government possibly say – what kind of tax break could the government possibly offer – that would make the prospect of having 5, 8, 12 kids appealing? Also, as an educated woman, you are aware that the world is over-populated. Having more children to solve short term demographic problems is not the answer.

@name

I think the solution is to let in more immigrants every year. Why should we? Simple: Because they're people! They're people who pay taxes (and, if they're here legally, pay even more taxes).

@name

We don't want more immigrants coming over here and taking our jobs and stealing our stuff and sponging on benefits. The government is already making emergency plans to cope with the influx of migrants and the meltdown of the school, health and police systems. When they get here they end up stealing and getting involved in crime because they have no idea how to behave, and then we end up supporting them in luxury in prison.

@Spindrift Seafoam

Migration is the answer to many of the world's demographic problems. Populations in the rich west are shrinking and aging – we need more young people to work, to pay taxes and to fund pensions. Populations in the poor south are growing, and there is an explosion of young workers who need work. It makes sense for the workers to move to where the work is.

Question 1

Refer to Sources 1 and 2

a) Identify the trend in different age groups' beliefs about
    vaccinations. [1]

b) Identify two trends in beliefs about evolution according to
    age group. [2]

c) Explain the likely causes for one of these trends. [3]

d) Are Wyoming's problems mostly personal, regional, national
    or global? Justify your answer. [6]

Question 2

a) In order to decide whether people will go back to Wyoming,
    what do you need to know? [6]

b) How would you test the theory that Russia's population is
    declining because of economic recession? [8]

Question 3

a) Identify one prediction given by @Educated Mother.
    Explain why it is a prediction. [2]

b) "Populations in the rich West are shrinking and ageing."
    Is this a fact or an opinion? Justify your answer. [3]

c) Whose reasoning is more effective – @Educated Mother's,
    @our country first's or @Spindrift Seafoam's? [15]

Your answer should consider all three arguments, and you should support
your point of view with their words. You should also consider:

● the strength of their reasoning and evidence

● their use of language

● different types of information.

Question 4

How can places with shrinking populations most effectively attract
young people? [24]

You could consider:

● Incentives for migrants

● Investments in new technological industries

● Encouraging young people to have more children

In your answer you should

● state your conclusion

● give reasons to support your choice

● use the material in the Sources and/or any of your own ideas

● consider different arguments and perspectives.

2 Education

- Right to education
- Quality of education
- Funding for education
- Education-business partnerships

- Assessment
- Purpose of education
- Equality in education
- Education and development
- Education technology

> Do some of these comments and questions raise more than one issue?

Activity 1

1. Match the comments and questions below to the issues listed above.

   a) Private corporations are being called upon to increase their financial support of education as the world faces a global learning crisis, an education forum heard on Sunday.

   b) Ms Bokova spoke of the urgent need to address the global lack of access to education faced by girls and other disadvantaged populations. Poor quality education costs governments $129bn a year, according to the Education for All Global Monitoring Report.

   c) We all know that gut-wrenching feeling the day exam results come out. It's one of those days where you get to either gloat to your friends about your good results, or go home as fast as you can.

   d) When I was appointed deputy education minister in 2013, I decided to continue the Caring Schools Programme, since it was also in line with the ministry's Caring Teacher programme. It is expected that problems that exist in the schools involved can be reduced by the cultivation of the caring attitude.

   e) Why do I always have to think about the future, about what's good for me? People go on about the right to education – what about the right to live my life now?

2. Identify at least one comment or question which comes from a

   a) personal perspective

   b) national perspective

   c) global perspective.

Discussion

1. Choose an issue, comment or question that interests you and discuss it with a partner.

   a) Think about personal, local/national and global perspectives on this issue. For example, think about the perspectives of a worker, a company boss, a head of government, an international charity worker, and so on.

   b) What information do you need to help you discuss this?

Key vocabulary and language exercises

Activity 2

1. Use internet resources to help you complete the mind map with different words and ideas relating to education. Use dictionaries and online resources to help you make lists of new vocabulary and technical terms.

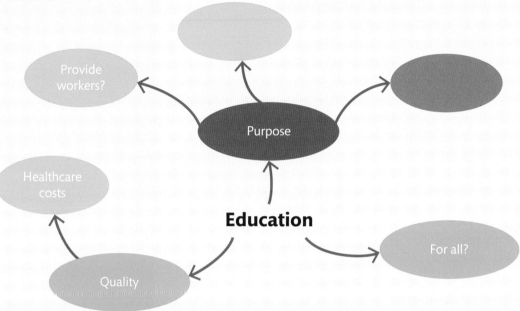

Activity 3

Complete the sentences below using the correct tense in each case.

1. If we invest in education now, _____ next generation able to compete in world economy.

2. If the government provided incentives for businesses to invest in education, _____ improve education system and provide workers with the skills businesses need.

3. If I had only worked harder at school _____ have a better life now.

Stimulus material

Document 1

Exam pressure has primary pupils flocking to tutorials

Kenneth Lau

Monday, July 06, 2015

Hong Kong: Five in every six Primary Six students attend tutorial classes, with a quarter of these spending at least nine hours a week or an average of 1.1 to 2.2 hours a day, according to a survey.

Caritas said 85.4 percent of the 1,677 Primary Six students polled from March to May this year go to tutorial classes after school or during the holidays.

Chan said there is no evidence to prove that spending more time in tutorial classes could lead to a better academic performance. Instead, parents should spend more time with their children.

"Every child is an independent individual. If they cannot feel that their parents are pushing them for their own good ... it will create conflict and a dislike for learning," Chan said.

Social worker Shirley Chow Man-wai said the territory-wide assessment system should be cancelled as it has put immense examination pressure on students.

http://www.thestandard.com.hk/news_detail.asp?pp_cat=11&art_id=158728&sid=44790018&con_type=1

Document 2

@Tishan

I would love to study to be a doctor. But my family need the money I can earn. I'm working in a bank now. It's a good job but I hate it. It's like living in a box when I dream of the sky. It seems so unfair that some of my friends are at school and hating it, while I can't go.

@Colin

In my opinion, we should change the education system. School should be free, but only for people who work hard and get good results. Then no one would waste time or misbehave, and those of us who want to learn could get on with it.

@Ruby

My parents have made me stay at school to do maths. I'm lucky to have parents who value education, but this is the wrong education for me. All I want to do is work in my uncle's goldsmithing business. I should be able to choose my own future.

Document 3

The global talent pool has taken on a dramatically different look

by Dirk Van Damme
Head of the Innovation and Measuring Progress division, Directorate for Education and Skills

The location of human capital matters: in the 20th century, the United States and several other countries were able to benefit from the pool of skilled people in their populations to progress economically and socially at a much higher rate than their competitors.

In the first decades of the 21st century, things look much different. The latest Education Indicators in Focus brief provides a prediction to 2030 based on current trends (see the

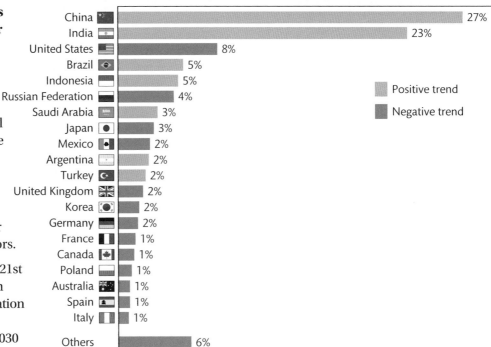

Global talent pool in 2030
Projected share of 25–34 year-olds with tertiary degree across OECD and G20 countries

- China 27%
- India 23%
- United States 8%
- Brazil 5%
- Indonesia 5%
- Russian Federation 4%
- Saudi Arabia 3%
- Japan 3%
- Mexico 2%
- Argentina 2%
- Turkey 2%
- United Kingdom 2%
- Korea 2%
- Germany 2%
- France 1%
- Canada 1%
- Poland 1%
- Australia 1%
- Spain 1%
- Italy 1%
- Others 6%

Positive trend
Negative trend

chart on the right). In 2030, China would be home to 27% of the global pool of highly educated people, and India to another 23%. The United States would follow with only 8%. And of the emerging economies, Brazil and Indonesia would follow with 5% each. Together China and India would be home to half of the world's highly educated youth.

http://oecdeducationtoday.blogspot.co.uk/2015/04/the-global-talent-pool-has-taken-on.html

Skills practice exercises

Activity 4

1. Refer to Document 1.

   a) What percentage of Primary 6 children in Hong Kong attend tutorial classes?

   b) How does this compare to your country (or another country if you are from HK)?

   c) Do you think it is a good thing for primary age children to be attending tutorial classes as well as school?

2. Chan suggests that pupils spend more time with their parents instead of tutors.

   a) Do you think this would be an effective alternative?

   b) What sort of evidence would you need to establish whether tutorial classes or time with parents is more effective?

   c) Using online resources, can you find any evidence to show what the most effective way to raise attainment is?

   d) Find out about the primary assessment system in Hong Kong (or another country if you are from HK).

   e) How does the HK primary assessment system compare with the system in your country?

   f) How important is it to have a high stakes national assessment at the end of primary school?

   g) What are the advantages and disadvantages of high stakes primary assessment?

Activity 5

1. a) Tishan says, "My family need the money I can earn." Is this a fact or opinion? Explain your answer.

    b) Identify one opinion that Tishan gives. Explain your answer.

    c) Whose view is closest to yours? Why? Discuss this.

    d) Identify one value judgement and one prediction that Colin makes.

    e) Identify one opinion and one value judgement in Ruby's words. Explain your answers.

    f) What might be the consequences if everyone/no one had to pay for education?

    g) What might be the consequences if education was free only for people who worked hard and got good results? Think about the national and global perspectives as well as the personal.

    h) What do you think are the causes of bad behaviour in schools?

    i) From a national perspective, is it more important to train people to be economically productive or to be personally fulfilled? Give reasons for your answer.

Activity 6

1. Refer to Document 3.

    a) Are any of the following statements true, according to the table?

        i) In 2030, 2% of the UK population will be graduates, whereas 23% of the Indian population will be graduates.
        ii) In 2030, fewer people in the US and Europe will be graduates.
        iii) We don't know what proportion of each country will be graduates.

    b) Describe the trends shown in the table.

    c) What do you think are the likely consequences of this change?

Activity 7

1. a) Have you thought about education in any new ways? If so, what and why?

    b) Have you changed your mind about anything? Give your reasons.

    c) Which is more important and why:

        i) Personal fulfilment or a well-paid job? (Does it make a difference if you're young or old?)
        ii) Academic learning or learning for life?
        iii) A young person's aims for the future or a parent's aims for their child?

Ideas for discussion, debate and practice

- What are the most important education problems in your area?
- How should we deal with the problems in our education system?
- How do these compare to the education problems in a contrasting region?
- How can we ensure that young people realise the value of education?

Debate

1. Should education be free for all? If so, what steps can we take to achieve this?

2. How could we share resources out so that people who want to study can do so?

3. How should we provide the best opportunities for people who struggle at school?

4. "Education isn't about fairness. It's about maximising gain for you, your family and your country."

Examination practice

Source 1

Business survey: Which of the following would you say are the most critical skills for employees in your organisation to possess today? Select up to three.

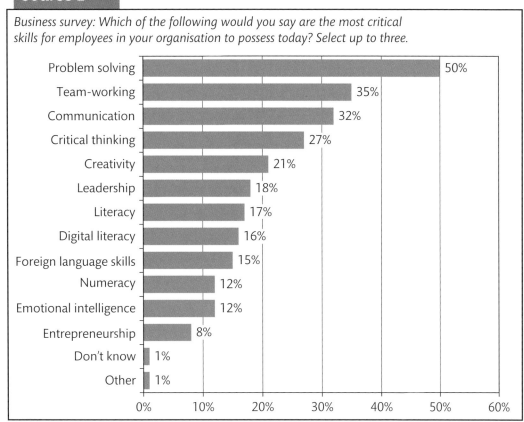

Skill	Percentage
Problem solving	50%
Team-working	35%
Communication	32%
Critical thinking	27%
Creativity	21%
Leadership	18%
Literacy	17%
Digital literacy	16%
Foreign language skills	15%
Numeracy	12%
Emotional intelligence	12%
Entrepreneurship	8%
Don't know	1%
Other	1%

Source 2

Quality is the biggest challenge facing UAE's education

Roberta Pennington

January 16, 2014 Updated: January 16, 2014 08:24 PM

DUBAI // The UAE has made a lot of progress toward meeting the 2015 goals set out by Unesco's Education For All Movement, but quality remains its greatest challenge.

"While the UAE has high literacy rates, you have high numbers of enrolment in primary education and secondary education, you have a good higher-education system, the quality remains a challenge," Dr Khan said after the Education For All forum.

"Despite the heavy investments, when you look at the Pisa (Program for International Student Assessment) and Timss (Trends in International Mathematics and Science Study) results, the UAE is not faring very high. You have to ask whether they are investing in the right things."

http://www.thenational.ae/uae/education/quality-is-the-biggest-challenge-facing-uaes-education

Source 3

Right to education is often ignored in troubled regions

Maysa Jalbout

July 12, 2013

Zeineb, a 13-year-old Syrian refugee, goes to school every day despite having to make her way past child predators promising a better life through marriage before she can reach a makeshift classroom tent in the Zaatari camp on the Syria-Jordan border.

Of the children at Zaatari aged 6 to 18, 76 per cent of girls and 80 per cent of boys do not go to school: some fear to leave their mothers, others share their parents' hopes of an imminent return to Syria. Zeineb thinks she is lucky, also, because many girls her age have fallen into the deep trap of child marriage.

Globally, the proportion of out-of-school children in conflict-affected countries rose to 50 per cent of all children in 2011, up from 42 per cent in 2008. The rise is in part attributed to three new countries joining the list of the 32 countries affected by armed conflict between 2002 and 2011. Two of the three are in the Arab region, Libya and Syria.

In contrast to this dramatic increase, the share of humanitarian aid that is devoted to education has declined. Education suffers from a double disadvantage: not only does it receive a small share of aid overall, but it also receives the smallest proportion of the amount requested of any sector, according to an analysis in the Education for All Global Monitoring Report. In 2012, of the modest amount requested for education during humanitarian crises, only 26 per cent was received.

http://www.thenational.ae/thenationalconversation/comment/right-to-education-is-often-ignored-in-troubled-regions#full

Source 4

Peter: Mass education doesn't work in the modern world. It's based on cramming our heads full of useless facts and figures. We learn stuff we don't need at work and the system doesn't make us useful to employers. I've been looking for a job for months, which just proves how rubbish education is. We should go back to the old system of masters and apprentices to make sure that everyone learns something useful.

Andi: There are children around the world who would love to go to school and get an education. You're privileged and all you can do is moan about the opportunities that have been given to you.

Imi: I think the answer is to work together to improve education. The people who run schools and education systems need to listen to business leaders and young people to find out what is needed. But most of all, people like us, who are lucky enough to have a good education, should share our talents and contribute to improving education around the world.

Question 1

Refer to Source 1.

a) What are the three skills that business leaders most want in employees?   [1]

b) Are these skills that are well developed in your school? Explain your answer. [2]

c) "Only 12% of business leaders are interested in numeracy, so I don't have to worry about doing well in maths." Is this a reasonable conclusion to draw from the table? Explain your answer.   [3]

Refer to Source 2.

d) Identify two ways in which the UAE is meeting UNESCO targets.   [2]

e) To what extent do you think that the quality of education is a personal, national or global?   [4]

Question 2

According to Source 3, 50% of children in conflict-affected countries are not going to school.

a) What do you think are the likely personal and national consequences of this? [2]

b) Choose one of your predicted consequences. Describe how you would test it. [5]

According to Source 3, "the share of humanitarian aid that is devoted to education has declined."

a) What do you think are the likely global consequences of this?   [2]

b) Choose one of your predicted consequences. Describe how you would test it. [5]

Question 3

Refer to Source 4.

a) "Mass education doesn't work in the modern world." Is this a fact or an opinion? Justify your answer.   [3]

b) Why might Miguel's statement be biased?   [2]

c) Whose reasoning is most effective?   [15]

Your answer should consider all three arguments, and you should support your point of view with their words. You should also consider:

● the strength of their reasoning and evidence

● their use of language

● different types of information.

Question 4

Explain what you think is the most pressing problem in education today, and suggest a solution. In your argument you should:

● state your conclusion

● give reasons to support your choice

● use the material in the source and/or any of your own ideas

● consider different arguments and perspectives.

3 Employment

Some of the key issues include:

- Fairness
- Equality
- Profit
- Globalisation
- Unemployment
- Job Creation
- Young People
- Job as Identity

Do some of these comments and questions raise more than one issue?

Activity 1

1. Match the comments and questions below to the issues in the diagram above.

   a) I just want a fair day's pay for a fair day's work.

   b) I used to be a miner, but the mines closed. Now I can't feed my family – what kind of a father does that make me? It's like my place in the world has just closed up and I'm no use for anything. That's why I want my son to get a good education: so he's got choices.

   c) One of the most important causes of the Arab Spring rebellions was the high proportion of young, unemployed men.

   d) "In our discussion on 'World Today' we will be asking: who should create jobs? Individual entrepreneurs? Governments? Local businesses? Multi-national corporations? Phone in and let us know what you think."

   e) Businesses in this country can't afford the extra costs involved in equality and minimum wages. When these companies go bankrupt, there won't be any jobs at all for our people.

   f) Affirmative action – for example quotas for the number of women and ethnic minorities in senior jobs – is necessary.

   g) The world needs flexible, well-educated young people to do the jobs of the future.

2. Identify at least one comment or question which comes from a

   a) personal perspective

   b) national perspective

   c) global perspective.

3. Choose an issue, comment or question that interests you and discuss it with a partner.

   a) Think about personal, local/national and global perspectives on this issue. For example, think about the perspectives of a worker, a company boss, a head of government, an international charity worker, and so on.

   b) What information do you need to help you discuss this?

Key vocabulary and language exercises

Activity 2

1. Complete the table using the answers below. Use a dictionary/the internet if you need to.

CEO

Multi-national corporation

Employee

Employer

Affirmative action

Economic recession

Entrepreneur

> If English is not your first language, avoid using online translation tools. They are often not very good! Your language skills will develop better if you use dictionaries.

1	A worker
2	Someone who provides workers with a job
3	A person who sets up a business, taking the risks and gaining any rewards.
4	A big business which operates in many different countries
5	A period of general economic decline. A local, national or global economy stops growing and may shrink. This usually comes together with high unemployment.
6	Chief Executive Officer – the highest ranking person in a company.
7	Action which favours groups of people who usually suffer from negative discrimination.

2. Fill in the gaps, using the words on the right.

The local area used to have a lot of small, local businesses, run by local _____. However, two _____ have recently arrived. In some ways this is an advantage for the community, because there is lower _____. On the other hand, people who used to own their own companies now have to _____ and work for someone else. Probably the biggest problem, is that all the senior management jobs go to foreigners. We need _____ to ensure that local people are fully represented at management level.

apply for a job

unemployment

entrepreneurs

multi-national corporations

affirmative action

Stimulus material

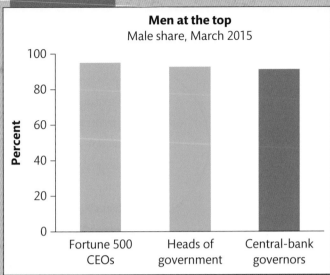

Men at the top
Male share, March 2015

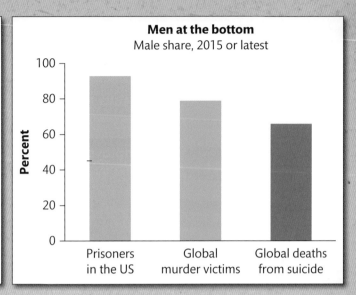

Men at the bottom
Male share, 2015 or latest

Poorly educated men in rich countries are having difficulty coping with the enormous changes in the labour market and the home over the last century. As technology and trade have made strength less valuable, less educated men have struggled to find a role in the workplace. Women, on the other hand, are surging into expanding sectors such as health care and education. Men who lose jobs in manufacturing often never work again. And men without work find it hard to attract a permanent mate. The result, for low-skilled men, is a poisonous combination of no job, no family, and no prospects.

Tallulah, in the Mississippi Delta, USA, is picturesque but not prosperous. Many of the jobs it used to have are gone. In Madison Parish, the local area, only 47% of men of prime working age (25–54) are working.

The men in Tallulah are typically not well educated. This would have mattered less, in the old days. A man without much book learning could find steady work in the mill or in the fields. But the lumber mill has closed, and on nearby farms "jobs that used to take 100 men now take 10," observes Jason McGuffie, a pastor. A strong pair of hands is no longer enough. If you want to answer the phone, you need to speak proper English. If you want to be a truck driver, you need at least an eighth-grade education to handle the paperwork.

What can be done?

Cultural attitudes must shift. It has become acceptable for women to become surgeons or physicists without losing their femininity. It needs to become culturally acceptable for young men to become hairdressers, nurses or receptionists without losing their masculinity. Young men need to be prepared to work hard at school to gain the skills they will need. Policymakers also need to lend a hand, because foolish laws are making the problem worse. Even more important than this, we need to improve the education system, and young men need more positive role models.

Document 3

The biggest challenge in the Middle East is that the region's economies do not create enough jobs, especially for highly skilled workers. What affects job creation is the business environment dominated by micro, small and medium-sized enterprises, and high agricultural employment in some countries. Of the 4.8 million formal enterprises in Algeria, Egypt, Jordan, Lebanon, Morocco, Syria and Tunisia, 98% employ fewer than 50 workers.

Youth unemployment disproportionally affects young women whose unemployment rates typically double the average. Job opportunities are rare for young men and almost non-existent for young women, as most employers openly give preference to male job-seekers. Some employers do prefer female workers, but the jobs which they offer are low-skilled and low paid, and hence not attractive to the few educated women seeking employment.

According to the World Bank, 42% of private enterprises in the region point to the formal schooling system that does not respond to their skills needs as the main obstacle to hiring young people. The mismatch is particularly high in Lebanon (56%) and Egypt (50%).

http://jobmarketmonitor.com/2013/11/22/after-the-arab-spring-youth-unemployment-still-the-most-urgent-challenge/

Document 4

We aim to contribute a minimum of 25% of our company's profits directly to charitable projects in Sri Lanka, specifically those projects which are aimed at giving educational opportunities to underprivileged children or young people.

At the same time, our ultimate goal is to establish a separate foundation which will provide investment and donations to charitable projects and social enterprises over the long term.

To generate the profits from which we make charitable donations, Nineteen48 operates as a commercial entity, with a clear focus on trading in gemstones sourced primarily from Sri Lanka.

By trading with Sri Lanka in this way, we are also helping the local economy and specific communities within the country.

http://www.nineteen48.com/about-us/our-values/

Skills practice exercises

Activity 3

1. What trend can be identified in the charts in Document 1?

2. From Document 2, identify

   a) one problem for men in rich countries

   b) three parts to a complex solution to this problem.

3. Document 2 gives the example of Tallulah, USA. Do you think the problems in Tallulah are mostly personal, local, national or global? Explain your answer.

4. In Document 3 identify

   a) one problem for all skilled workers

   b) one problem for skilled female workers.

5. What do you think are the causes of the employment problems you have identified?

6. What might be one possible solution for skilled women in Middle Eastern countries?

7. What kind of solutions do you think Middle Eastern countries should consider?

Activity 4

1. Make a business plan for a small, ethical business.

   a) Make a list of all the things you need to find out about.

   b) Set some aims for your business.

   c) What exactly will ethical mean for your business?

   d) Write a budget plan.

2. You have been offered a job with a company in the capital city. What do you need to find out?

Activity 5

1. "The men in Tallulah are typically not well educated." Is this fact, opinion or prediction? Explain your answer.

2. "We aim to contribute a minimum of 25% of our company's profits directly to charitable projects in Sri Lanka." Is this fact, opinion or prediction? Explain your answer.

3. "The main purpose of a business is to make a profit."

   How far is this statement in conflict with the values statement from Nineteen48 in Document 4? Justify your answer.

4. Read the comments below, which respond to the documents. Then answer the questions.

   @Savannah Susie

   Those men in Tallulah need to try harder to look for work. It's no good sitting around waiting for someone to come and give you a solution. It's not reasonable. You have to get in there and work for what you want. And if that means book learning – then they need to get some book learning and stop wishing for the past.

   @Septimus Drake

   There's an easy solution. The men should send the women back to working in the kitchen and looking after babies where they belong. Then there wouldn't be any more problems with not enough work for the men.

@ Puteri 24_7

It looks to me as if this is a whole world problem. Now that we have a global economy, we have regions where skilled workers are needed, and regions where workers need low skills. The problem is that people are varied. So Americans need a mixture of highly skilled and low skilled jobs to match the people they have. And in Middle Eastern countries, they also need a mixture of highly skilled and low skilled jobs to match the people they have. So either we need mass migration of skilled people to skilled job regions, and low skilled people to low skilled regions, or we need to change the way the global economy works.

a) "And if that means book learning – then they need to get some book learning and stop wishing for the past." Is this fact, opinion or prediction? Explain your answer.

b) Whose reasoning is most effective? You should consider:

- Knowledge claims
- Predicted consequences
- Suggested solutions
- Values

Activity 6

1. Who is, and who should be, responsible for creating jobs? Are governments, companies or individuals responsible?

   In your answer you should

   - state your conclusion
   - give reasons
   - give examples where relevant
   - show that you have considered at least one other viewpoint.

Ideas for discussion, debate and practice

- What difference does having a job make to an individual?
- What difference do unemployment rates make to communities/countries?
- How important is fairness? Is it more important than economic growth?
- Is it better to have local companies creating jobs or multinational companies? Are personal and national perspectives different?
- Is it right to define or judge people by their jobs?
- What are the employment problems in your area? What are the possible solutions?

Reflection

1. Reflect on the issues you have considered in this chapter.

   a) Have you changed your opinions or formed new opinions? If so, how?

   b) Are there any issues that you can't find an answer to?

   c) How has your own performance improved in this section?

   d) What can you do to improve your performance?

Examination practice

Thread: rude colleague

@sadandunhappy

I'm having problems with a colleague at work and I want some advice on how to deal with him. John is rude and unpleasant most of the time. A lot of it is just little things – he'll stand in the doorway and not let me through, or make comments about my personal hygiene. The thing is, I do quite a lot of his job as well as my own, but our boss doesn't realise this. She believes John when he says that I am lazy. For example, I came in at 10am after seeing a client, and John said, "What time do you call this? Can't you get to work on time and help those of us doing the real work?" I'm getting more and more stressed and I don't even want to go to work anymore.

@juniperberry

Well, you could try turning up on time and doing your fair share of the work. If you were actually doing your share of work your boss would notice. This country is suffering a real decline in productivity because of layabouts like you who don't pull their weight and this is going to lead to economic recession and unemployment, and that will cause a huge rise in the crime rate. So do some work and stop being so sad and unhappy.

"I just don't get it. I've applied for over 200 jobs, but I've never even got a call back."

@teeniusgenius

I think you're being unfair @juniperberry. Teachers don't always notice who is working hard and who is messing around – they have their favourites and some of them make judgements based on what they already think about people, not on what people are actually doing. So why not bosses? @sadandunhappy,

I had a similar situation in my part time job this summer. I think you should try having a calm chat with your boss and explaining the situation. Ask for advice about how to deal with the situation rather than being personal and complaining, because this is more likely to get results.

@hairyjumper

I think you should treat your colleague just exactly the way he treats you, @sadandunhappy. Be rude, be strong, and make sure you keep telling the boss

what you think of John. And stop doing his work. This will make both him and your boss realise how much you are actually doing.

@diamondlight

@sadandunhappy, talk to your boss in a calm way. I work in human resources, and I see this all the time, the way people's perspectives are skewed by fear and

uncertainty and partial information. If you explain your perspective to your boss, she will make a better decision because she will have more evidence.

Source 3

The International Labour Organisation (ILO) recently released its 2015 World Employment and Social Outlook (WESO) report, and presented the findings to the United Nations Friday. One of the report's major findings is the worldwide unemployment rate among 15 to 24-year-olds of 13 percent, or 74 million youths, is set to rise.

William Reese, CEO of the International Youth Foundation, thinks that figure is significantly underestimated.

"I'm not surprised by that number, because it is probably much higher than they state. We've seen reports of over 70 million young people unemployed, but the real number is probably six or seven times that," Reese said.

He said a flawed system of assessing unemployment led to employment figures far below the reality.

"Those statistics are typically assessing people who are looking for jobs, so if you're not looking for work, you're technically not unemployed. People in poor countries are often underemployed or underpaid," Reese told IPS.

"Unemployment statistics don't take that into consideration. People in poor countries do work; if they didn't, they would die. But in poorer countries, data is even worse."

http://www.mintpressnews.com/global-youth-unemployment-rate-rising-rapidly/201978/

Question 1

Consider Source 1.

a) What employment issues does the cartoon raise? [3]

b) Explain how and why the perspectives of the teenager and the employment adviser might be different. [3]

Consider Source 2.

c) Identify three possible solutions to @sadandunhappy's problem. [3]

d) To what extent do you think this problem can be explained by different perspectives? Justify your answer. [3]

Question 2

a) @sadandunhappy says his boss, "believes John when he says that I am lazy." What evidence would you need to decide whether this is true? [4]

b) How would you gather this evidence? [2]

Consider Source 3

c) How effective is the use of evidence in Source 3 to support the claim that youth unemployment is significantly underestimated? [8]

Question 3

a) How reliable is the ILO as a source of information? [2]

b) How reliable is @teeniusgenius as a source of advice for @sadandunhappy? Explain your answer. [3]

c) How good is @juniperberry's reasoning? [6]

In your answer you may consider some of:

- Are reasons given to support an opinion/conclusion/proposal?

- Is the reasoning logical?

- Does this use emotion to persuade me instead of reason?

- Are there gaps in the reasoning?

- Are the facts and evidence used well?

d) How likely are the consequences suggested by @juniperberry, @teeniusgenius and @hairyjumper? [9]

Question 4

How well does modern education prepare young people for the work in today's global economy? [24]

In your answer you should

- state your conclusion

- give reasons to support your choice

- use the material in the sources and/or any of your own ideas

- consider different arguments and perspectives.

4 Fuel and energy

Some key issues include:

- Fossil fuels
- Renewable energy
- Nuclear energy
- Sustainability
- Climate change
- Infinite demands, finite resources
- Energy and development
- Inequity
- Energy security
- Fuel poverty
- Access to energy
- Energy as a right

Activity 1

> Do some of these comments and questions raise more than one issue?

1. Match the comments and questions below to the issues in the diagram above.

   a) "We should catch the train. It's more sustainable than going by car."

   b) "In 2014 Energy Ministers of the G7 signed a joint statement in Rome on energy security. The fundamental principle they subscribed to was that energy security is a common responsibility. Each country's energy security relies on that in neighbouring countries."

   c) "The UN Sustainable Energy for All process has declared the objective to provide universal access to electricity by 2030, recognising that access to energy is a fundamental enabler for economic development and prosperity. However, our World Energy Scenarios have highlighted that unless drastic measures are taken the number of energy poor will only decrease from today's 1.2 billion figure to between 300 to 500 million in 2050, with most of the energy poor expected to reside in the African continent."

   d) Presently, the most important global issue is the role of energy in climate change.

   e) There are people in rich countries who have to make decisions between heating a room and heating their dinner. This is wrong. Everyone should have access to energy.

2. Identify at least one comment or question which comes from a

   a) personal perspective

   b) national perspective

   c) global perspective

Discussion

1. Choose an issue, comment or question that interests you and discuss it with a partner.

    a) Think about personal, local/national and global perspectives on this issue. For example,

    think about the perspectives of a worker, a company boss, a head of government, an international charity worker, and so on.

    b) What information do you need to help you discuss this?

Key vocabulary and language exercises

Activity 2

1. Use internet resources to help you complete the mind map with different words and ideas relating to fuel and energy. Use dictionaries and online resources to help you make lists of new vocabulary and technical terms.

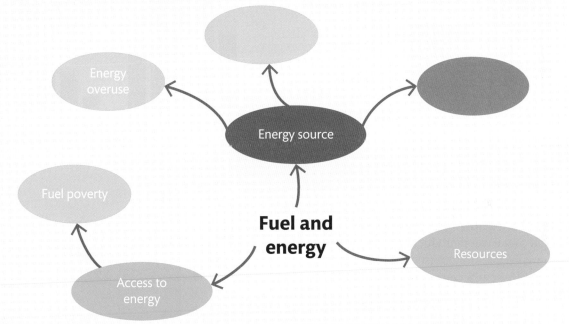

Activity 3

Complete the sentences below using the correct tense in each case.

1. Even if we reduce carbon emissions now, _____ be too late to save the planet.

2. If the government provided incentives for companies to reduce energy use, _____ be more likely to adopt energy efficient practices.

3. If we had actually changed our energy use in the 1980s, _____ not have such a big problem now.

Stimulus material

Document 1

Non fossil fuels

Energy consumption growth

Annual change, Mtoe

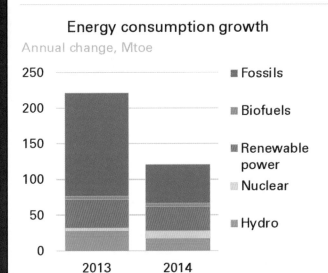

Legend:
- Fossils
- Biofuels
- Renewable power
- Nuclear
- Hydro

Renewable power growth

Annual change, TWh

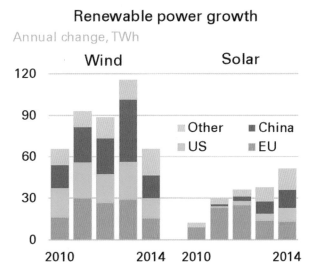

Wind   Solar

Legend:
- Other
- China
- US
- EU

Document 2

Energy companies have announced plans to build or convert power stations which altogether would burn 81 million tonnes of wood every year. The UK's total wood production (for all purposes) is only 10 million tonnes annually. Planning consent has been granted for five coal power stations to partly or fully convert to wood. Those power stations alone will burn almost five times the UK's annual wood production every year.

Not surprisingly then, 80 per cent of biomass is expected to be imported. Most imports so far are from British Columbia and the southern US, two regions where highly biodiverse and carbon-rich forests are being clearcut at an ever faster rate. And one scientific study after another confirms that burning trees for electricity results in vast carbon emissions which cannot possibly be absorbed by new trees for decades or centuries, if ever. So the government's renewable energy strategy will continue to make climate change, deforestation and air pollution ever worse.

http://www.redpepper.org.uk/biomass-the-trojan-horse-of-renewables/

Document 3

A child born today may live to see humanity's end, unless...

By David Auerbach*, Reuters

Friday, June 19, 2015 09:56

Humans will be extinct in 100 years because the planet will be uninhabitable, according to Australian microbiologist Frank Fenner, one of the leaders of the effort to eradicate smallpox in the 1970s. He blames overcrowding, denuded resources and climate change.

Fenner's prediction is not a sure bet, but he is correct that there is no way emissions reductions will be enough to save us from our trend toward doom. And there doesn't seem to be any big global rush to reduce emissions, anyway. When the G7 called on Monday for all countries to reduce carbon emissions to zero in the next 85 years, the scientific reaction was unanimous: That's far too late.

A couple hugs while standing on a hilly area overlooking Cairo on a dusty and hazy day where temperatures reached 46 Celsius (114 Fahrenheit)

At this point, lowering emissions is just half the story — the easy half. The harder half will be an aggressive effort to find the technologies needed to reverse the climate apocalypse that has already begun.

Lowering emissions and moving to cleaner energy sources is a necessary step to prevent catastrophic temperature rises. The general target is to keep global temperatures from rising more than 2 degrees Celsius. Higher increases — like the 5°C increase currently projected by 2100 — run the risk of widespread flooding, famine, drought, sea-level rise, mass extinction and, worse, the potential of passing a tipping point (frequently set at 6°C) that could render much of the planet uninhabitable and wipe out most species. Even the 2°C figure predicts more than a meter's rise in sea levels by 2100, enough to displace millions.

Apart from coordination to cope with climate-driven crises and associated instability, climate-change leadership needs to encourage and fund the development of technologies to reverse what we are unable to stop doing to our planet. Many of these technologies fall under the rubric of "carbon sequestration" — safely storing carbon rather than emitting it. Riskier strategies, like injecting sulfates into the air to reflect more of the sun's heat into space and ocean iron fertilization to grow algae to suck in carbon, run a high risk of unintended consequences. Better and safer solutions to reduce CO_2 concentrations in the atmosphere don't yet exist; we need to discover them and regulate them, to avoid the chaos of what economists Gernot Wagner and Martin L. Weitzman term "rogue geoengineering" in their book Climate Shock.

None of these approaches are substitutes for emissions reductions. Achieving a carbon-neutral society is a necessary long-term goal regardless of other technological fixes. Technology could buy us the time to get there without our planet burning up.

David Auerbach writes the Bitwise tech column for Slate Magazine. He previously worked as a software engineer at Google and Microsoft.

http://www.thanhniennews.com/commentaries/a-child-born-today-may-live-to-see-humanitys-end-unless-46859.html

Activity 4

Refer to Document 1.

1. What is the average GDP produced per unit of energy use by advanced economies?

2. What is the average GDP produce per unit of energy use by BRIC economies?

3. What can be concluded from the difference between these figures?

4. What proportion of the 125 countries assessed are net energy importers?

5. Why does it matter if a country has to import energy?

6. How reliable is WEF as a source of information?

Activity 5

Refer to Document 2.

1. Look up http://www.redpepper.org.uk. How reliable is this as a source of information? Explain your answer.

2. The article predicts that, "80 per cent of biomass is expected to be imported." How likely is this consequence? Explain your answer.

3. The article concludes that, "the government's renewable energy strategy will continue to make climate change, deforestation and air pollution ever worse."

    a) How likely is this consequence? Explain your answer.

    b) How good are the reasons and evidence given to support this conclusion? Go to the original article, and click on the link to the scientific studies.

4. What alternative forms of renewable energy can you think of? Would they have better consequences in your opinion than biomass?

Activity 6

Refer to Document 3.

1. Summarise Document 3 using your own words. Think about

    a) Predicted consequences

    b) Possible solutions

2. How effective do you think the reasoning is in this passage? Think about:

    a) Use of evidence

    b) Likeliness of consequences

    c) Exaggeration

Discussion

1. What are the personal, local/national and global consequences, issues and perspectives that arise from the following?

   a) There is significant opposition to a biomass power station planned for the docks.

   b) Wind turbines will ruin the view.

   c) It's raining so I'll drive to work.

   d) It would be wonderful to have electricity in our village.

   e) Why should I cut down my fuel use when big industries are using more and more?

> Remember that other people have personal and local perspectives too.

Ideas for discussion, debate and practice

- What are the most important fuel and energy problems in your area?

- Choose a city or country in a very different part of the world. What are their most important fuel and energy problems?

- What are the similarities and differences in the fuel and energy problems experienced by these two areas?

What kinds of fuel should governments invest in for the future?

How can individuals contribute to national efforts to reduce fuel use?

Suggestions for research

Is it reasonable for nations to keep using oil, even though this contributes to climate change?

Discussion

Debate: Nuclear waste will destroy the planet as surely as carbon emissions.

Reflection

- Have you thought about fuel and energy in any new ways? If so, what and why?

- Have you changed your mind about anything? Why (not)?

- Do you think that more resources should be put into finding renewable energy?

- How can we all reduce our energy use without harming the economy?

- How does your personal perspective link with different national and global perspectives?

- Is your personal perspective well thought through? What evidence and reasons can you give to support your perspective?

Examination practice

Source 1

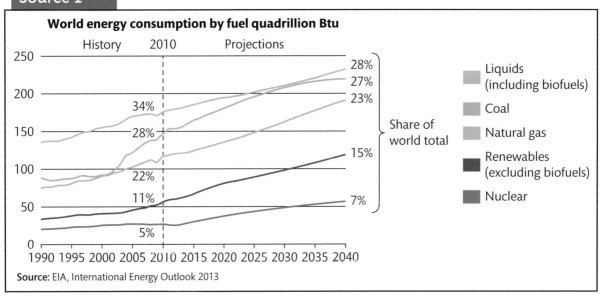

World energy consumption by fuel quadrillion Btu

Source: EIA, International Energy Outlook 2013

Source 2

Nuclear evacuees face dilemma over returning home

by Natsuko Fukue

NARAHA, FUKUSHIMA PREF. – More than four years since Satoru Yamauchi abandoned his noodle restaurant to escape radiation spreading from the tsunami-wrecked Fukushima No. 1 nuclear plant, the central government is almost ready to declare it is safe for him to go home.

But like many of the displaced, he's not sure if he wants to. "I want my old life back, but I don't think it's possible here," he said on a recent visit to the dusty *soba* buckwheat noodle restaurant in Nahara that he ran for more than two decades.

The father of four has lived in Tokyo since evacuating from his home to escape toxic pollution spewing from the crippled reactors hit by gigantic tsunami in March 2011.

Meltdowns in three of the reactors — 20 km away — blanketed vast tracts of land with isotopes of iodine and cesium, products of nuclear reactions that are hazardous to health if ingested, inhaled or absorbed.

Of the municipalities immediately surrounding the nuclear plant, which were totally evacuated, Naraha will be the first where people will be allowed to return.

After years of decontamination work, where teams remove topsoil, wash exposed road surfaces and wipe down buildings, the government will in September lift the evacuation order and declare it a safe place to live.

http://www.japantimes.co.jp/news/2015/07/23/national/social-issues/nuclear-evacuees-face-dilemma-returning-home/#.Vbl_3_nCefg

Source 3

Energy poverty and a lack of access to energy services by billions of people needs to also be seen as a cause of unrest and instability, especially in the context of urbanization and youth unemployment. Energy poverty affects both lives and economies. Consider emerging-tech hubs in cities such as Nairobi. Without power, or with poor quality power, the internet cannot support the platforms and aspirations of young Africans carving out new careers and innovations. The same is true of businesses and industries that rely on energy services to maintain productivity. To stay operational they have to buy their own generators; nearly 50% of sub-Saharan African companies own or share a generator.

https://agenda.weforum.org/2015/03/why-energy-poverty-is-the-real-energy-crisis/

Source 4

 Hassan We have been suffering severe fuel shortages here in Pakistan for two weeks now. Nearly every fuel station in our major cities has been closed. It is completely unacceptable. Businesses are failing because of this shortage. Family men, peaceful men, have been fighting on the forecourts. I am a strong supporter of our government, but even I think that the government needs to act now, and it needs to act decisively. The ambulances cannot get to sick people! This is no good.

 Mohammad "We need the army to take control of the country. This fuel crisis only shows that democracy is not a good form of government. It leads to weak governments which only want to please people, not strong governments which take action. We need fuel to keep our country going, there is no other alternative than getting fuel flowing again in our petrol pumps.

 Iqbal This fuel crisis will pass, like all the other crises. Instead of panicking we should take this time to think of how we can reduce our dependence on fossil fuels. There are many ways to use less fuel – I for example, have bought a bicycle recently. We have plenty of sun in Pakistan, so we should be erecting more solar panels to take advantage of this natural resource.

Question 1

Refer to Source 1.

a) Describe the trends you see in the graph in Source 1. [6]

Refer to Source 2.

b) The Japanese government is declaring Fukushima a safe place to live four years after a Tsunami damaged the nuclear plant. To what extent is this a personal, national or global issue? Justify your answer. [6]

Question 2

In 2011 an earthquake and tsunami damaged a nuclear power plant in Fukushima, Japan. Homes and businesses were evacuated because of nuclear radiation.

Mr Satoru Yamauchi is considering returning home.

a) What questions would you ask to find out whether Mr Yamauchi's home really is safe to return to? [6]

b) How would these questions help you to make a decision about whether he should return home? [8]

Question 3

a) Refer to Source 4. "The fuel crisis will pass, like all other crises." Is this a fact or an opinion? Explain your answer. [2]

b) Refer to Source 3. "Nearly 50% of sub-Saharan African companies own or share a generator." How reliable do you think this figure is? Justify your answer. [3]

c) Refer to Source 4. Whose reasoning is most effective – Hassan's, Mohammad's or Iqbal's? [15]

Your answer should consider all three arguments, and you should support your point of view with quotes from the source. You should also consider:

- use of evidence
- knowledge claims
- possible consequences
- how logical the reasoning is.

Question 4

In your opinion, what is the most significant global energy crisis? [24]

You could consider

- global energy use
- nuclear disasters
- energy shortages threatening democracy
- energy shortages threatening economic growth
- energy poverty.

In your answer you should:

- state your conclusion
- give reasons to support your choice
- use the material in the sources and/or any of your own ideas
- consider different arguments and perspectives.

5 Globalisation

Some key issues include:

- Economic globalisation
- Cultural globalisation
- Political globalisation
- Social globalisation
- Globalisation vs. localisation
- Core and periphery
- Human effects of globalisation
- Globalisation and development
- Globalisation and inequality
- Global and national governance

Discussion

1. Choose an issue, comment or questiaon that interests you and discuss it with a partner.

   a) Think about personal, local/national and global perspectives on this issue. For example, think about the perspectives of a worker, a company boss, a head of government, an international charity worker, and so on.

   b) What information do you need to help you discuss this?

Activity 1

1. Match the comments and questions below to the issues listed above.

   a) "We had a great time on our world tour. We went to McDonald's and Starbucks in every city we visited. You can go to Gap or Zara. I bought some Nikes in Singapore and got my iPhone replaced in Beijing."

   b) "Globalization is facing a big problem – slow world economic growth, which is fueling anti-global sentiment in key parts of the world."

   c) "Globalisation leads to multi-national corporations having huge power over the lives of individuals around the world, and it exaggerates inequality. The rich get richer and the poor get poorer."

   d) "The social implications of globalization have so far been seen as an unfortunate consequence of progress. The ability to continue to think and feel and dream seems somehow threatened. But we can shape the forces of globalisation with human hands."

   e) "Nations are going to become less important, as economies become more global."

2. Identify at least one comment or question which comes from a

   a) personal perspective

   b) national perspective

   c) global perspective.

Do some of these comments and questions raise more than one issue?

INDIAN OCEAN

Key vocabulary and language exercises

If English is not your first language, avoid using translation tools. They are often not very good! You language skills will develop better if you use dictionaries.

Activity 2

1. Use dictionaries and online resources to find definitions of these words and phrases.

Words and phrases	Definition
a) Social globalisation	
b) Political globalisation	
c) Cultural globalisation	
d) Economic globalisation	
e) Localisation	
f) Nationalism	
g) National sovereignty	
h) Governance	
i) Outsource	
j) Exploit	
k) Core	
l) Periphery	

Activity 3

1. Use internet resources to help you complete the mind map with different words and ideas relating to globalisation. Use dictionaries and online resources to help you make lists of new vocabulary and technical terms.

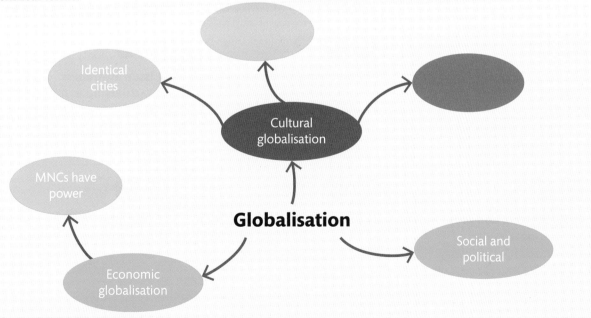

OCEAN

Stimulus material

For just as in the years of the Industrial Revolution people turned to political nationalism to protect and shelter their communities against the uneven and inequitable patterns of growth so, too, people seem to be turning back to – and mobilizing around – old loyalties and traditional identities as they seek to insulate themselves; whether it be in Catalonia or Belgium or Lombardy, they are demanding protection against what seems to be the economic disruption and social dislocation of globalization, which threatens to sweep aside long-established customs, values and ways of life.

How has the electoral performance of nationalist parties in Europe changed over time?

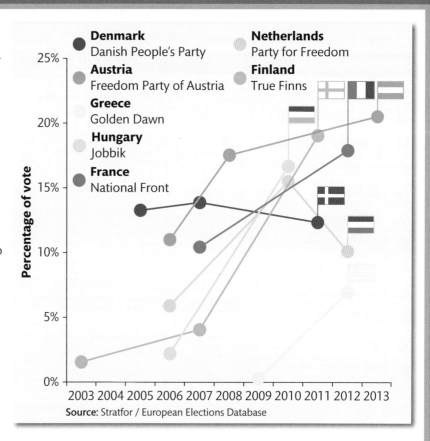

Source: Stratfor / European Elections Database

What are the top solutions to intensifying nationalism?

Asia

#1 **Partnership and cooperation**
#2 **Issue awareness**
#3 Education for citizenry

Middle East & North Africa

#1 **Partnership and cooperation**
#2 **Issue awareness**
#3 Education for citizenry

Europe

#1 **Issue awareness**
#2 **Partnership and cooperation**
#3 Education for citizenry

North America

#1 **Partnership and cooperation**
#2 **Issue awareness**
#3 Education for citizenry

Latin America

#1 **Partnership and cooperation**
#2 **Issue awareness**
#3 Education for citizenry

Sub-Saharan Africa

#1 **Education for citizenry**
#2 **Issue awareness**
#3 Stakeholder forums

Source: Survey on the Global Agenda 2014

Document 2

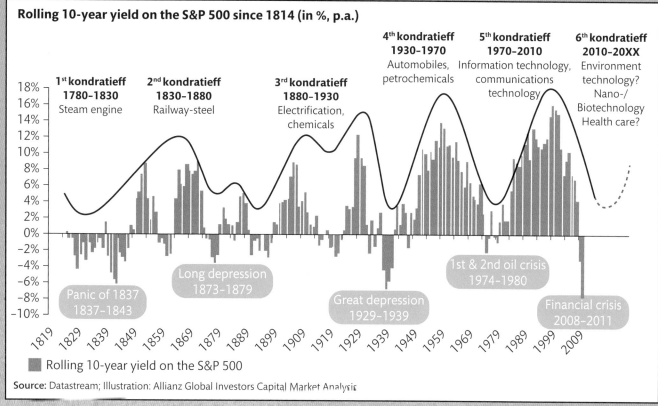

Figure 1 Kondratieff cycle – long waves of prosperity.

Skills practice exercises

Activity 4

1. Summarise Document 1 in your own words.

2. Do you agree that nationalism is more a threat to global prosperity and cooperation?

3. What are the probable consequences of the solutions to nationalism suggested in the document?

4. Why do you think that different regions suggested different solutions?

5. Which of these solutions do you think is likely to be most effective? Why?

Activity 5

Refer to Document 2.

1. Document 2 shows cycles of prosperity and recession linked to major innovations.

   a) What was the first of these innovations?

   b) Which of the innovations mentioned do you think has been the most significant for a globalising world? Explain your answer.

   c) What do you think will be the next major innovation? How global will it be? Explain your answer.

Activity 6

1. What are the probable effects of globalisation on each of the following individuals?

   a) Banker in the USA.

   b) Kenyan flower farmer selling to a European market.

   c) American tourist on holiday in Kenya.

   d) Student in a school.

   e) Aeroplane pilot.

2. Think about the different perspectives these people have. What are the needs, expectations, beliefs and desires that make their perspectives different?

Reflection

- Have you thought about globalisation in any new ways? If so, how and why?

- Have you changed your mind about anything?

- Do you think that globalisation is beneficial for both core and periphery?

- Do you think that we could make globalisation fairer – more human? If so, how?

- Do you think that development is possible without increasing globalisation?

Ideas for discussion, debate and practice

- What are the most important globalisation problems in your area?

- What are the similarities and differences in the globalisation problems experienced by these two areas?

- Choose a city or country in a very different part of the world. What are their most important globalisation problems?

- How should we minimise the negative impact of globalisation?

Discussion

"We should protect our national sovereignty from international interference."

"Nations are an old fashioned way of running things. We need global and local governance."

Examination practice

Source 1

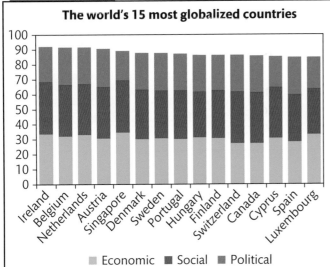

The world's 15 most globalized countries

The world's 15 least globalized countries

■ Economic ■ Social ■ Political

"The internet means we can organise anti-globalisation demos across the planet."

Source 3

The most serious threat to the stability of Europe, however, remains Russian nationalism. The biggest security question facing Europe—and perhaps the world—will be whether President Putin rides the nationalist wave he has helped to create, and continues to threaten Ukraine and even the Baltic states.

The relationship between nationalist rhetoric and territorial disputes will also be critical to the future of Asia. Mr Modi of India, Shinzo Abe of Japan and Xi Jinping of China are all energetic nation-builders who have used nationalism as a spur to domestic reforms. But their nationalism also has an outward-looking face. Asia's big question in 2015 is whether the urge to get on with domestic reforms in China, India and Japan will trump international rivalries. There are grounds for optimism. Though tensions remain high over issues such as the dispute between China and Japan over islands, political leaders are likely to try to manage their differences without conceding on basic issues of principle.

Overall, however, the resurgence of nationalist politics will make 2015 a bad year for international co-operation.

http://www.economist.com/news/21631966-bad-news-international-co-operation-nationalism-back

Source 4

Irina: I think globalisation is a good thing. We are all richer because of it. Globalisation means that there is more trade overall, and especially more international trade. We all benefit from this because there is more money moving around the world. I don't see how coffee farmers in Kenya, for example, would be better off if we stopped buying their coffee. Companies can also make more money, because they can outsource expensive services to cheaper areas of the world, and this also brings employment to those areas. It's a win-win situation.

Kwame: Income equality is growing, and this is partly because of globalisation, where core countries exploit the countries in the periphery. The World Bank and the International Monetary Fund are evil organisations that loan money to poor countries, but insist that they engage in free trade, allowing open competition, which effectively means that companies from rich countries can exploit the poor countries.

Rennick: I don't think globalisation is that great for rich countries either. All our jobs are outsourced to cheap countries. And migrants come over here and take the jobs that are left, so ordinary folk are left with nothing much. The big companies do great, but the rest of us? I think we're better off sticking to ourselves.

Question 1

Refer to Source 1.

a) Identify the world's most globalised country. [1]

b) Describe a trend you see in the chart relating to social, political and economic development. [3]

Refer to Source 2.

c) Choose one cartoon and explain the issue or issues it raises. [4]

d) Do you think that the effects of globalisation are mainly global, or are they also significant on a personal and national level? [4]

Question 2

Refer to Source 3.

a) How effectively is evidence used in Source 3 to support the prediction that 2015 will be a bad year for international co-operation? [6]

b) How would you find out whether 2015 was in fact a good or a bad year for international cooperation? You may consider the types of information, sources of evidence or methods you might use. [8]

Question 3

Refer to Source 3.

a) Identify one prediction in Source 3 (apart from the last line). [1]

b) "Income equality is growing." Is this a fact or an opinion? Justify your answer. [3]

Refer to Source 4

a) Why might Irina be biased? [1]

b) Whose reasoning is most effective, Irina's, Kwame's or Rennick's? [15]

Your answer should consider all three arguments, and you should support your point of view with their words. You should also consider:

- the strength of their reasoning and evidence

- their use of language

- different types of information.

Question 4

Do the advantages of globalisation outweigh its disadvantages? [24]

In your answer you should:

- state your conclusion

- give reasons to support your choice

- use the material in the Sources and/or any of your own ideas

- consider different arguments and perspectives.

6 Law and criminality

- Preventing crime
- Rehabilitating criminals
- Justice
- Justice and development
- Punishing crime
- Dealing with international crime
- Funding the criminal justice system
- Surveillance

Activity 1

1. Match the comments and questions below to the issues listed above.

   a) "Hong Kong's police are one of the reasons for the low crime rates and high level of safety in Hong Kong. The police are often described as very helpful, polite and omnipresent, which gives many people a general feeling of safety in Hong Kong, but also of surveillance."

   b) "Four billion people around the world live without the protections of the law. They live without access to their rights, vulnerable to exploitation and violence. Poverty will only be defeated when the law works for everyone."

   c) "Some people think that we need more police to ensure that we are safe from criminals. But who is going to pay for this? I don't want to pay higher taxes; I already give the government enough money."

   d) "Crime Prevention through Environmental Design is an international crime prevention strategy which considers how physical environments can be designed in order to reduce crime. It includes things like lighting, security cameras but also other changes to an area that change the decisions people make. It makes sense to me. I remember when I was about four, I was sitting on the kitchen table, and I kept putting my finger in the sugar bowl. My mother punished me. But now I wonder why she didn't simply move the sugar bowl so that I wasn't tempted. I think often, it is opportunity and temptation that makes people do criminal things. I don't think they are necessarily bad people."

2. Identify at least one comment or question which comes from a

   a) personal perspective

   b) national perspective

   c) global perspective.

> Do some of these comments and questions raise more than one issue?

Discussion

Choose an issue, comment or question that interests you and discuss it with a partner.

a) Think about personal, local/national and global perspectives on this issue. For example, think about the perspectives of a worker, a company boss, a head of government, an international charity worker, and so on.

b) What information do you need to help you discuss this?

Activity 2

1. Use internet resources to help you complete the mind map with different words and ideas relating to law and criminality. Use dictionaries and online resources to help you make lists of new vocabulary and technical terms.

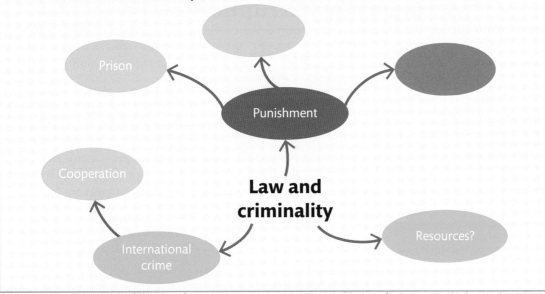

Prison

Punishment

Cooperation

Law and criminality

International crime

Resources?

Activity 3

Complete the sentences below using the correct tense in each case.

1. If we cooperate with Interpol, _____ able to track international criminals more closely.

2. If the government provided enough jobs, _____ be less crime.

3. If Daria had not paid the people smugglers, _____ be in prison for expressing her opinion.

Stimulus material

Document 1

At 16.30 on Monday, a man with a scarf wrapped around his face walked into Treasure jewellery shop with a shotgun and stole $20 000 worth of diamond jewellery. Darius left work at the bank near Treasure at 16.20. He is seen on CCTV with a scarf wrapped around his face at 16.25. At 18.45 Darius met his girlfriend at a restaurant, asked her to marry him. He gave her the ring she had spent many hours admiring in the window of Treasure. The police inspector decided that Darius must be the thief.

Statement:

I left work at about 16.15. It was a really cold evening so I wrapped up well, and put my scarf around my face. Otherwise the cold air gives me a really bad cough. After walking home, I got ready to meet my girlfriend. I took a long time because I was nervous and wanted to look good because I had planned to ask her to marry me. Yes, I bought the ring at Treasure. I went in last week. On Tuesday. No, I didn't go in today, I didn't need to.

Document 2

In Vietnam, death penalty cannot be a remedy for corruption

As legislators in Hanoi consider removing "war crimes" and "surrendering to the enemy" from Vietnam's list of capital offenses, ongoing debates at the National Assembly suggest that "corruption" is likely to remain a capital crime. This is mistaken – corruption should not be a capital crime.

Proponents of the death penalty say it needs to remain in place to fight corruption and overhaul the business climate. But with corruption remaining massive and the death penalty clearly being no deterrent, holding on to it as a panacea seems naïve.

The 2014 Corruption Perceptions Index (CPI) ranked Vietnam 119 out of 175 countries with a score of 31/100 – a ranking the country has retained since 2012. Study after study has proved that the practice of giving and taking bribes is so common that it is understood to be a routine and infamous part of doing business here in Vietnam.

Repeated rhetoric from the top leadership notwithstanding, the commitment to address corruption has apparently failed to trickle down the system. Meanwhile, the state sector, notorious for its less-than-efficient performance, has done nothing to assuage the fears that it is the bane of the economy and a major source of corruption.

It is in this context that the idea of simply killing a person while leaving a broken system untouched seems ineffective and wrong.

A number of lawmakers have also objected to scrapping the death penalty for corruption on the grounds that doing so would go against the will of the people.

But this misses the larger point. The bottom line is people are sick of greasing official palms to get through their lives.

Businessmen cannot countenance paying "informal charges" to complete mundane licensing and tax procedures; ordinary people are sick of paying "informal charges" to see a doctor or get their child into kindergarten.

Lawmakers cannot pretend they are addressing these issues by killing those who lack political connections or financial resources to weasel their way out of capital punishment. Lawmakers just cannot ride this backlash to insist that the death penalty should remain in place, claiming they are merely speaking for their constituents.

What the public longs to see is a no-holds-barred crackdown on corruption and real political will to tackle the root causes. There is no point in carrying out a few high-profile executions and then continuing with business as usual.

Proponents of the death penalty are also convinced that it would play a crucial role in repairing the shattered trust of foreign investors as the country is in the middle of implementing major financial reforms. Again, it is unlikely that many would buy into this. Foreign investors and members of the public want to see a crackdown on corruption – one that brings economic reforms and respect for the rule of law.

The death penalty may help to placate concerned citizens in the short run. But it cannot be used in place of larger, more comprehensive long-term moves to weed out corruption.

So if Vietnamese lawmakers want to show their constituents that they are not lame-duck representatives, it is time they directed their efforts and endeavors toward amending laws and rectifying deep-seated ills that allow widespread corruption instead of noisily advocating the death penalty as a remedy.

http://www.thanhniennews.com/commentaries/in-vietnam-death-penalty-cannot-be-a-remedy-for-corruption-46817.html

Document 3

RECENTLY passed laws in Malaysia restrict fundamental liberties.

The Prevention of Terrorism Act (PoTA) passed by Parliament earlier this year provides for detention without trial. This means that the person accused of committing a terrorist act need not be charged in Court for him to be detained under the Act.

There is even a provision in PoTA stating that any decision of the Prevention of Terrorism Board (the body empowered to issue detention orders under PoTA) cannot be judicially reviewed by the Courts. This means that those aggrieved by any decision of the Board have no recourse through the Courts, unless it relates to non-compliance of procedure.

According to the doctrine of separation of powers, power in a State resides in three separate and independent bodies – the legislature that enacts laws, the executive that implements and executes laws, and the judiciary that interprets laws.

[These three bodies] of the State each have their own functions and responsibilities. Their powers are limited and they act as a check and balance mechanism to each other. This ensures that the institutions act in accordance with their constitutional roles, and do not abuse their power. None of these bodies have absolute power.

The judiciary is the last bastion of fundamental liberties, the wall between the citizen and the excesses of the State. If a person's rights are violated by the Government, the judiciary is responsible to ensure that the person has an avenue to enforce his or her rights.

This is one the reasons why laws such as Pota and the amended Sedition Act are at odds with democracy, the rule of law and the constitutional framework of our country.

We should not allow for power be taken away from the judiciary. Yes, the laws have been passed and it is only a matter of time before they come into force. But that does not mean that all hope is lost. We must continue to push for the government to respect and uphold the role of the courts in our constitutional framework.

http://www.thestar.com.my/Opinion/Online-Exclusive/A-Humble-Submission/ Profile/Articles/2015/06/29/Upholding-the-role-of-the-judiciary/

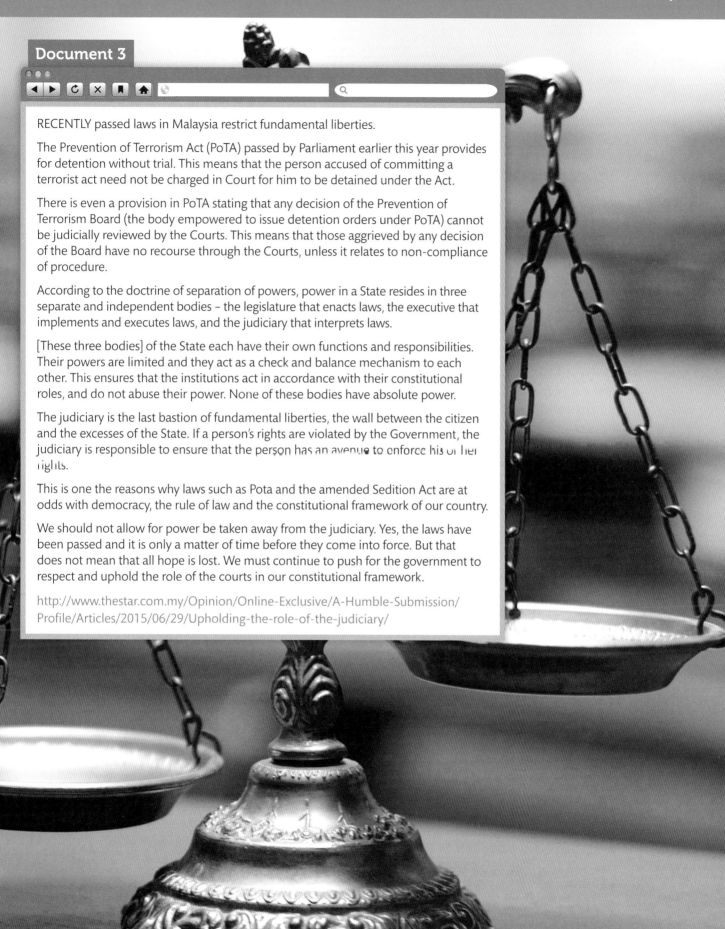

Skills practice exercises

Activity 4

Refer to Document 1

1. How reliable are the claims that Darius makes? Justify your answer.

2. What do you need to know to decide whether Darius was the thief? How will this information help?

3. Do you think that Darius was the jewel thief? Justify your answer.

Activity 5

Refer to Document 2

1. According to the Document, Vietnam has the death penalty for corruption.

   a) Is the death penalty in place in your country?

   b) If so, for which crimes?

   c) Find out what other crimes attract the death penalty in countries around the world.

2. Use the article to complete the table:

Arguments in favour of death penalty for corruption	Arguments against the death penalty for corruption
Fight corruption act as a deterrent	It doesn't work.

3. To what extent is the death penalty a personal, national or global issue?

4. What is your personal opinion on the death penalty?

Activity 6

1. According to Document 3, Malaysia has introduced a Prevention of Terrorism Act which allows for detention without trial.

   a) Very briefly summarise why the author thinks this is such a bad thing.

2. The UN Declaration of Human Rights says, "No one shall be subjected to arbitrary arrest, detention or exile."

   "Everyone is entitled in full equality to a fair and public hearing..."

   a) Do you think that it is right to take away fundamental human rights from people suspected of terrorism? What if they are wrongly suspected?

3. What laws has your government introduced to prevent or deal with terrorism?

4. What is your opinion about the government taking away people's rights?

> Document 3 contains some complex language. Remember that you do not need to understand every word. Focus on understanding the main ideas, and concentrate on important passages.

Examination practice

Source 1

Gun murder compared by country

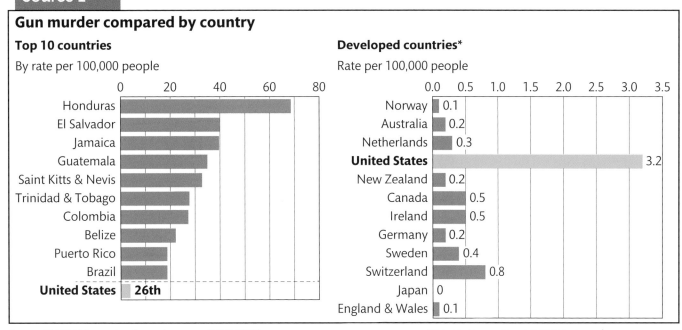

Top 10 countries

By rate per 100,000 people

Developed countries*

Rate per 100,000 people

Source: UNODC. Latest data for each country (2004–2010)

*Listed in Human Development Index order

Source 2

Public outrage as judges pass unfair sentences

Our criminal justice system has been called into question today by the punishments handed down by judges in three different cases.

Case 1:
Person: Banker
Offence: Fraud. He was convicted of using $10million of clients' money to fund his own extravagant lifestyle.
Plea: Guilty
Sentence: 15 months in prison

Case 2:
Person: Migrant agricultural worker
Offence: Armed burglary. He was convicted of breaking into and entering the home of a millionaire with a gun and stealing $50, 000 of valuables.
Plea: Not guilty
Sentence: 10 years in prison.

Case 3:
Person: Farmer
Offence: Shooting and killing a burglar
Plea: Not guilty
Sentence: 15 years in prison

What do you think? Are these sentences fair?

@amazinggrace

This just shows what this country is coming to when you can't even defend your home any more. It's the burglar that should be sent to prison, not the person he burgled. There's no hope for us in this day and age. It's like that case where the teenager sued a business because he fell through their roof, and the judge said the business should have kept the roof safe for burglars. It's being so soft on kids that leads to all this crime. What I say is, spare the rod and spoil the child – but these days they'll lock you up for trying to instil proper discipline into your kids.

@be reasonable

Defending your home is acceptable, but killing the intruder is a bit extreme. Why not disable them and call the police?

@hope for the future

The real outrage is that the rich banker who stole $10 million got 15 months but the poor agricultural worker got 10 years for stealing much less. This is social inequality at its worst. Fraud and burglary are both forms of theft and the punishment should reflect the amount stolen. This would lead to a fairer criminal justice system. We should pay bankers and agricultural workers the same amount of money. This would lead to less greed, a happier society and much less crime.

@cynicalrealist

You are naive and wrong on two counts, @hope for the future. First, if bankers aren't happy with the millions they already get, how would paying them less reduce their greed? Second, there's an important difference between using a computer to move money that doesn't really exist from one bank account to another, and invading someone's private home with a gun, going through their things and stealing things they really care about.

@innocentbanker

Not all bankers are greedy and not all of us take criminal actions or make irresponsible decisions. Personally I think that the criminal, irresponsible few should be punished much more harshly. This is partly because it would make other bankers realise they can't get away with crime, and partly because it gives us all a bad name when criminal bankers seem to get away with it. We should make it quite clear that they are criminals just as much as burglars are. If you break the law you are a criminal. And fraud is breaking the law.

Question 1

Consider Source 1.

a) Which country has the highest gun crime rate?
[1]

b) Which country has the lowest gun crime rate?
[1]

c) Suggest one reason for the difference in gun crime rate between the lowest and highest countries. [1]

Consider Source 2

d) Explain briefly why the three sentences have caused outrage. Use your own words but refer to the article and online comments. [6]

e) Identify three possible solutions for the future which are mentioned in the online comments. [3]

Question 2

The migrant agricultural worker claims that he is not guilty of the armed burglary, but he was convicted because one of his hairs was found at the crime scene.

Suggest two pieces of evidence that would help to show that he was in fact not guilty. How would this evidence help? [14]

Question 3

a) @be reasonable says, "Defending your home is acceptable, but killing the intruder is a bit extreme."

Do you think this is fact, opinion, prediction or value judgement? Explain your answer. [2]

b) Does @hope for the future suggest likely consequences? Justify your answer. [3]

c) @cynicalrealist says, "there's an important difference between using a computer to move money that doesn't really exist from one bank account to another, and invading someone's private home with a gun, going through their things and stealing things they really care about."

Do you accept this value judgement? Justify your answer. [3]

d) Whose reasoning is better – @amazinggrace's or @innocentbanker's? [12]

You should also consider:

- the strength of their reasoning and evidence
- their use of language
- different types of information.

Question 4

The following actions are being considered to reduce gun crime:

- Make it illegal for anyone to own a gun.
- Restrict gun ownership to farmers, hunters and the police.
- Make killing someone with a gun a capital offence.
- Community action groups in areas with high levels of gun crime.

You must recommend a course of action to the government. In your answer you should

- state your recommendations
- give reasons
- give examples where relevant
- show that you have considered at least one other viewpoint. [24]

7 Migration

- Reasons for migration
- Types of migration
- Effects on host country
- Effects on country of departure
- Anti-migration sentiment
- Migration and development
- Migration and criminality
- Managing migration
- Migration and families

Do some of these comments and questions raise more than one issue?

Activity 1

1. Match the comments and questions below to the issues in the diagram above.

   a) According to the Geneva Convention, which most governments signed in 1951, governments should take in refugees and cooperate internationally to make sure that refugees find asylum.

   b) Migrants get treated better than people who were born here. It's not fair.

   c) Spending money on military personnel and equipment to tighten borders is a waste of taxpayers' money. It only means that refugees pay increasingly professional people smugglers to find other ways into a country. It does not stop migrants from crossing borders.

   d) Migrants often send remittances home to their families. This money is often an important part of the economy for poor countries – half of the GDP of Tajikistan, for example, comes from migrant remittances.

   e) Many people blame migrants for increasing crime levels. But research shows that areas which have large migrant populations actually have lower crime rates. Of course, international crime gangs are a problem, but these gangs are not necessarily composed of migrants.

   f) Identify at least one comment or question which comes from a

   i) personal perspective

   ii) national perspective

   iii) global perspective.

2. Choose an issue, comment or question that interests you and discuss it with a partner.

Discussion

Think about personal, local/national and global perspectives on this issue. For example, think about the perspectives of a worker, a company boss, a head of government, an international charity worker, and so on.

What information do you need to help you discuss this?

Key vocabulary and language exercises

Activity 2

1. Use internet resources to help you complete the mind map with different words and ideas relating to Migration. Use dictionaries and online resources to help you make lists of new vocabulary and technical terms.

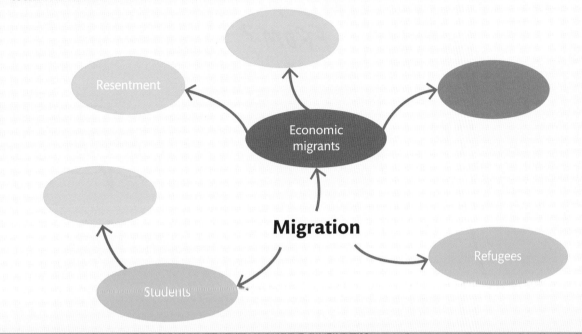

Activity 3

Complete the sentences below using the correct tense in each case.

1. If we welcome migrants now, _____ reduce the risk of terror attacks.

2. If the government provided incentives for educated migrants to come, _____ develop thriving economic communities.

3. If I had stayed in the town where I was born _____ not have a good job in the bank.

Stimulus material

Document 2

GENEVA — The United Nations warned on Friday that Greece and its Balkan neighbors were being overwhelmed by the flood of migrants arriving from Syria and other areas of conflict, and it urged European countries to step forward with aid to avert a looming humanitarian crisis.

With Greece's economy in crisis and negotiations over a bailout seemingly headed toward the final stage, the United Nations refugee agency said Europe had a responsibility to help the nation deal with the surge in migrants trying to reach safety. More than 77,100 people have reached Greece by sea since the start of the year, 60 percent of them from Syria, and 1,000 are arriving daily, the agency said.

The influx is creating "an unprecedented refugee emergency" at a time when Greece is financially unable to cope, William Spindler, a spokesman for the United Nations High Commissioner for Refugees, told reporters in Geneva.

"We would expect the E.U. to activate its emergency response because Greece is part of the European Union," he said. "Greece urgently needs help, and we expect Europe to step forward."

European leaders who are facing mounting resistance to immigration reluctantly agreed last month to take in 40,000 migrants and asylum seekers, although a plan sought by Greece and Italy for mandatory quotas across the European Union was abandoned. The refugee agency welcomed that development, but described it as a "modest" first step. The agency emphasized on Friday that "as needs continue to grow, these measures must be expanded."

Despite the economic crisis, communities on the Greek islands, particularly Lesbos, Samos and Chios, have used their own resources to assist the migrants, Mr. Spindler said. Islanders have bought and distributed bread, provided clothes, and donated milk powder for infants. Local doctors have volunteered to treat migrants who are ill, exhausted and, in some cases, wounded from conflicts back home.

The scale of the arrivals, however, has far outstripped the capacity of local authorities, and thousands of migrants are now camped in conditions that are "deplorable," Mr. Spindler said.

Greece has been the arrival point for roughly half the 155,000 people who have reached Europe this year, according to the International Organization for Migration.

Although most of the 1,914 reported deaths have occurred along the Mediterranean route from North Africa, the Aegean Sea is not without peril. The Greek Coast Guard reported that a boat that left Turkey with up to 40 migrants on Tuesday had capsized. Though 19 people were rescued, the remainder were feared to have died.

The pressure has spread throughout the region as migrants and asylum seekers try to make their way to Europe through Macedonia, Serbia and other western Balkan countries, the refugee agency said. About 45,000 people have sought asylum in those countries so far this year, nine times the number over the same period in 2014.

"The tightening of borders and the building of walls is not the solution," Mr. Spindler said.

http://www.nytimes.com/2015/07/11/world/europe/un-warning-of-migrant-crisis-in-greece-urges-europe-to-take-action.html?_r=0

Document 3

Don't let them drown: Campaigning to stop the deaths in the Med

In April 2015, more than 1,000 people drowned in one week as several overcrowded boats sank in the Mediterranean and Aegean Seas.

"The equivalent of five passenger planes full of people have drowned last week alone, and this is only the start of the summer. If they had been holiday makers, instead of migrants, imagine the response."

— Kate Allen, Amnesty UK Director

Tackling the wider issues

Meanwhile, EU leaders are discussing how to address wider issues – both the causes of the tragic deaths we have seen at sea and how to respond to the needs of those rescued. We expect these discussions will continue through June and July.

A comprehensive solution to this crisis will require co-operation and solidarity – both across Europe and with much poorer countries outside of Europe.

The absence of safe and legal routes for refugees to seek and receive asylum in Europe has forced tens of thousands of people into the hands of people smugglers, and in turn onto overcrowded and unseaworthy boats. We're calling on European countries to make safe and legal routes available for asylum-seekers.

Most people making the dangerous crossing or rescued at sea will first arrive in Italy or Greece – responsibility for refugees must be shared more fairly among European countries.

Poorer countries continue to accommodate and support the greatest number of refugees. We're calling for European countries to provide more resettlement places.

http://www.amnesty.org.uk/dont-let-them-drown-mediterranean-europe#.VaD3cU3JCdw

Skills practice exercises

Activity 4

Refer to Documents 1.

1. What issues do the graphics and the cartoon raise about global migration crises?

Activity 5

Refer to Document 3.

1. Identify the causes of migration mentioned in the document.

2. Are these mainly personal, national or global causes?

3. Find out about the causes of the South East Asian Migrant crisis.

4. Are these mainly personal, national or global causes?

Activity 6

Refer to Document 4.

1. What possible solutions are suggested to the migrant crisis?

2. How effective do you think these solutions will be?

3. Find out what other solutions people have proposed.

4. What do you think of these other solutions?

Activity 7

1. In your opinion, what is the best way to deal with migration crises?

Ideas for discussion, debate and practice

If you were a migrant, how would you want to be treated?

Think about the benefits and the costs of each of these migrants to the host country and the country of departure:

- Student doctor

- Nurse

- Traumatised woman from a war zone

- Seven year old child from a war zone

Examination practice

Source 1

Trafficking in human beings is a multi-billion-dollar form of international organized crime, constituting modern-day slavery.

Victims are recruited and trafficked between countries and regions using deception or coercion. They are stripped of their autonomy, freedom of movement and choice, and face various forms of physical and mental abuse.

The main types of human trafficking include:

- Trafficking for forced labour;
- Trafficking of organs.

Closely connected is the issue of people smuggling in which smugglers are paid to help individuals enter a country illegally.

http://www.interpol.int/Crime-areas/Trafficking-in-human-beings/
Trafficking-in-human-beings

Source 2

Iran's Deputy Ambassador to the UN, Gholam-Hossein Dehqani urged the international community to take action on human trafficking. Poverty, unemployment, discrimination, a lack of social and economic opportunities, and global financial crises are among the factors making individuals vulnerable to human trafficking, Dehqani said. He stressed the responsibility of wealthy nations.

http://www.presstv.ir/detail/2013/05/15/303607/iran-urges-action-on-human-trafficking/

Source 3

A migrant domestic worker recounted her friend's experience of trying to escape from a situation of forced labour: "She managed to escape through a window, from the family that treated her like a slave. She was terrified and had bruises on her body. Her passport was locked in the house. The policeman at the station asked her for her documents. She of course did not have them and wanted to tell him what had happened, but he insisted on her documents first and said he must know who she was."

http://www.antislavery.org/english/slavery_today/trafficking.aspx

Source 4

Libya's people smugglers

The head of the European commission, Donald Tusk, confirmed the European plan to "capture and destroy vessels used by the smugglers before they can be used".

But interviews with smugglers show there is a problem with this. Smuggling boats start life as fishing trawlers. Smugglers do not maintain a separate, independent harbour of clearly marked vessels, ready to be targeted by EU air strikes. They buy them off fishermen at a few days' notice. To destroy their potential pool of boats, the EU would need to raze whole fishing ports.

"One of the reasons why [Libyan] fish is expensive is the lack of fishing boats going out to sea to fish," a people smuggler who wanted to be known as Hajj explains later. "They're all being used by smugglers."

"Who? Where?" asks a friend of Hajj's when contemplating the potential targets of EU anti-smuggling operations. "No one has the name 'smuggler' written on their chest. Anyone here who has no money can sell their apartment, buy a boat, and organise a smuggling trip. By the time of the next trip you'd already have regained half the cost of the apartment. It's a very easy formula."

What you pay depends on who you are. At the moment, says Hajj, a sub-Saharan African is expected to pay "no more than $800 or $1,000. A Syrian would pay no more than $2,500. A Moroccan no more than

€1,500". Because of the saturated market, prices are lower than usual – and as a result smugglers are trying to fill their ships with larger numbers to make up the shortfall.

That more disasters are happening this year is partly a result of the lower price for a seat on a boat.

"It's ridiculous," says Hajj. "Three hundred passengers is the maximum for a 17-metre boat. But people are sending out boats loaded with 350, 700, 800. They are being overloaded because the price of an individual has gone down."

But beyond the destruction of specific boats, conversations with smugglers, refugees and coastguards along the shores of west Libya suggest there are other, more long-term strategies for curbing the flow of people across the Mediterranean. The message from refugees is clear: find us a safer option. Often fleeing dictatorship, war or hunger at home and faced with further conflict and exploitation in supposedly safer havens like Libya, to many refugees the Mediterranean seems the least bad option.

While the world fails to address the root causes of the biggest wave of mass migration since the second world war, the business of people smuggling will continue.

Extracts from: http://www.theguardian.com/world/2015/apr/24/libyas-people-smugglers-how-will-they-catch-us-theyll-soon-move-on

Question 1

Refer to Source 1.

a) Explain in your own words the difference between human trafficking and people smuggling. [3]

Refer to Source 2.

b) Give three factors that make people vulnerable to people trafficking. [1]

c) Explain why one of these factors might cause people to be more vulnerable to human trafficking. [4]

Refer to Source 4.

d) Explain why targeting people smugglers' boats is unlikely to be successful. [4]

Question 2

a) What questions should the police ask the young women in Source 3 to find out whether she really is a legal migrant? Explain how her answers might help. [6]

b) How effectively is evidence used in Source 4 to support the claim that "the business of people smuggling will continue"? [8]

Question 3

Refer to Source 3.

a) How reliable is Interpol as a source of information? Explain your answer. [3]

b) How reliable is the migrant domestic worker in Source 3 as a source of information? Explain your answer. [6]

c) How reliable is Hajj as a source of information in Source 4? Explain your answer. [6]

d) "Europe cannot help all the refugees in the world. Europe simply isn't big enough to offer a home to everyone who needs one, and it isn't rich enough to solve all the world's problems. Of course we want to help people in need. But we are drowning in other people's problems, and we have enough problems of our own."

How effective is this reasoning? You should support your point of view with their words. You should also consider: [5]

- the strength of their reasoning and evidence

- their use of language

- different types of information.

Question 4

What do you think is the best way to reduce people smuggling?

You could consider some of the following:

- Try to prevent people from leaving conflict zones.

- Provide troops and arms to end the conflict more quickly.

- Refuse to let smuggled and trafficked people into the country.

- Try to solve the problems at the source.

You must recommend a course of action to the government. In your answer you should

- state your recommendations

- give reasons

- give examples where relevant

- show that you have considered at least one other viewpoint. [24]

What else do I need to know?

You have already thought about filling the gaps in your knowledge when you are researching a topic. In the exam, you may be asked about gaps in your knowledge. These are likely to be small, focused pieced of information. They may be important pieces of information that you need to come to a conclusion or to make a decision, for example.

It is important to think about how this information will help you to come to a conclusion or to make a decision. Let's look at an example:

> You are a police constable on duty. A young woman, bruised, bleeding and very upset comes up to you in the street. She says that she is a legal migrant cleaner and her employer is beating her. She wants to press charges against her employer.
>
> What do you need to know to decide whether the employer is guilty? How will you find the information you need? How will this help you to decide whether the employer is guilty?

I need to know how the woman got her injuries. So I will ask a doctor to examine her to find out what sort of injuries the woman has, and whether they are the sort of injuries that could come from being beaten. This will help me to decide whether the woman is telling the truth about how she was injured. For example, if her injuries could have come by falling or by being run over, I will question whether the woman really got her injuries from her employer. But if they are the sort of injury you get from a beating, it is more likely that she is telling the truth about being beaten.

> *Do think about alternative possibilities. Do not jump to conclusions.*

This is a very thorough answer which focuses on the precise information needed, identifies a reliable way of getting the information, and explains how this will help to make a decision. It is clear that the information from the doctor will help to make a decision, but won't give certainty.

I need to know if the employer really beats his cleaner. I will ask a doctor to examine her. If the doctor says the injuries were made by a beating I will know that the woman is telling the truth and the employer is guilty. If the doctor says the injuries came from being run over, I will know that the cleaner is lying to get her employer in trouble.

This answer does identify an important piece of information that the police constable needs to know. Asking a doctor to examine the woman is a good way of getting useful evidence about the injuries. But in this answer, the comments about how the information will help are too extreme. For instance, even if the doctor agrees that the injuries could be caused by a beating, the woman's employer is not the only person who could have beaten her. So "I will know the woman is telling the truth" is too extreme. We can't know this. Also, if the woman's injuries came from being run over, we can *suspect* that the woman is lying, but she might be confused or mistaken (perhaps if she has been hit on the head) and we need much more information to be sure *why* she is lying.

I need to know whether the woman really is a cleaner. So I will ask her for details of her employer and interview the employer to find out what the woman does in her job. Then I will also ask the employer whether she beats her cleaner and why she does this.

This answer focuses on irrelevant information. It is not important to know whether this woman is a cleaner in order to decide whether her employer is guilty of beating her.

8 Transport systems

- Aging transport systems
- Efficiency of transport systems
- Transport and development
- Environmental issues
- Who should fund transport systems?
- Comfort and convenience
- Airports

Key vocabulary and language exercises

Activity 1

1. **a)** Public transport systems should work like road systems. Here in the UK – and in many other countries – we pay a tax once a year to use the roads, and using each road is free of charge when you use it. If buses, trains and trams worked in the same way, more people would use public transport, which would benefit the environment and reduce congestion.

   b) I think that people who drive their cars short distances are selfish. They should think more about clean air and the future of the planet than their own convenience.

   c) Aging transport infrastructures are a significant problem in many cities around the world. There needs to be constant maintenance, which is expensive and causes frustrating delays. There are also the inevitable debates about upgrading the infrastructure – should we prioritise the needs of the economy or the environment? Who should pay for the expensive upgrade?

   d) We think of congestion as a modern, global problem which results from more people owning and using cars. But it is actually one of the oldest problems facing cities – even the Ancient Romans had problems with congestion. This means that we are wrong about the causes of congestion, and that we need to rethink our solutions to this problem.

   e) Around the world, cities with efficient transport systems are becoming wealthier.

Key vocabulary and language exercises

Activity 2

1. Use internet resources to help you complete the mind map with different words and ideas relating to demographic change. Use dictionaries and online resources to help you make lists of new vocabulary and technical terms.

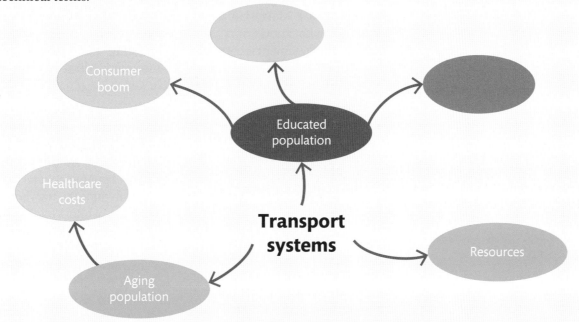

Stimulus material

Document 1

 XueFei: "In Shanghai, where I work, the transports systems are new and growing fast. But the pace of change is too fast, and the pollution is often so bad you can hardly breathe or see. This is going to get worse. By contrast, in my home village, my parents don't have running water or electricity, and there is no public transport."

 Mark: "Here in the UK our infrastructure is getting old. It can't cope with the demands of modern life. Some of our sewers are over 150 years old and our trains are twentieth century. We need a new airport to keep business growing, but people oppose this because it might damage the environment."

 Alina: "I want to sell the jewellery I make online. But our internet connection is so unreliable, and the postal service is terrible. Half the things I post are lost and never get to my customers. We need to invest a lot of money in this country's infrastructure. But who's going to pay for it?

Activity 3

Complete the sentences below using the correct tense in each case.

1. If we go by car instead of by train, _____ (arrive much sooner)

2. If the government provided incentives for people to use public transport, _____ fewer people drive their own cars.

3. If the government had started to plan the public transport system earlier, _____ not be so inefficient.

Document 2

Controversy in Northern Malaysia over an airport shows political rift

Luc Citrinot – 18 June 2014, 07:01

A project of building a new airport in Kedah (Malaysia) in direct competition to Penang shows that infrastructure development in Malaysia is all about political games and ambitions…

KUCHING – The Chief Minister of Kedah State in Malaysia bears a famous patronym: **Mukhriz Mahathir**. Son of ex-Prime Minister of Malaysia **Mahathir Mohammad**, he certainly looks to emulate his illustrious father in the State of Kedah.

Like his dad who turned the Island of Langkawi into a tourist destination in the late eighties, Kedah Chief Minister dreams to turn himself into the driving force of economic development in his State and Northern Malaysia. His latest project is to build a brand new international airport in Kulim equipped with two runways on 600 hectares of land. It would then became the main gateway not only for Kedah but also for the neighbouring State of Penang – located 40 km away and have a catchment area stretching up to Southern Thailand, indicated earlier in the month the Premier.

"This is just 'rubbish'. Who would like to fly in the middle of nowhere in Kedah to then further go to Penang", asks a Malaysian travel journalist, who knows very well the area. His statement is certainly shared by the Penang government. Officially Penang Chief Minister **Lim Guan Eng** does not reject the idea of constructing a new airport in Kedah – although it would then be the fourth one in the region next to Penang, Langkawi and Alor Setar. But he also immediately asks why there is no commitment to expand first Penang international airport in Bayar Lepas before to process with any new airport. **Penang International Airport** is Malaysia third busiest airport welcoming close to 5.5 million passengers in 2013, up by 15% over 2012.

The claim by Mukhriz Mahathir that Penang airport has no space to expand is regarded with skepticism by Penang government, reported on Monday Malaysian newspaper the Star. Chief Minister Lim Guan Eng opposed the idea, talking about possibility to reclaim up to 500 acres of land for an expansion south of the airport. Speaking with local media, Penang Chief Minister questioned the wisdom of such a proposal. *"Penang is the largest recipient of Foreign Direct Investments in the country from 2010 to 2013 and Kedah does not even come close,"* Lim said, then suggesting that Penang should consequently have three airports like Kedah.

They are however some explanation behind Kehad push to fund an airport which would probably cost around US$ 700 million. Penang is one of the Malaysian States being run by the opposition while Kedah belongs to the current coalition in power. The plea of Mukhriz Mahathir to get the new airport would in fact revive a former proposal from Mohammad Mahathir to [build] such a facility in Kedah.

The idea dates back to 1997. At the time, Mahathir had even suggested that once the future **Northern Malaysia Central Airport** would have been built, Penang Airport could then eventually close its doors. The 1997 economic crisis in Asia put however a spell on the ambitious project by then. Ambitions are hard to die.

http://www.traveldailynews.asia/news/article/55856/controversy-in-northern-malaysia-over

Skills practice exercises

Activity 4

Refer to Document 1.

1. Find and write down one fact, one opinion and one prediction in what XueFei says.

2. XueFei says, "the pollution is so bad you can hardly breathe or see." Do you think this is a fact or an exaggeration?

3. How would you check what the pollution is like in Shanghai? See if you can find out.

4. Mark says that infrastructure in the UK "can't cope with the demands of modern life." Is this a fact or an opinion? Why do you think this?

5. How would you find out more about whether UK infrastructure can cope with modern life? See how much information you can find in ten minutes.

6. Do you think business or the environment is more important? What are your reasons?

7. "Half the things I post are lost and never get to my customers." How far do you think this is a fact and how far an opinion? Why?

8. How would you check this claim to see if it is a fact?

9. Do you think Alina lives in a high, medium or low economic development country? Why? Does everyone in the class agree?

> Remember, facts can be verified and opinions cannot.

> Think about your search terms. If "UK infrastructure modern life" doesn't work, what other search terms could you try?

Activity 5

Refer to Document 2.

1. Use Document 2 to identify the following.

   a) Reasons for building a new airport in Kedah, Malaysia.

   b) Positive consequences of building the new airport in Kedah, Malaysia.

   c) Negative consequences of building the new airport in Kedah, Malaysia.

2. In your opinion, are these personal, national or global reasons and consequences?

3. Use Document 2 to identify possible alternative solutions:

   a) Reasons for the alternative solution

   b) Reasons against the alternative solution

4. Use the information in the document to draw a mind map of challenges and possible solutions.

5. Choose a proposed airport construction in another part of the world and research the issues. Compare the issues with those in Malaysia.

6. Do you think that Kedah airport should be built? Write an argument to support your view.

Activity 5

1. What types of transport does each of these individuals need?

   a) Subsistence farmer in Kenya.

   b) Kenyan flower farmer selling to a European market.

   c) American tourist on holiday in Kenya.

   d) Student in a school.

   e) Teacher in a school.

2. Think about the different perspectives these people have. What are the needs, expectations, beliefs and desires that make their perspectives different?

3. To what extent are transport systems a personal, national or global concern? Think about the needs of business, government, tourism and ordinary people.

Ideas for discussion, debate and practice

- What are the most important transport and infrastructure problems in your area?

- Choose a city or country in a very different part of the world. What are their most important transport problems?

- What are the similarities and differences in the transport and infrastructure problems experienced by these two areas?

Discussion

Choose a contentious airport construction programme (such as Kedah, London, Nantes, Turkey, and so on.). Debate whether the airport should be built.

Examination practice

Source 1

Rail and bus rapid transit (BRT) infrastructure

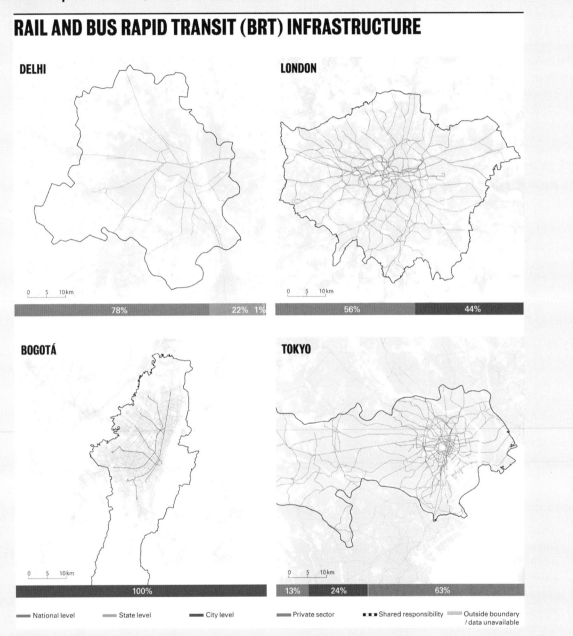

RAIL AND BUS RAPID TRANSIT (BRT) INFRASTRUCTURE

DELHI
78% | 22% 1%

LONDON
56% | 44%

BOGOTÁ
100%

TOKYO
13% | 24% | 63%

National level | State level | City level | Private sector | Shared responsibility | Outside boundary / data unavailable

The four cities have varied levels of authority over key infrastructure, like rail and bus rapid transit

Delhi, Bogotá, London and Tokyo, have pioneered innovations in transport in the last few decades, from Tokyo's highly integrated transport system to Delhi's new Metro, London's Congestion Charge, Boris Bikes and CrossRail to Bogotá's Bus Rapid Transit (BRT) and ciclovías. The colours of routes on the maps identify which level of government – national, state, city, local and shared responsibility -owns and manages different parts of the network. The bar charts indicate the percentage of the type of city transport infrastructure managed by each government level.

http://www.theguardian.com/cities/2015/feb/11/tale-four-cities-london-delhi-tokyo-bogota-data

Source 2

@frustrated and angry

The public transport system in this country is a disaster. If I wanted to take a bus, I would take a bus. I want to take a train, so I turn up at a railway station. But they tell me that there is a bus "over there" somewhere, with a vague hand wave. It is cold, wet and dark. The football fans are singing. I can't find a bus. Apparently it isn't here yet. On the train this part of the journey would take fifteen minutes. After twenty minutes a bus arrives. The driver takes my bag and stows it, which makes me feel insecure and unhappy. What if someone else takes it? The bus travels slowly, and I start to feel sick. The football fans are still singing. Eventually, we get to the next train station. There should be a train waiting on Platform 2. There isn't. Next time, I am going to drive. In my own car. Whatever the costs.

@frequent traveller

Ah the replacement bus.

For about 6 months I travelled by train at weekends to a faraway place that has only a single line working on the final stretch.

Every single journey has involved a replacement bus. A wide variety of "operational" reasons were given, all of them bogus.

The simple truth is that passenger traffic is so low at weekends that it is being shut down and replaced by a shuttle bus, because bus + driver costs a lot less than running diesel trains through four stations.

If they were upfront about it would not be so bad, but not a word about it to be found until you get there.

And yes, the rail company owns the bus company.

@business realist

Bus + driver costs a lot less than running trains. Granted. So, why should trains be run? This shows up the complete stupidity of a heavily subsidized railway system. Now the train companies have found a way to collect the subsidies without wasting money on running actual trains. Good show!

> @business realist, it is a train *service*. It is not a profit maximising company. Sometimes there are not enough passengers to make a profit, it is true. But at other times, such as commuter times, there are more than enough passengers. So it can even out – because the company can make money at peak times, it should offer a service to a smaller number of travellers at other times.

@impressed tourist

You are very lucky to have such an efficient and thorough public transport system. Yes, it sometimes has problems, but on the whole it is very good.

Source 3

Name	Description	Advantages	Disadvantages
Fare increases	Increase fares or change fare structure to increase revenues	Widely applied. Is a user fee (considered equitable).	Discourage transit use. Is regressive.
Discounted bulk passes	Discounted passes sold to groups based on their ridership	Increases revenue and transit ridership	Increases transit service costs and so may provide little net revenue
Property taxes	Increase local property taxes	Widely applied. Distributes burden widely.	Supports no other objectives. Is considered regressive.
Sales taxes	A special local sales tax	Distributes burden widely.	Supports no other objectives. Regressive.
Fuel taxes	An additional fuel tax in the region	Widely applied. Reduces vehicle traffic and fuel use	Is considered regressive.
Vehicle fees	An additional fee for vehicles registered in the region	Applied in some jurisdictions. Charges motorists for costs.	Does not affect vehicle use.
Utility levy	A levy to all utility accounts in the region	Easy to apply. Distributes burden widely.	Is small, regressive and support no other objectives.
Employee levy	A levy on each employee within a designated area or jurisdiction	Charges for commuters.	Requires collection system. May encourage sprawl if only in city centers.
Road tolls	Tolls on some roads or bridges	Reduces traffic congestion.	Costly to implement. Can encourage sprawl if only applied in city centers.
Vehicle-Km tax	A distance-based fee on vehicles registered in the region	Reduces vehicle traffic.	Costly to implement.
Parking taxes	Special tax on commercial parking transactions	Is applied in other cities.	Discourages parking pricing and downtown development.
Parking levy	A special property tax on parking spaces throughout the region	Large potential. Distributes burden widely. Encourages compact development.	Costly to implement. Opposed by suburban property owners.
Expanded parking pricing	Increase when and where public parking facilities (such as on-street parking spaces) are priced	Moderate to large potential. Distributes burden widely. Reduces driving.	
Development or transport impact fees	A fee on new development to help finance infrastructure, including transit improvements	Charges beneficiaries.	Limited potential.
Land value capture	Special taxes on property that benefit from the transit service	Large potential. Charges beneficiaries.	May be costly to implement. May discourage transit-oriented development.
Station rents	Collect revenues from public-private development at stations	Charges beneficiaries.	Limited potential.
Station air rights	Sell the rights to build over transit stations	Charges beneficiaries.	Limited potential.
Advertising	Additional advertising on vehicles and stations	Already used.	Limited potential. Sometimes unattractive.

http://www.vtpi.org/tranfund.pdf

Question 1

a) Which two cities have the most developed public transport systems? [2]

b) Which city has the most public transport owned and operated at national level? [1]

c) Which city has the highest proportion of its public transport owned and operated at city level? [1]

d) Which public transport system would you expect to be most efficient? Give your reasons. [4]

e) To what extent is public transport a personal, local or national issue? Justify your answer. [4]

Question 2

How could you test which of these cities had the most efficient public transport systems? Would you try them for yourself or conduct a survey? Explain the difficulties of both methods and explain your reasoning. [14]

Question 3

a) "The public transport system in this country is a disaster." Is this a fact or an opinion? Justify your answer. [3]

b) Why might @frustrated and angry be biased? Explain your answer. [2]

c) Refer to Source 2. Whose reasoning is most effective? [15]

You should support your point of view with their words. You should also consider

- the strength of their reasoning and evidence

- their use of language

- different types of information.

Question 4

How should public transport be funded?

You are in charge of a public transport project. You have to decide how it should be funded. Put forward a proposal and support it using evidence from the documents.

In your answer you should

- state your recommendations

- give reasons

- give examples where relevant

- show that you have considered at least one other viewpoint. [24]